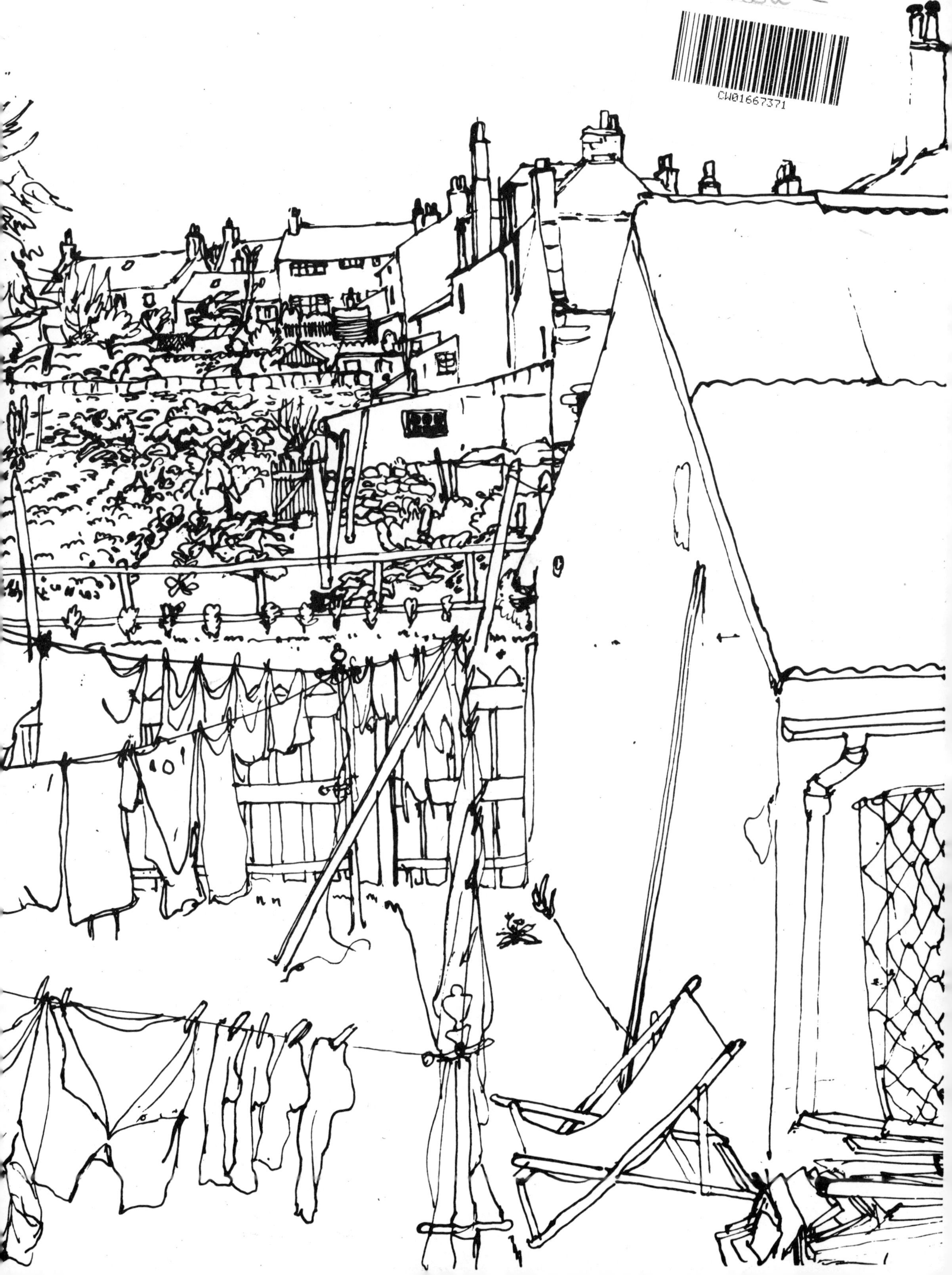

W G GILLIES

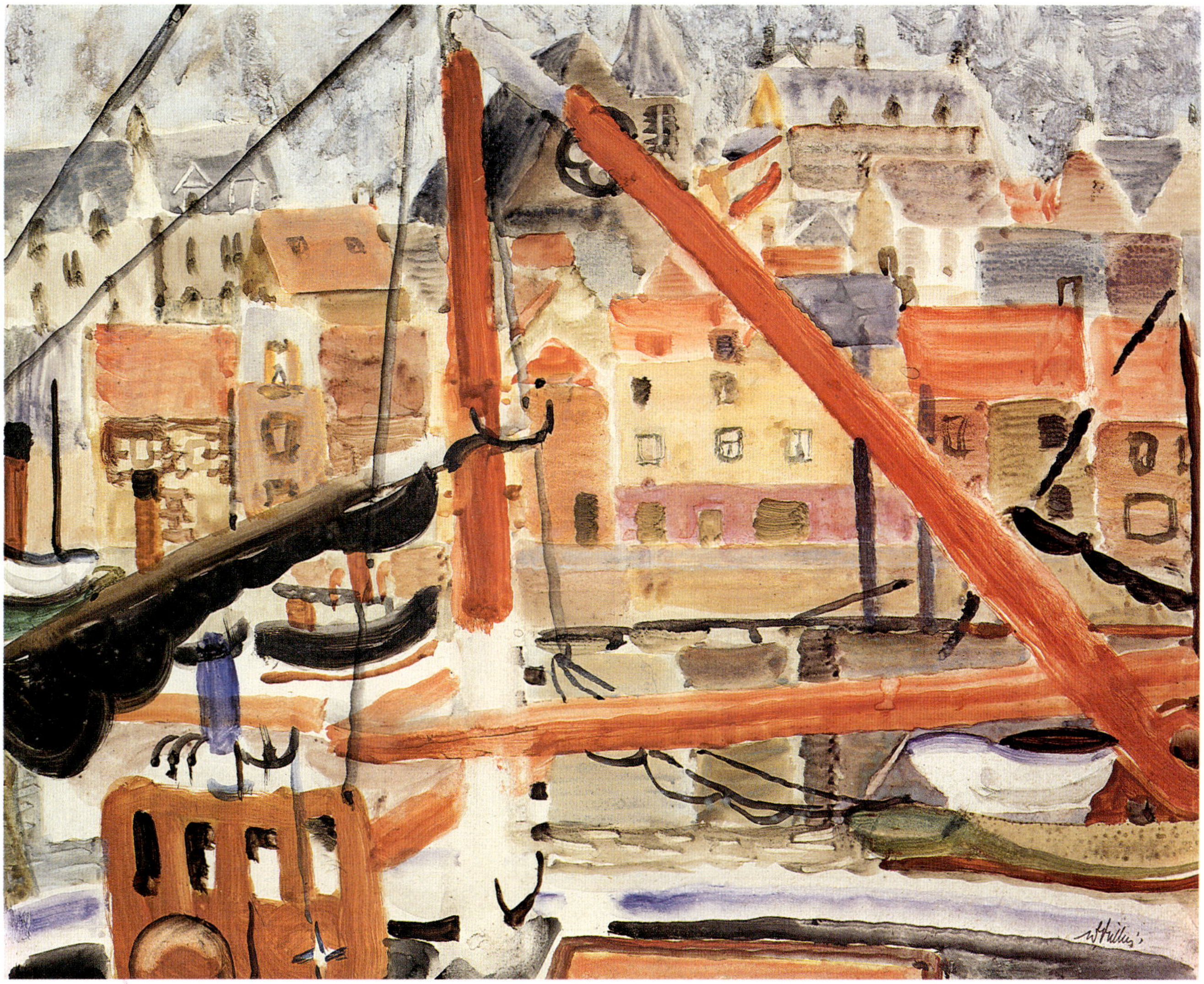

St Monance 1935 watercolour on paper 51 × 90 cm

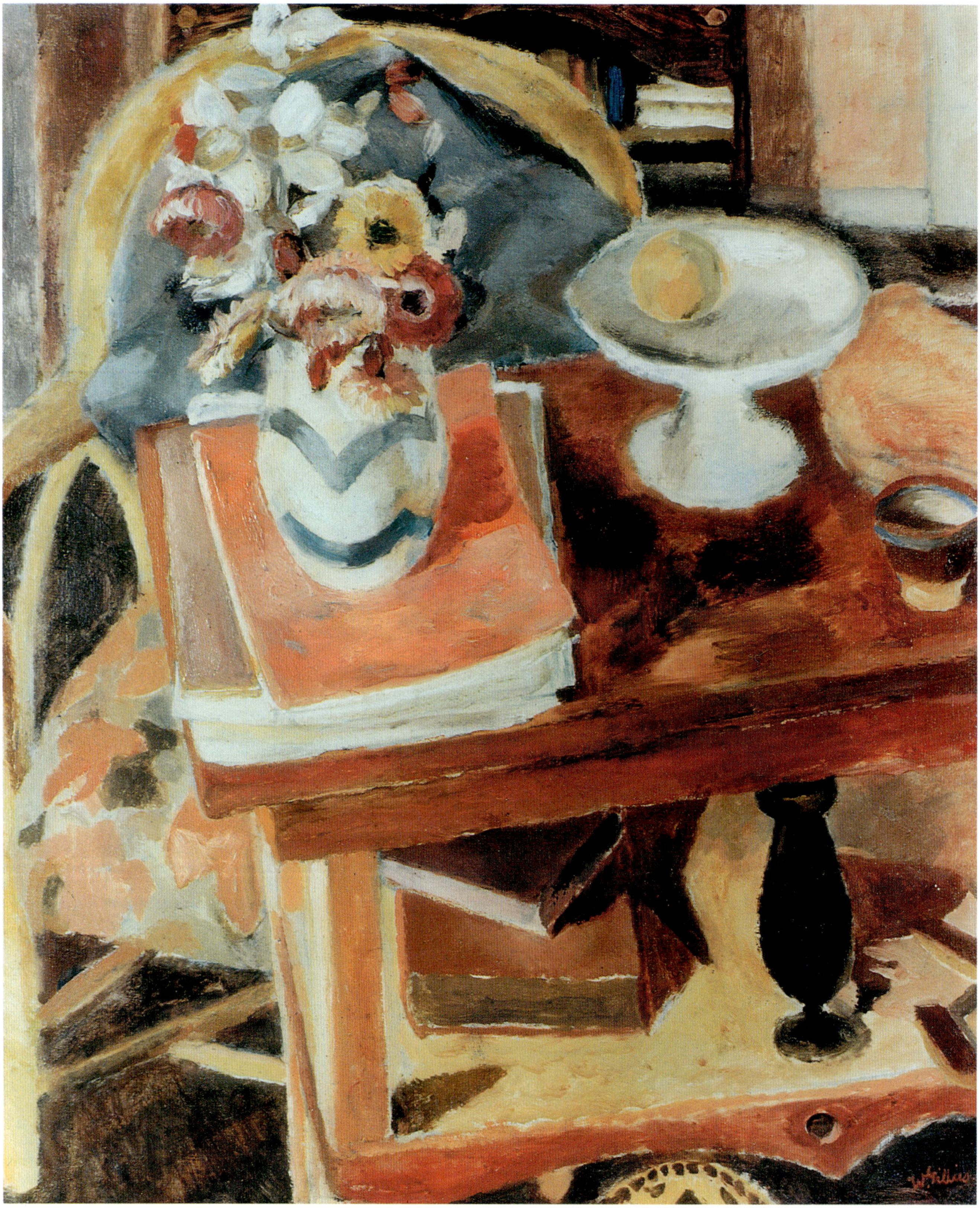

Interior, Flowers and Books c.1940 oil on canvas 92 × 71 cm

W G GILLIES

A Very Still Life

W Gordon Smith

Atelier Books

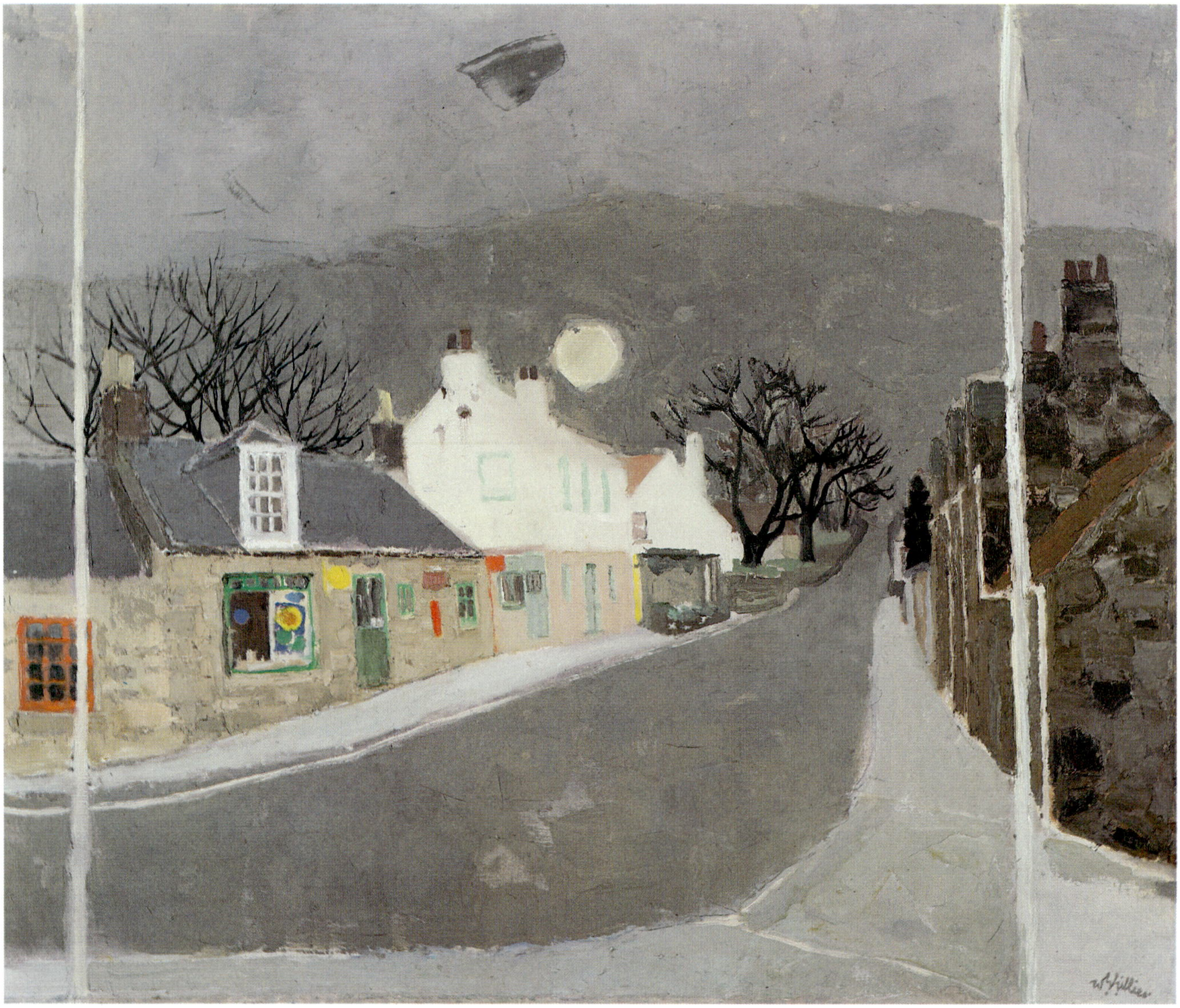

Temple-Dusk 1968 oil on canvas 86 × 100 cm EDC

First published 1991 by
Atelier Books
4 Dundas Street
Edinburgh EH3 6HZ

ISBN 1 873830 00 9

Production and publishing consultant, Paul Harris
Whittingehame House, Haddington EH41 1QA

Typeset by Falcon Typographic Art Ltd, Edinburgh & London
Printed in Yugoslavia by Gorenjski Tisk

Soup and Sherry

It was 3.30 in the afternoon, mid-November
and I was calling on Bill Gillies.
(Sir William Gillies, R.S.A., R.A. etcetera.)
"Come in," he says, "We'll have soup.
You won't be drinking and driving
so we'll have sherry." Didn't like
the idea of the combination, but
the lentil soup was hottering
on the stove so there was nothing for it
but swallow it with the sherry.
There was a painting on the easel
of Temple, the village where we were.
It didn't look like the rainy street
off which I'd just come. In it
the moon was up and silvering
the length of it, pavement, tarmac road,
squat houses, and touching up
two black trees, winter trees,
but each twig starting from its branch
as if Spring were in it. I looked out
the window. Nothing like the painting.
No glimmering windows along the street.
He was stirring the soup. He didn't look up.
"I catched a painting last night."
I could see him casting on the Esks,
North Esk, South Esk, Leithen Water, Falla.
How many paintings got away? "Soup's ready."
How many poems slip back into my dark sea?

George Bruce

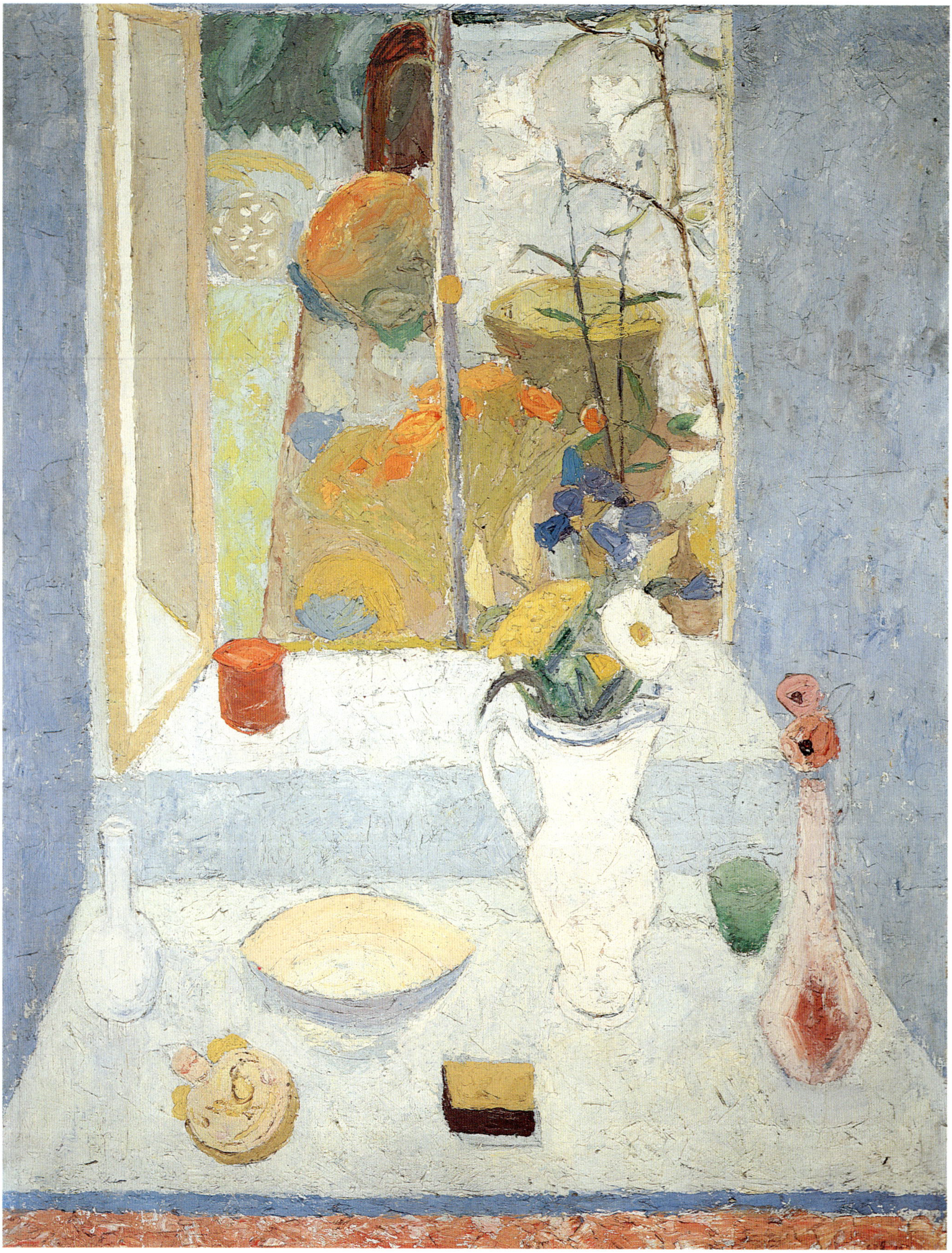

The Blue Window 1940 oil on canvas 127 × 70 cm RSA

Sir William Gillies, A Memorial

I first met him when I went up to Edinburgh in 1933 although I already knew a little about him from Robert Westwater who had taught at my school in London. It was a splendid privilege to be an art student in Edinburgh in the Thirties because there was a talented group of painters at the Art College. This included not only Gillies but William MacTaggart, John Maxwell and Robert Westwater. From time to time Peploe *père* looked in.

Gillies style of teaching was what would be called 'hands-off' nowadays, I suppose. He said little, but if he commented it was always positive. He was generous with encouragement and his own bubbling enthusiasm was infectious. He became Head of the Painting School and eventually Principal of the entire College. He never did anything less than wholeheartedly but it seems a pity that such a talent should have spent so much time on the oversight of a fairly complex organisation. But he seemed actually to enjoy it.

By the time we met he was already a mature painter and he seemed so much at ease in the way he was worked that it never occurred to me at the time to wonder what influences had shaped him. Looking back over half a century with hindsight and with a little wider knowledge one can see that Nature and Munch must have been abiding influence. But he was also alert to new ideas and I remember the delight with which he greeted a roomful of works by Klee which were shown at the Royal Scottish Academy in the mid-thirties.

When we first knew Gillies his mother was still alive. He called her 'Birdie' which was very apt because she was tiny with bright and darting eyes so like his own.

Gillies was fortunate, or inspired in his choice of Temple as his home – not all that far from Haddington where he was born. I think one could say, as with Constable, that his native countryside made him a partner. The main street of Temple runs downhill and the three cottages which Gillies made into one stepped downhill in keeping with the road. The interior was like an Aladdin's Cave, rich in pots and dishes made by his talented sister, and yellow ochre furniture, as I remember, which echoed the rich ochres and reds of the landscape glimpsed through the windows.

Sir Norman Reid

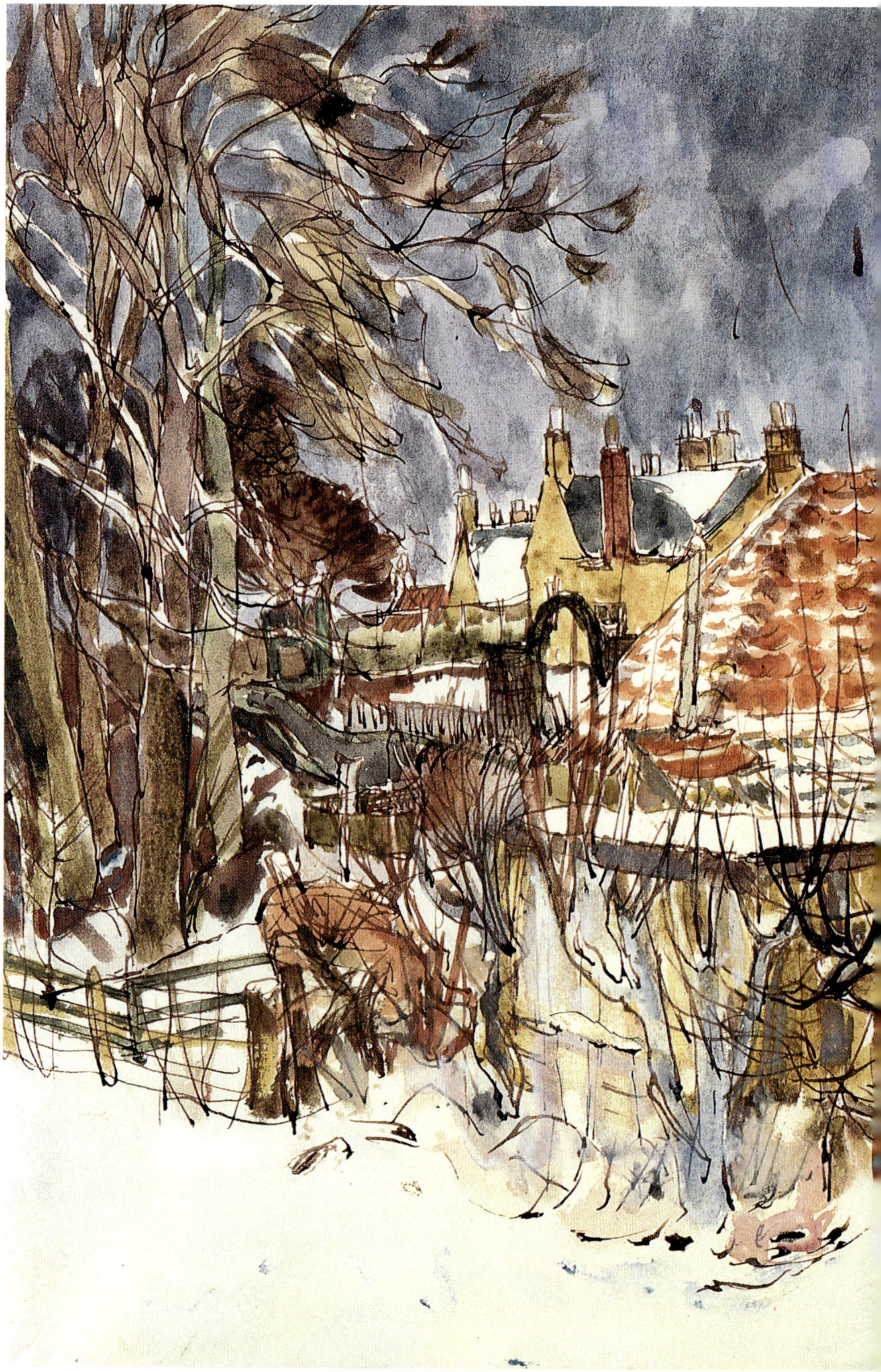

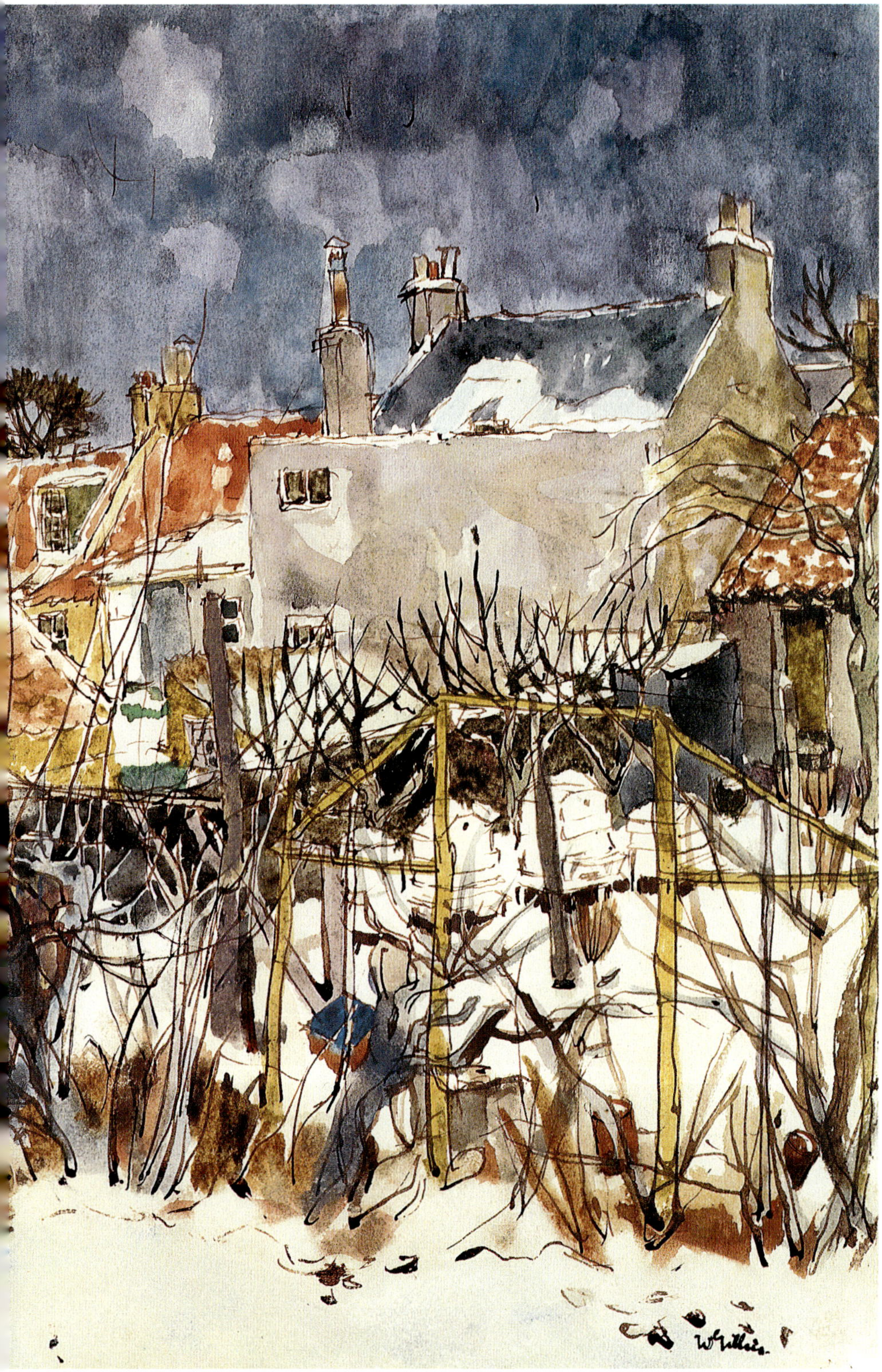

Winter, Temple, Back of Houses c.1948 watercolour and ink on paper 50 × 32 cm SNGMA

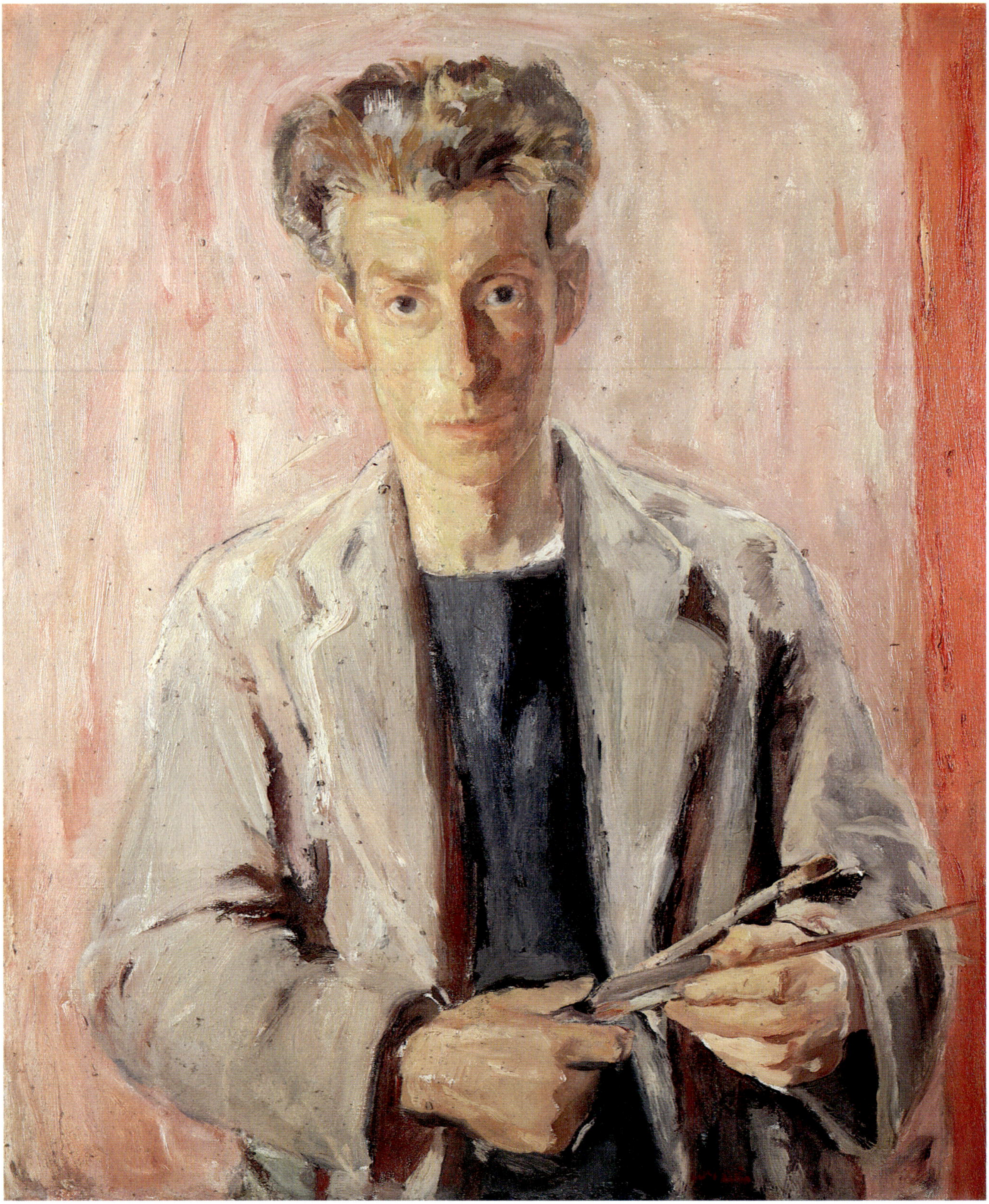

Self-Portrait 1941 oil on canvas 86 × 70 cm SNGMA

Prelude

He was born in a pretty little Scottish market town on the south side of the River Forth estuary on 21 September, 1898. Kitchener was defeating dervishes at Omdurman. Radium was discovered that year. Oscar Wilde wrote *The Ballad of Reading Gaol* and Rodin sculpted *The Kiss*. Beardsley, Gladstone and Bismarck died. He shared the year of his birth with Paul Robeson and Hemingway.

None of this, if it was known at all, was momentous news in the royal burgh of Haddington, noted for its grain market, its imposing Town House, a fine old kirk, a Mercat Cross topped by a goat, two bonny old bridges over the River Tyne, and the bustle and clash of its ritual feeing-days, when farm-servants hired themselves out for another year of hard labour.

A clever Scottish king, Alexander II, had been born there in 1198, the English had burnt the place down more than once in the Middle Ages, and John Knox was also born there, or thereabouts, in 1513. Sitting on the Great North Road – with Edinburgh a few miles to the west and London a long way south – perched on the brink of the twentieth-century, Haddington was not distinguished by very much else.

Criss-crossed by bewildering by-roads, it stood at the heart of some of Scotland's richest agricultural acres. The gentle Lammermuir hills ranged the southern skyline. Only ten miles away the open sea gnawed at the eastern coastline. The town itself and the tranquil villages and tidy farm steadings, scattered across the rolling patchwork landscape, bore none of the scars of the industrial, or any other, revolution. It would be many decades before the petrol tractor, invented in Ohio that year, disturbed the peace of East Lothian's fertile fields.

He grew up in the town, round his father's shop in the High Street, and out by the trout burns and meadows of a somnolent countryside. Almost as soon as he could grip a pencil he could draw. A diligent and inquisitive pupil, he 'stuck in' at school – fulfilling the first ordinance of the Protestant work ethic – but a compulsion to observe and record what he liked about the world around him ran like a *leitmotiv* through his young life and would, before long, seem to him to be the only reason for his existence.

That enthusiasm for drawing and painting took him to the art college which he would serve as a teacher and administrator for most of his adult life. As a painter he never stopped working and selling and learning. His output was prodigious, his influence incalculable. By 1970, when his gifts were celebrated by a huge retrospective exhibition which spilled across two galleries, this quiet, intensely private man was already recognised as one of the great Scottish painters of the twentieth century. He was knighted for his services to art in Scotland and elected Academician of the Royal Academy.

The quiet lad from Haddington, Sir William George Gillies, CBE, RA, RSA, PPRSW, D.Litt, FEIS, died in his modest cottage at Temple, Midlothian, on 15 April, 1973.

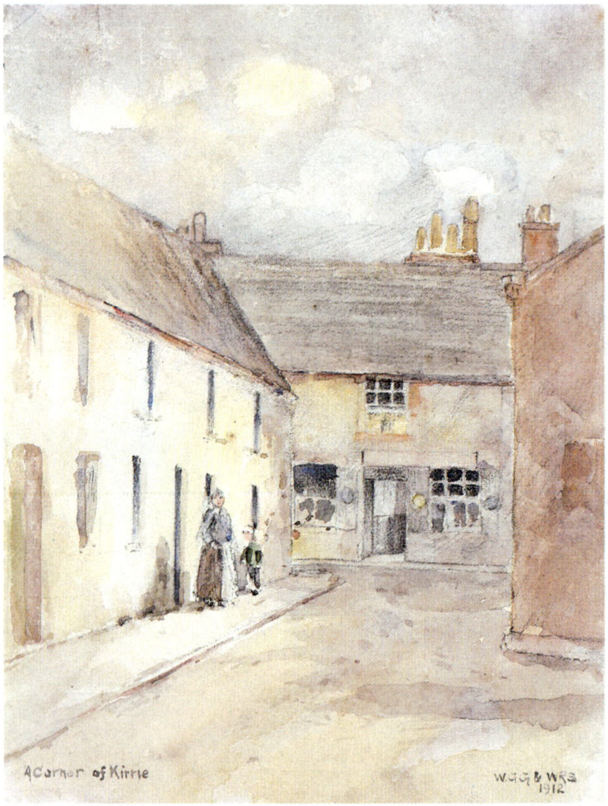

A Corner of Kirrie 1912 watercolour on paper
23 × 18 cm RSA

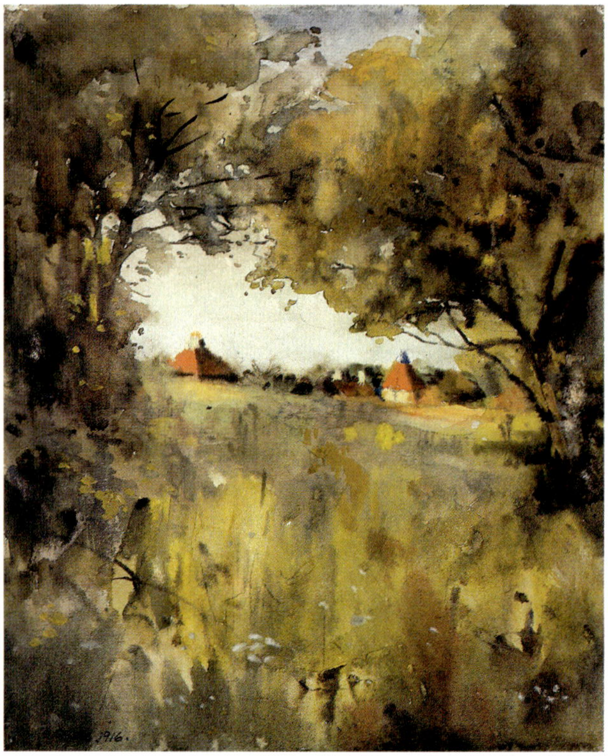

Spillsmerford, Pencaitland 1916 watercolour on paper
30 × 24 cm RSA

Chapter 1

John Gillies, a tailor to trade, owned a tobacconist business in Haddington and when his son was born lived above the shop with his wife Emma Smith, who hailed from Kirriemuir, and their infant daughter Janet, or Jenny as she came to be called. Another daughter, Emma, was born in 1900. They lived a cosy, uncomplicated life. As the business prospered, John Gillies built a new house on the outskirts of town.

Fortuitously, in these less-enlightened times, when attainment in mathematics or physics was more desirable than anything as frivolous as the arts, the boy's aptitude for drawing was actively encouraged. There was no genetic artistic legacy that anybody in the family knew about, but he was fortunate in having an uncle, his mother's brother, who taught art at a school in Broughty Ferry, near Dundee.

William Ryle Smith spent summer holidays indulging Sunday-painter enthusiasms among the closes and pends of Haddington, registering in swift watercolours the vernacular charm of the old town's seventeenth-century architecture – its squat gables, dank wynds and closes, its pantiles and corbie-steps. His nephew became an avid companion in these shared summers. Man and boy struck up a happy relationship, stoking each other's enthusiasms, enjoying their easy friendship. They would venture further afield to Edinburgh on day-excursions to the classical salons of the National Gallery of Scotland and visit the annual exhibitions of new work at the Royal Scottish Academy and by the Society of Scottish Artists.

Although the growing lad's secondary school, Knox Institute, did not take art seriously enough to employ a specialist teacher, he did receive encouragement. There are few Scottish poets, painters, writers or musicians who cannot summon one source of early persuasion and support, usually at school, often by a member of that dedicated band of formidable spinsters who, before and after the archetypal Miss Jean Brodie, formed the backbone of the educational system. At Knox Institute it was Miss Fordyce, a teacher of English who took art classes as a second subject. She had enough confidence in the talent and character of an exemplary pupil to allow him to sketch and draw on his own and even bicycle off into the fields and hedgerows during school hours in search of suitable subjects.

For six years Willie sat in class beside Norman W. Porteous, son of the headmaster, and they attended the same Sunday school. They were within a week or two of being the same age. In his 93rd year (in 1991) Professor Porteous recalled with unconcealed pleasure their happy boyhood: 'We were the best of pals, although our interests were very different. Willie was always drawing and that made him a bit special. I don't remember a time when he wasn't keen on art. I wanted to learn Greek and my father didn't have time during school hours to teach me, so he gave me the books and told me to teach myself. In the sense that even then, at such a young age, we wanted to learn something out of the ordinary, I suppose that set us both apart from the rest and drew us together. I kept in touch with him throughout his life, over all these years. There was never a breach in our friendship, and it was a great joy to me when he got one honour after another.'

When Professor Porteous, formerly Professor of Hebrew at Edinburgh University, retired as Principal of New College he was presented with a Gillies watercolour, *Fir Tree by Lochside*. Anyone charting its provenance should not overlook the fact that the painting links two school chums from Haddington who became the Principals of two of Scotland's most important colleges.

Whenever he could, young Willie caught a train to Dundee's seaside suburb overlooking the Tay and plundered the delights of the Orchar Gallery in Beach Crescent – an important small collection of mainly Scottish paintings – from a holiday base in his uncle's home. He discovered even greater riches at Broughty Ferry. Ryle Smith subscribed to the lavishly-produced monthly art magazine *The Studio*, which ranged across the spectrum of European art and crafts with good illustrations in colour and monotone supporting informed criticism, features and analysis. Shelves of back-numbers conjured exotic worlds – the classical and the avant-garde of Paris, London, Berlin and Vienna, but also, and remarkably, regular despatches about the burgeoning Glasgow Style and even reviews of exhibitions he had enjoyed with his uncle in Edinburgh. Scottish art, the magazine revealed, occupied a small, but proud place in world culture.

The house at Broughty Ferry boasted some genre paintings by local artists, including a few sensitive watercolours by James Waterston Herald, the Arbroath painter of the 'blottesque' school whose delicacy and decorative style owed something to Arthur Melville and is now much admired by collectors.

Back in Haddington his sketching forays into the countryside continued to be his most ardent pastime. This enthusiasm undoubtedly set him aside from other boys of his age, but did not exclude him from their company or the normal rituals of a happy boyhood. All was well in their simple world as seasons slipped by and fused the years together. If his head was often in the clouds, his feet remained firmly on the ground. One of his earliest 'artistic' commissions came about through his friendship with a local farmer, the proud breeder of a registered herd of Friesian cattle. When calves were born their characteristics had to be noted for the thoroughbred record. Young Willie carefully sketched each calf's markings in the stock book.

Asked, as youths often are, what he wanted to do with his life, he responded, as youths usually do, with vagueness and uncertainty. He secretly hoped that he could emulate his uncle and teach art. By his mid-teens, doing well at school and seeing his industry rewarded, he had made up his mind, particularly after a local amateur painter, R.A. Dakers, recognised his ability and took him under his wing. Dakers was editor of *The Haddington Courier*, a cultivated man of affable temperament, and his accomplished oil paintings, usually in heavy gestural impasto applied with the palette knife, were hung regularly at the big annual shows in Edinburgh. His painting interests, chiefly in landscape and flower studies, chimed with those of his young protégé, and they would pedal into the Lammermuirs or follow the Tyne in search of subjects. Their painting sessions in Dakers' attic studio, working up pencil sketches on to canvas, were a revelation and inspiration to a lad who, up to that time, had no experience of oil techniques and to whom the palette knife seemed a strange and magical tool. However, in one of his first experiments with oil paint, a portrait of his mother, dated 1916, he confined himself to brushwork.

The practical influence and coaching of Dakers had a profound effect on a pupil whose devotion to drawing and painting did not, however, divert him from the more rigorous demands of the school curriculum. He became dux of Knox Institute. For the first – but certainly not last – time in his life, intelligent curiosity, equable temperament, and single-minded application took him to the top of his class.

A Haddington watchmaker and dedicated art collector, Alexander Wright, responding to the young man's precocious talent and growing local reputation, gave up a window of his shop on the High Street to mount the first exhibition of his watercolours. These simple representations of recognisable East Lothian topography and landscape caught the fancy of Wright's customers and passers-by, to the extent that some of them were not only praised but purchased. A watercolour landscape from this period is a treasured possession of today's Knox Academy, as the Institute became.

About this time he also read the first public appreciation of his work in a *Haddington Courier* article about a school roll of honour, a list of former pupils serving in the war

> . . . which has been very cleverly designed and executed by Mr W.G. Gillies, Haddington, a junior student who, although only 17 years of age, displays quite exceptional artistic ability. The design consists in the main of a border beautifully executed in watercolour, embodying conventional laurel wreathing, Celtic corner-pieces, and old-style lettering. The names are in script . . . The scale of colouring comprises various subdued tones of brown, green, blue, red, buff and black, the whole work in every way reflecting great credit upon the youthful artist, who is a son of Mr Gillies, tobacconist.

Young Mr W.G. Gillies was accepted as a student at Edinburgh College of Art at the start of the 1916 autumn term. Just turned eighteen, he was due for military service, and for a short time the war left him alone to enjoy the heady excitements of his first formal training as an artist.

Not in any sense a bumpkin, he was nevertheless a countryman, with an intense affection for the red earth of East Lothian, its high skies and far horizons, and shy and socially reserved in the urban clash of Scotland's capital city. He lived in lodgings but spent most of his waking hours at day and evening classes. For the first time his natural skills as a budding artist would be examined and tested alongside the talents of his peers. Unlike many of his fellows

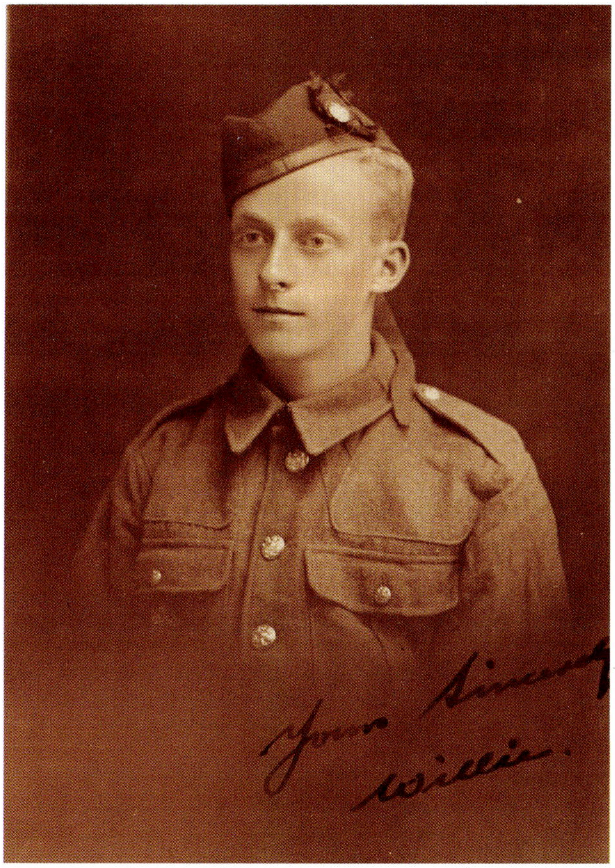

William Gillies in the uniform of the 10th Scottish Rifles, 1917
(Photo: RSA Archives)

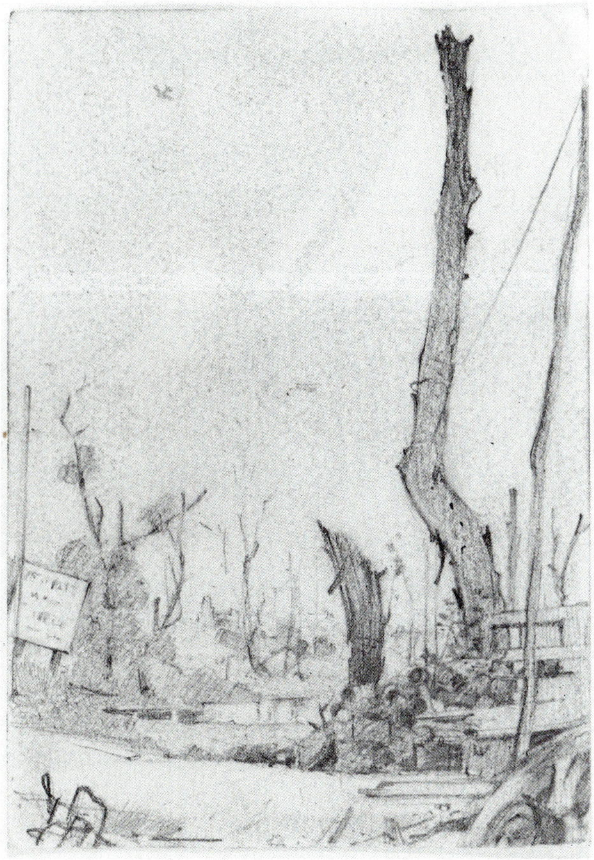

Our Post Behind Our Wire 1918 pencil on paper 9 × 13 cm RSA

he arrived at college with his mind firmly set on a vocation, his intuitive skills nurtured by good advice, and fortified by deep-seated – if diffident – confidence. In the face of stern competition and exacting standards, however, he soon realised that ambition, the guidance of Ryle Smith and Dakers, and faith in his own ability might not be enough. At ECA a probationary system meant that formal admission to the Diploma Course depended on an assessment of work in preliminary studies.

Towards the end of his second term, in the spring of 1917, his world was shattered one morning by the arrival of his call-up papers. As a sensitive young man, thirled to nature and seduced by its beauties and wonders, he lacked the fervour of those who, despite the war's terrible toll, the solemn lists of the dead that filled every newspaper, answered the call to arms so readily and followed the drum. He was neither pacifist nor unpatriotic. His background and upbringing told him where his duty lay, and his response was instinctive and positive, but the threat to his future as an artist, the abandonment of his training at such a crucial time, threw him into deep despair.

After square-bashing and initial infantry training he joined the Scottish Rifles, was soon drafted with the 10th Battalion to France, and saw active service in the battles which raged round the Hindenburg Line near Arras. He was wounded twice, and gassed, but like so many lucky survivors of that hideous war, lived not to tell the tale. Asked about life in the trenches, he cursed the 'whole ghastly experience,' and spent much of his life trying to forget its horrors. He told T. Elder Dickson, whose fine 1974 monograph is an essential source for all commentators on Gillies' life and work, that his fellow soldiers had no interest in art. 'There was no one to discuss art with, no opportunity to keep your hand in. I did an occasional portrait sketch or a pencil scribble of trenches and war-blasted landscapes – that was all. It was two years of wasted time.' Some private memories of his two years of military service must have been important to him, however. Alongside a few notepad drawings which he had sketched at the front he kept his campaign medals and photographs of comrades who, like himself, 'had not yet grown up.'

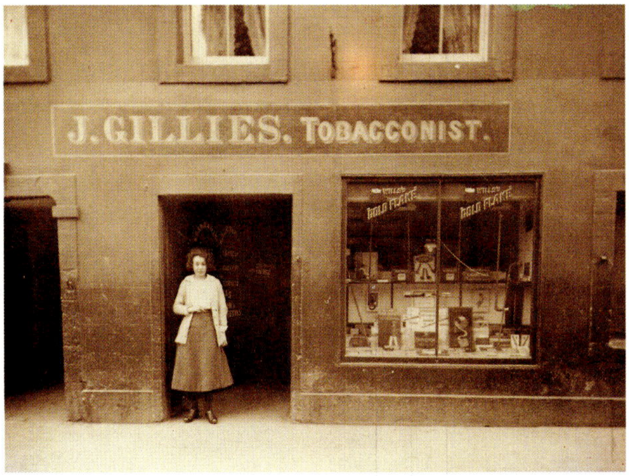

Emma Gillies in front of the family tobacco shop, Haddington
(Photo: RSA Archives)

Chapter 2

Discharged from the army in the spring of 1919 after a lengthy period of hospitalisation in the west of Scotland, he was fit enough to go back to art college at the start of the autumn term. His record as a diligent and accomplished student during his interrupted first year stood him in good stead. He was allowed to go straight into the second year of his four-year course, joining a huge intake of ex-Servicemen in crowded classes. Many of them had left for the war as callow youths and returned as men who had already seen too much. Some were bitter and disillusioned, others politically committed to creating a better world, many so relieved to be alive that they celebrated the arrival of each fresh day with playful exuberance.

Schools of art, like most other institutions of learning, owe success or lack of it largely to the quality and dedication of their staff. Purple patches or grey areas – 'that's the place to be,' or not to be, as the case may be – come and go in cycles, regardless of adjustments to the curriculum, the lottery of student intake, or artistic vogue.

Gillies and his post-war fellows at Edinburgh were lucky. They became involved in a discreet aesthetic revolution. The young college, its development seriously hindered by the war, had as yet no reputation to uphold. Before 1908, the Academy School in the Royal Institution edifice on Princes Street (now the Royal Scottish Academy) was the nation's most prestigious seat of art education. It laid down exacting standards of academic discipline, technical skill and classical composition. These immutable values were championed by the new school, regardless of convulsions in foreign parts – which, for Edinburgh's purpose, usually includes Glasgow. All traditional teaching philosophies respond grudgingly to change, but the disruption of the war, the relative maturity of many students, a restless discontent with the social status quo, and healthy curiosity about the metamorphosis of art throughout Europe launched the ECA of the 1920s, better late than never, into the twentieth century.

Painters with new vision and even stranger grammar and vocabularies, like van Gogh and Seurat, Matisse and Derain, had thrown open the shutters, revealing worlds conquered by riotous colour, where line and form obeyed different laws. Impressionism – even Post-Impressionism – had been and gone. Modernism, with Picasso and Braque showing the way, was established. Mondrian's pioneering experiments with abstraction were more than a decade old.

In Gillies' day the four-year Diploma Course at Edinburgh allocated the first two years to preliminary studies, with heavy emphasis on drawing (and yet more drawing), composition and the disciplines of perspective. The place crawled with plaster casts of hands and feet. Copies of sculpted portrait heads and classical figures, part of the great Albacini Collection, had to be represented in line and tone over and over again. The 4H pencil ruled supreme. Drawing from life was an extra-curricular evening activity. Many students, faced with yet another plaster nose or ear to draw, must have felt the frustrated rage that drove Vincent van Gogh to throw a plaster head of Apollo through the studio window when his cousin Anton Mauve insisted, 'You'll do it until you get it right.' But by all accounts Willie Gillies, to whom drawing came as easily as breathing, plodded in his placid fashion towards the day when he would be free to specialise in his chosen subjects.

The Head of the Drawing and Painting School, David Alison (1882-1955), a gruff traditionalist, fearsome to some students, was not nicknamed 'Bouff' for nothing. Unapproachable and likely to be monosyllabic if you dared, his admiration of fine painting ended, more or less, with the eighteenth century masters. He stood second to none in his admiration of Henry

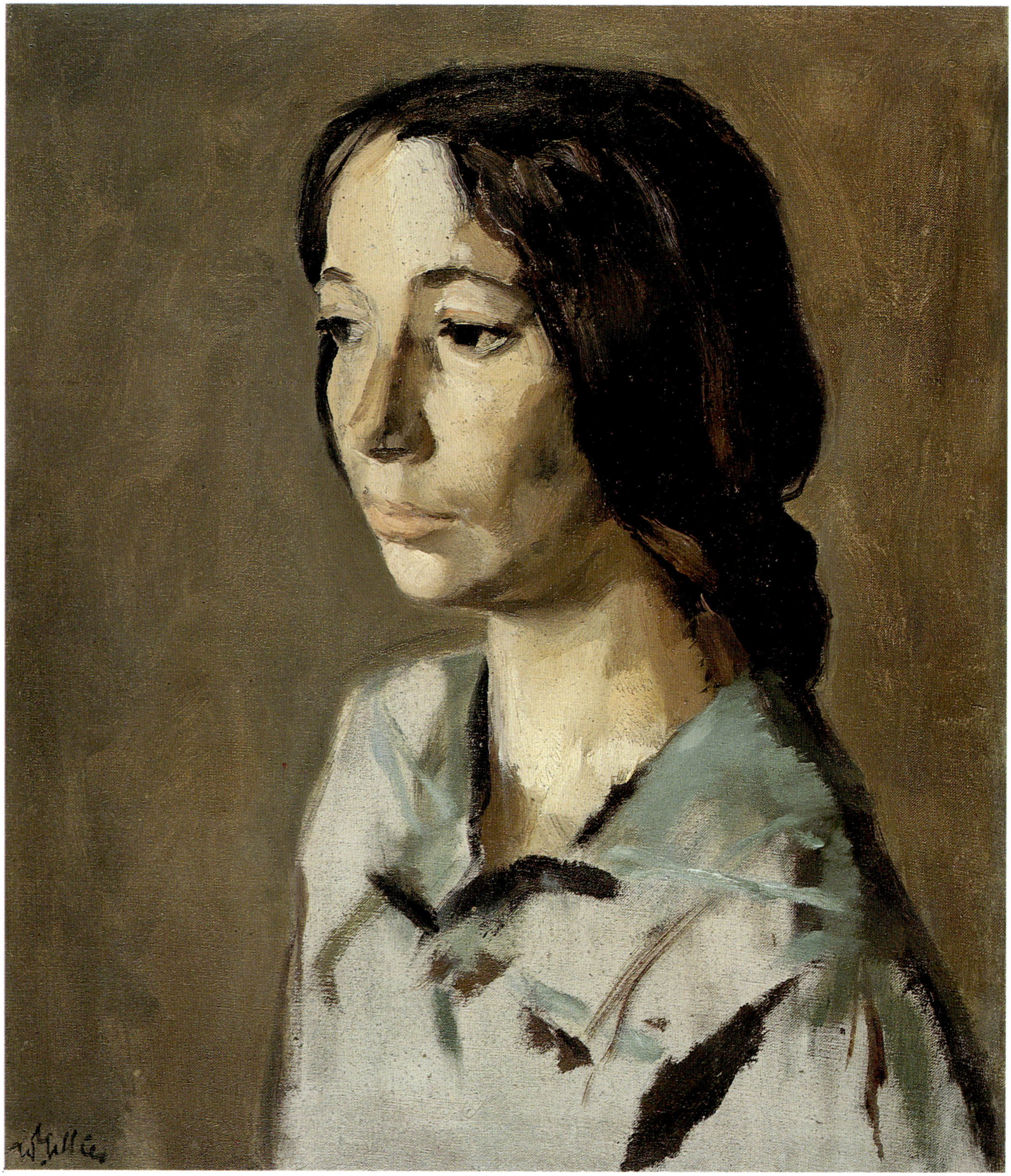

Portrait of Emma Gillies 1921 oil on canvas 76 × 64 cm RSA

Raeburn and venerated Velasquez, Rembrandt, Ingres and Goya. Yet Alison's theories of tonal harmony, founded on Raeburn's technique and laid down with trenchant authority, had a lifelong effect on the young Gillies. The influence is most obvious in his post-graduate portraits of fellow students – particularly those of R.H. 'Peter' Westwater and A.V. Couling – and echoes on into the family studies of the 30s, but his subtle adaptation of these early harmonic disciplines brought balance and lyricism to his landscapes and still lifes until the end of his days.

While classicism was being dinned into him with all the repetitious charm of multiplication tables he combed the pages of *Colour* magazine in the college library for reviews and pictures of the fresh excitements from France. He responded to Alison's teaching methods, spent extra hours learning as much as he could from him in evening life classes, but much later, in the prime of his painting life, conceded that *Colour* – like the back numbers of *The Studio* at Broughty Ferry – 'was a tremendous stimulus to me for years.' The painters of Paris had found ways to register emotion and create beauty in its most simple and elemental form. Moreover, they had found a way to translate experience into a visual language which he understood but could not yet speak.

The award of a travelling scholarship took him to London in the Easter vacation of 1920. Some sketches from that trip survive. His first visits to the National and Tate Galleries must have reinforced his sense of artistic schizophrenia, and a round of the fashionable commercial galleries served only to widen the gulf that stretched between classicism and modernism.

London deserved its reputation as one of the art capitals of the world, but its influence in those days of limited communication seldom spread beyond the Cheviots. A loud hurrah in the Metropolis was heard as a cheep – if that – in North Britain. It would be compounding a myth, however, and resurrecting an ancient wrong to dismiss Scotland at that time as an aesthetic wilderness.

In the remorselessly partial polemic of *Modern Scottish Painting* – commissioned in 1939 and surely one of the worst histories of art ever published – J.D. Fergusson quotes Fra Newbery, the influential principal of the Glasgow School of Art, writing in 1897:

> Glasgow has been extremely fortunate for the last twenty years. The finest examples of the work of the Barbizon School, and of the modern Dutch Masters, of Millet, Corot, Diaz, Monticelli. the Maris brothers, Israels and many others have been bought by Glasgow buyers, and were brought before the eyes of the Glasgow artists long before London had recognised even the existence of these continental influences.

The Glasgow Boys – and Girls, as has been so richly and recently demonstrated – began their march into art history in the early 1880s. Glasgow's civic temple to the arts, Kelvingrove Art Gallery and Museum, opened in 1901.

Samuel John Peploe (1871-1935), an Edinburgh artist who fell under the influence of French painting as early as 1894, was executing Fauvist panels in 1910. By the time Gillies went to art school Peploe had already absorbed the lessons of Cézanne and Matisse. In 1911, Edinburgh-born Francis Campbell Boileau Cadell (1883-1937), who had studied in France at the turn of the century, initiated the Society of Eight, an exhibiting group of kindred spirits who aimed to raise standards and, although based in Edinburgh, embrace the best work Scotland could produce. John Duncan Fergusson (1874-1961) was born in Leith, Edinburgh's seaport neighbour, which might account for a lifelong affection for Glasgow at the expense of the capital. As it happened, he spent his most productive working years in France, mounted his first one-man show in London in 1905, and four of his paintings were hung in the 1913 Post Impressionist and Futuristic Exhibition in London.

George Leslie Hunter (1879-1931), the only one of the gifted quartet who became known as the Scottish Colourists to have been born in the west – at Rothesay – should have had his first one-man show in San Francisco in 1906, but lost all his work in the earthquake. By 1916, a disciple of the Post Impressionists, he had established himself back in Scotland, but like the others, never lost his love of France and French painting.

T. J. Honeyman, without whom there would be less of a Burrell Collection, only a depleted Kelvingrove collection, and no Glasgow Citizen's Theatre, recalled in *Three Scottish Colourists* how Oskar Kokoschka paused in front of W.Y. MacGregor's magnificent *Vegetable Stall*, saying

'To think that that picture was painted before I was born, and I never knew.'

Scotland was also fortunate enough to have several enlightened art dealers, notably Craibe Angus and Alexander Reid (whose Burrell Collection portrait was painted by Vincent van Gogh) in Glasgow; John Forbes White in Aberdeen; and Peter MacOmish Dott in Edinburgh (his little Scottish Gallery was described by JDF as 'a charming oasis in the dried up desert and a great help to me'). They led public taste from the front, with what now seems scant attention to commercial opportunism.

David Alison, a founder member of Cadell's Society of Eight, dominated ECA in the inter-war years, guarding the citadel of the academic establishment while condoning the gentle revolution which transfixed the college's character for half a century and spread its influence throughout Scotland. There is evidence to suggest that he cleverly affected rigidity only as counterbalance to what might have become the subversive effects of Modernism. He swerved, but only to turn a Nelsonian eye. Strutting the studios in his Harris tweed plus-fours, 'bouffing' at skivers and backsliders, rewarding effort and talent with no more than a growled 'Aye, well done, a guid heid' – the 'heid' was always the first thing he noticed – he is remembered with affectionate respect. His method achieved spectacular results. During his long career at ECA – he retired in 1946 – the college produced colourists like Redpath, Maxwell, Gillies, MacTaggart, Beaton, McClure, Crozier, Philipson and Leishman, as well as innovators like Alan Davie, William Gear, Wilhelmina Barns-Graham, Margaret Mellis, Charles Pulsford and James Cumming.

David MacBeth Sutherland, who had won an ECA scholarship to Spain and Paris in 1911, then painted in Holland and Belgium in 1913, came home from war to join Alison's staff in 1918. A flamboyant, free-thinking liberal, he had trained initially at the Academy school but, affected by what he had seen abroad, became a confirmed Modernist. Gillies recalled to Elder Dickson: 'There was something exciting about him and his brilliant handling of colour . . . he was a tremendous stimulus to us all.' D.M. Sutherland was experimenting with broken-colour at that time, making different hues vibrate with each other to produce a unifying effect, and the way he emphasised pattern and structure while creating atmospheric tone made a vivid impression. Another adventurous colourist and superlative draughtsman, Donald Moodie, joined the staff in 1919 and stayed 36 years. Adam Bruce Thomson, a legendary teacher whose own painting style would become influenced by the freedom of Gillies, also nudged the college towards more liberal attitudes.

Lucky in his teachers, Gillies was also fortunate in the company he could keep. Fellow students enjoyed his convivial good nature, pawky sense of humour, and disarming modesty. He was a popular companion on weekend camping trips when, in high spirits, they would turn their backs on plaster casts and still-life bric-a-brac and wander off into the countryside in search of more challenging subjects. His college friends included William MacTaggart, grandson of the great Victorian landscape painter and a future President of the Royal Scottish Academy, and William Crozier, whose tragically early death denied Scottish art the promise of his mature output.

In 1920, just when his student life sailed along with confidence and equanimity – starting his third year and well set on his chosen course of Drawing and Painting – his father collapsed with a cerebral haemorrhage. He died the following year, while Gillies was on a sketching trip to the Solway. The shock of bereavement was bad enough, but the family's only source of income was the tobacconist's shop, and the changed circumstances threatened his future as a student. There were, after all, no State grants in those days and only token bursaries. Up to that time his young sister Emma had been working in the offices of *The Haddington Courier*. The family's confidence in Willie's artistic vocation, and their solidarity, can be measured by the 21-year-old Emma's instant decision to leave her job and take over the management of the shop.

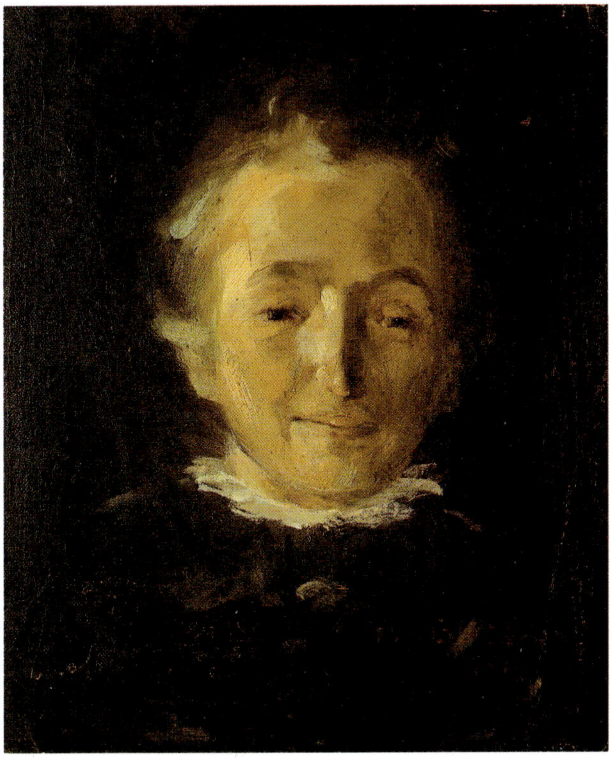

Portrait of Mother 1916 oil on canvas on board
37 × 31 cm RSA

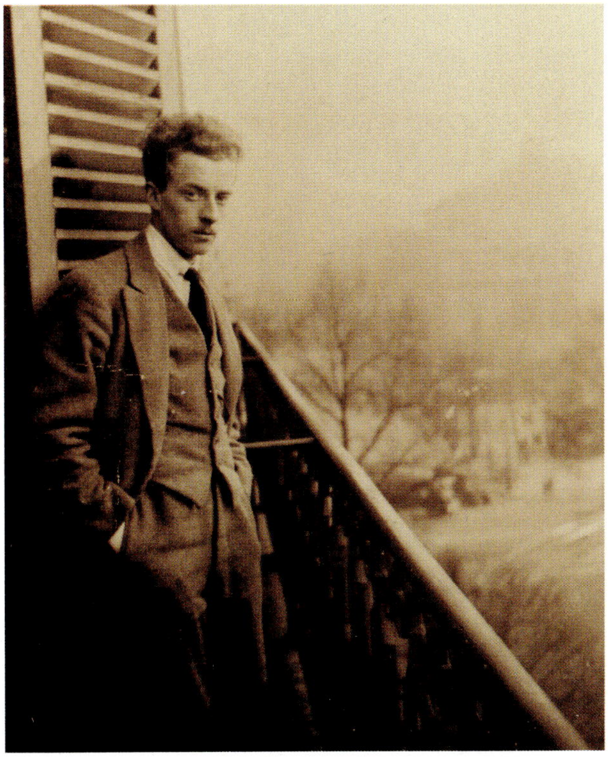

William Gillies, Paris, 1924 (Photo: RSA Archives)

Gillies qualified for a Certificate of Recognition from the Scottish Education Department which licensed him to teach art as a probationer in Scottish schools. 'Very promising,' was the examiners' judgment. He could have abandoned his course and found a job, but the family decided they would go on supporting him while he worked for his diploma.

Families – and, by ancient tradition, especially Scottish families – do not as a rule make social contracts with each other, or call in debts and obligations. Parents seek no reward for their investment in a child's education: the most they hope for is their offspring's happiness and advancement, and the chance that the gift might be handed on to another generation. The death of John Gillies passed the burden of support to the women in the family, but at the same time, by another tribal tradition, made the recipient of their good will the head of the household. This responsibility, as the family's putative decision-maker and future breadwinner, seems to have been accepted willingly by Gillies, forged even closer family ties, and drew him into a new and important bond with his mother that was to last for another forty years.

In 1922, aged 23, Gillies gained his Diploma in Drawing and Painting and was awarded, on merit, a scholarship for a year of post-graduate study. This gave him a small bursary, studio facilities, and freedom from the constraints of a curriculum. He did not take it to mean, as many did, that the hard work was over; on the contrary, he mapped out for himself a busy schedule of study and experiment, dabbled with engraving and other print techniques, and of course practised drawing daily as if he were a singer at his scales or a dancer at the barre.

His first love was still landscape – for the challenge it represented to him as an artist and for the response the countryside stirred in him the moment a horizon opened its arms to him and his feet touched turf. Whenever he could he camped and sketched and, pad and pencil at the ready, investigated the environs of Edinburgh. His curiosity about the nature of paint, how it could seem to take on a life of its own, and his tentative experiments with form and line and texture are revealed in the still-lifes of his post-graduate year. The convenience of a college studio and the availability of friends willing to act as models encouraged his interest

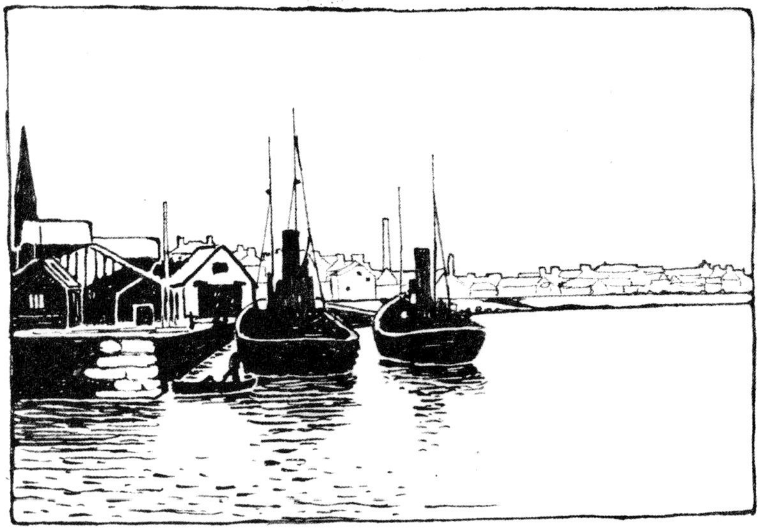

Anstruther 1915 ink on paper 8 × 12 cm RSA

in portraiture. I did not meet Peter Westwater, who was to become a distinguished portrait painter and critic, until thirty years after Gillies painted him in 1923 – and time had not been all that kind to that genial lover of life's extravagances – but the student portrait, as well as satisfying Alison's criteria for 'a guid heid,' pleases as a picture and cleverly caught essential characteristics of the man I came to know.

Gillies' precocious gift for portraiture – and even a degree of prescience in painting men who would go on to make their mark in the world – is most evident in the 1923 study of H. Harvey Wood. The high angle brings extraordinary focus to the sitter's warm, glancing eyes. Sharp planes accentuate the lean ascetic head of a sensitive, intelligent man who was responsible, more than anybody else, for the inauguration of the Edinburgh International Festival of Music and Drama in 1947.

The first post-war graduation from ECA, rich in mature ex-Service students who had begun to think of themselves as professional artists, produced the 1922 Group, a like-minded nine in number who banded together to mount their own annual exhibitions. Four Williams – Gillies, MacTaggart (not a diplomate, but an ECA student), Crozier and Geissler – were joined by George Wright Hall, George C. Watson, Arthur Couling, David Gunn and Alexander

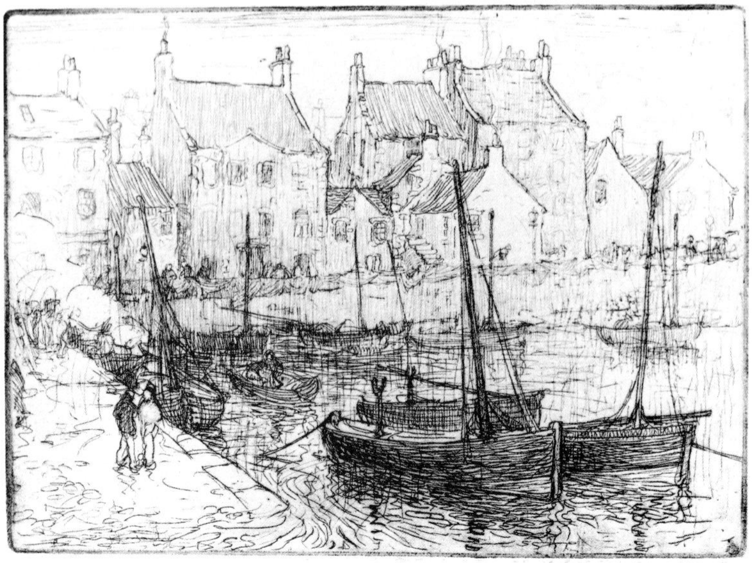

Newhaven Harbour 1922 etching 13 × 18 cm RSA

Graham Munro. They were all free, of course, to submit work to the annual shows of the RSA and SSA, but there was no guarantee that it would be hung. The group thought there was more chance of innovative work being seen and appreciated if they avoided the entrenched attitudes of selection committees. Between 1923 and 1928 the 1922 Group exhibited at the New Gallery, Shandwick Place, Edinburgh, and made a significant impact in a decade which saw a burgeoning of Scottish art.

Gillies told Elder Dickson that the only condition of 1922 Group membership was that the painters 'got on well together.' He enjoyed his role in it because 'it served a useful purpose in providing me with a motive for my intense concentration on painting. Besides, it was a salutary event for us all to be confronted with our work side by side with that of our fellow students – always a stimulating experience and a valuable spur to self-criticism.'

As evidence of his post-graduate year's industry at ECA, Gillies submitted a body of work which was accomplished enough to merit a 'highly commended' from the examining board and an enthusiastic citation from Morley Fletcher, the College Principal – 'Mr Gillies has a record of high distinction as a College student. He was first in his year, and in his subsequent work shows unusual promise as an artist.' The College backed its judgment with the award of a travelling scholarship to allow Gillies to study abroad.

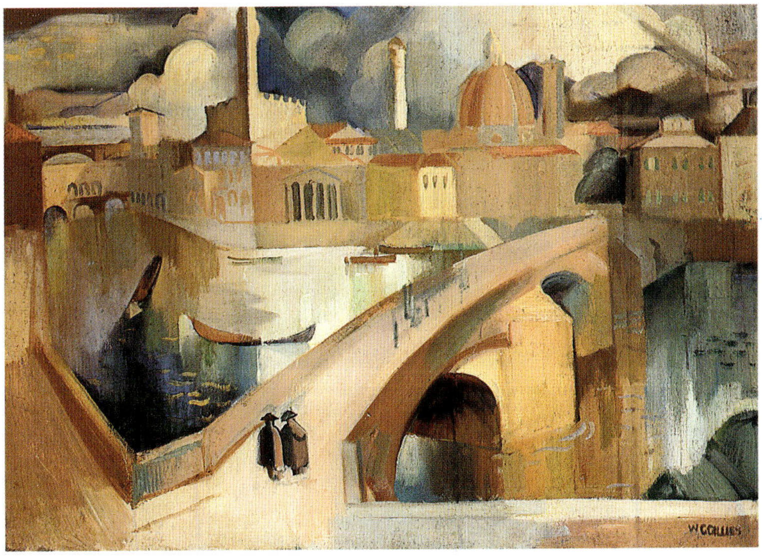

Florence 1924 oil on board 61 × 92 cm RSA

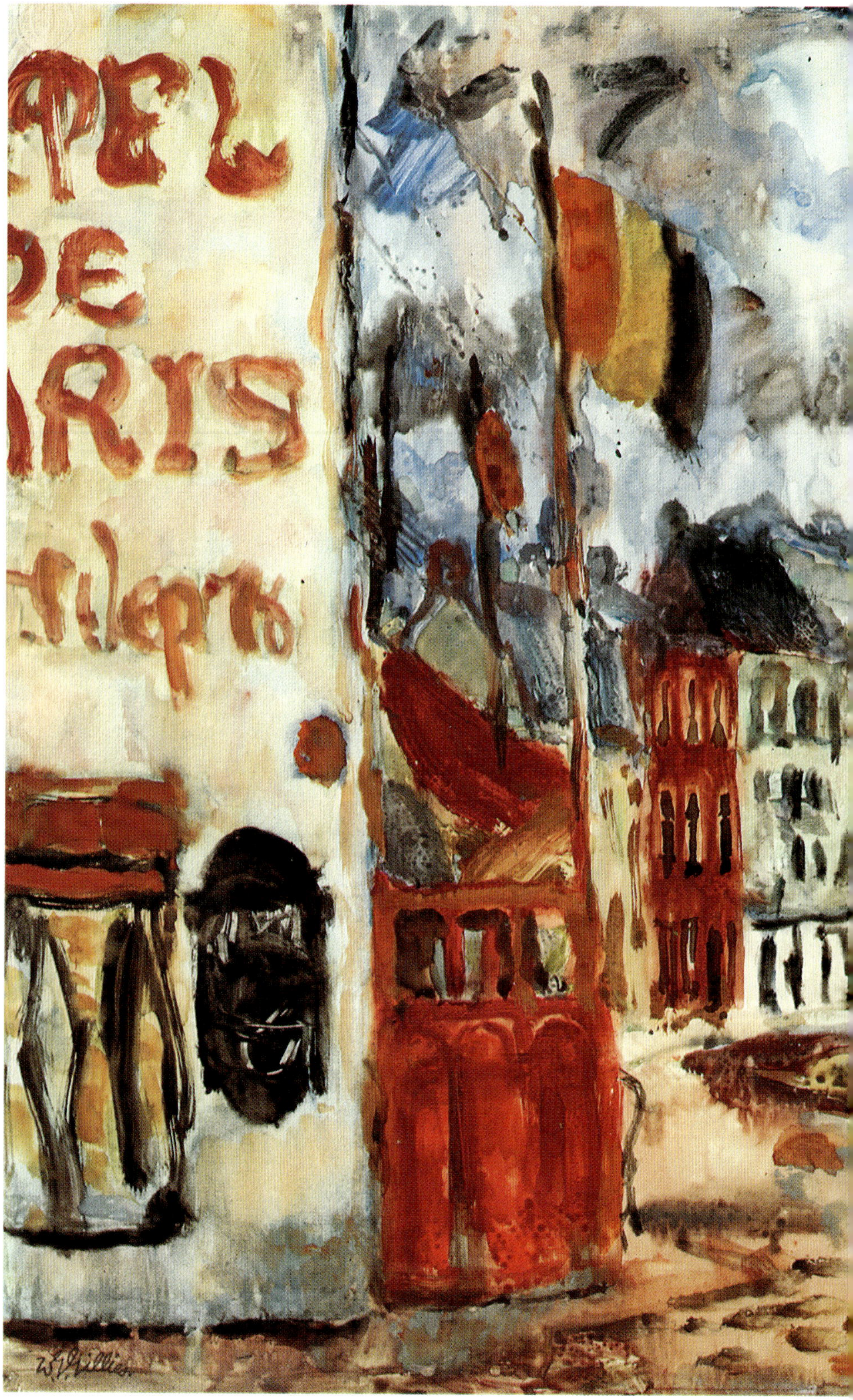

St Valery en Caux 1938 watercolour on paper 48 × 63 cm

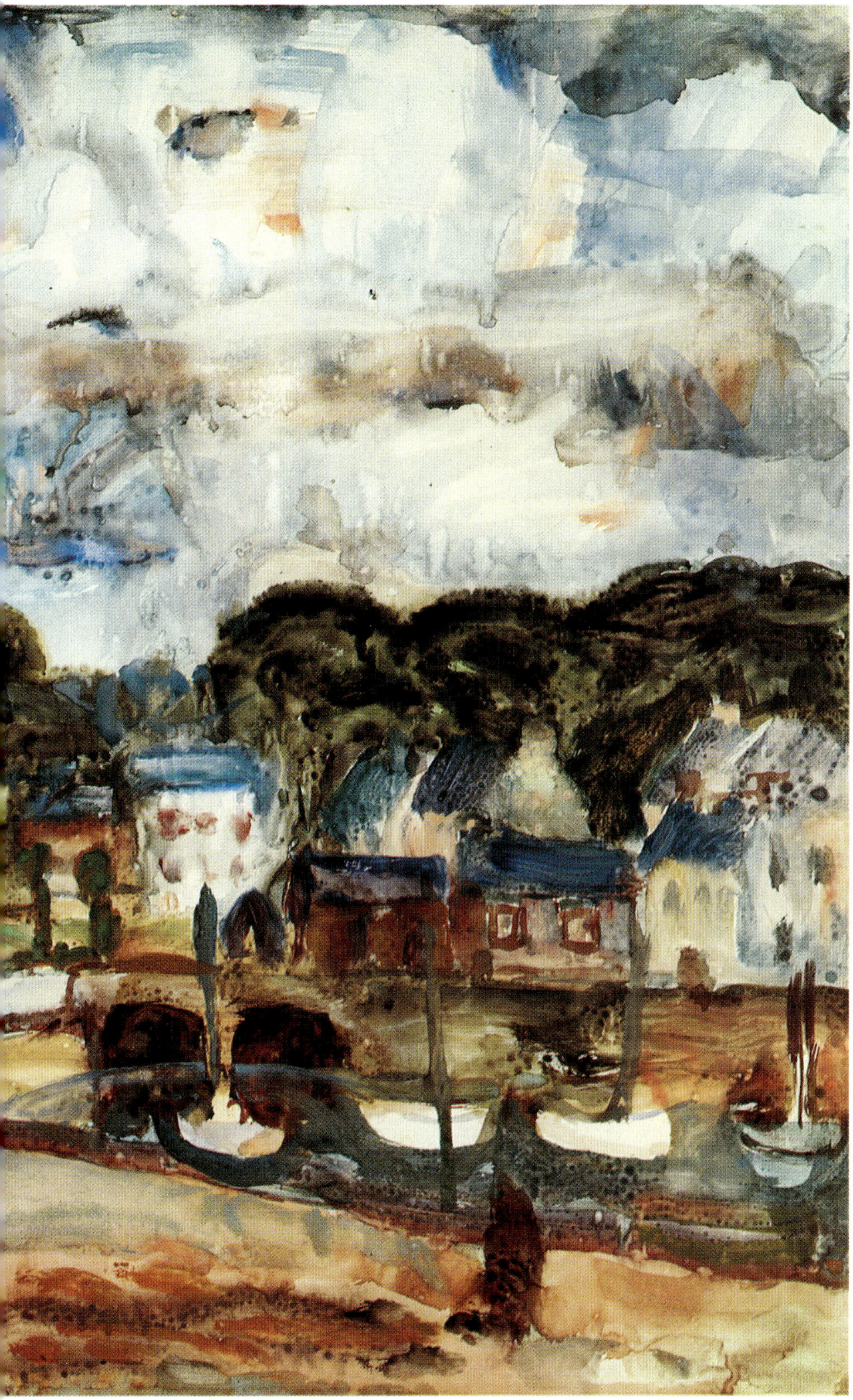

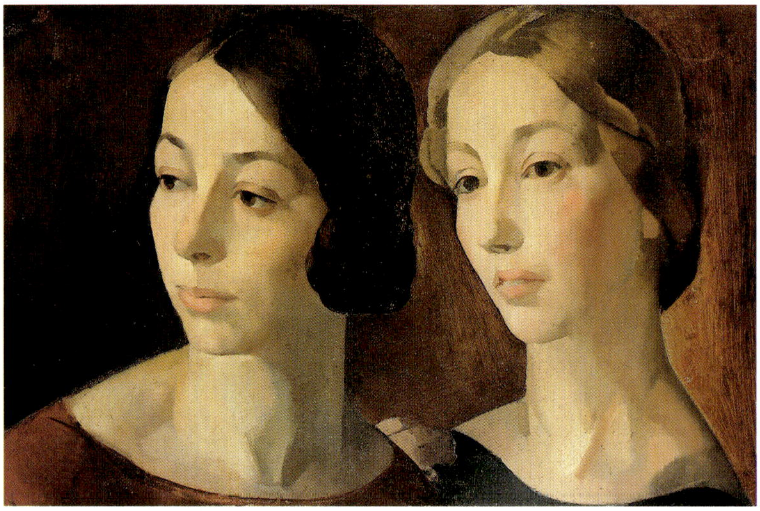

Sisters Emma and Janet c.1925 oil on board 33 × 36 cm RSA

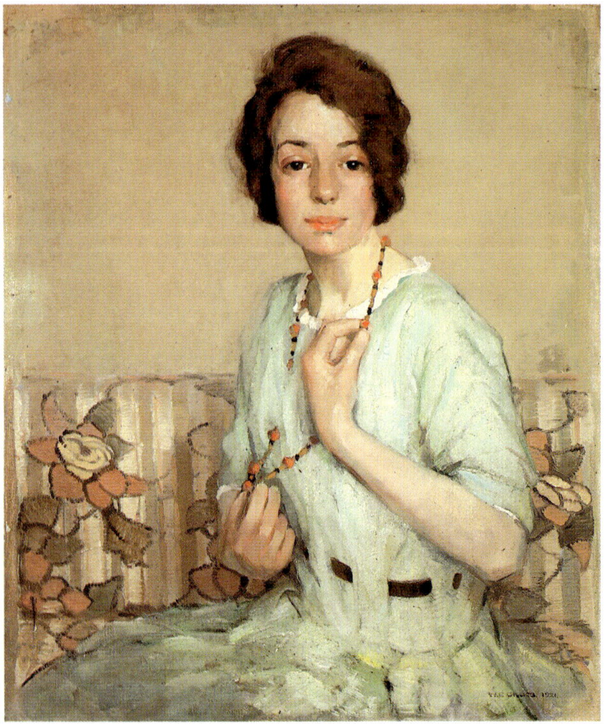

Portrait of Emma 1931 oil on canvas 61 × 51 cm

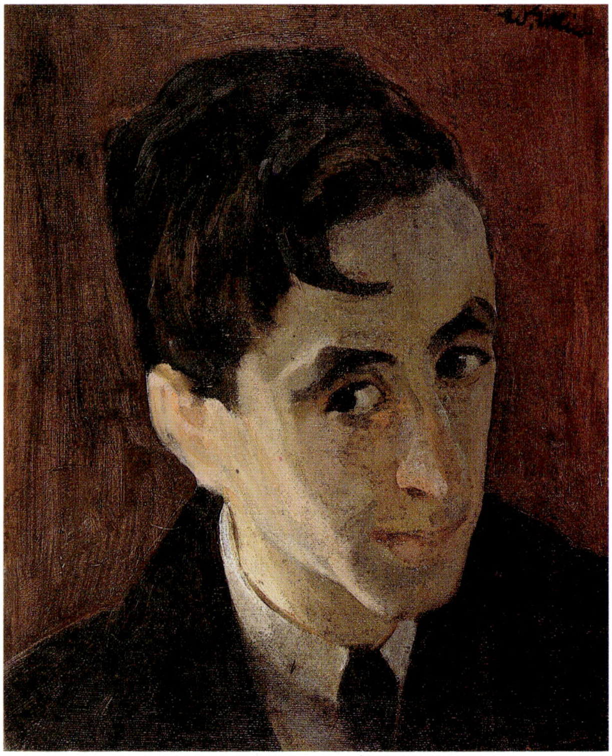

Portrait of H. Harvey Wood 1923 oil on board 38 × 28 cm RSA

Chapter 3

When Gillies and his fellow student William Geissler reached Paris in the autumn of 1923 to begin their study abroad, the chat in the boulevard cafés raged round Picasso's *Seated Woman*, Beckman's *The Trapeze*, and Utrillo's *Ivry Town Hall*. If Haddington seemed a long way away, David Alison's homilies on Titian and Rubens and Raeburn seemed like the Psalms of David.

At the instigation of the ECA Principal – Morley Fletcher had become enamoured of the Cubists – the two recipients of that year's travelling prize were persuaded to attend the newly-formed academy of André Lhote, a minor member of the Cubist school whose involvement in the famous 1912 Section d'Or exhibition guaranteed him a footnote to art history. By the time Gillies climbed the stairs to Lhote's *atelier*, the Frenchman's painting had become arid and academic, but he had earned widespread renown as a teacher and art commentator. The fact that Lhote taught Gillies in 1923 and had put many young Scottish painters through his studio when Jack Knox, the present Head of Drawing and Painting at Glasgow School of Art, studied in Paris in 1959, says much for his reputation and stamina.

Neither Gillies nor Knox set great store by anything they learned from Lhote. Gillies said the Paris experience had been a cruel disappointment. 'The hours of study were long and constant. We visited exhibitions at the weekend or went out sketching. That was all. We met no other French painter. What started off as appearing to be a new and exciting way of producing pictures, in the end turned out to be a dismal *cul-de-sac*. I did not long employ any of Lhote's principles in my paintings.'

The likely lads, honoured in their own country, found themselves in a familiar Scottish situation. Generations of lad-o'-pairts graduates, acknowledged prodigies and polymaths, sailed through Foreign Office examinations only to footer and fumble like gauche peasants at final interviews. And there they were, Edinburgh's chosen ones, transported to the Paris of the 20s, set down during that carefree decade in the crucible of the world's avant-garde art and music and literature. Buoyed up by the prospect of discovery, anxious to learn, hoping that they would find inspiration and encouragement, they got off to a squelching start. Lhote introduced himself by asking to see their portfolios – work that represented the best they could do, which had earned them their scholarships – then dismissed it, in an offhand and condescending manner, as 'accomplished but academic.' He made them feel provincial, inadequate and small.

What Gillies needed more than anything else at this time, after the constant grind of didactic instruction and technical exercise, was stimulus – a kick-start that would set his creative engine running. More importantly, he sought some method of aesthetic midwifery which would teach him how to feed the reality of what his eyes could see through the prism of his imagination. He realised that facility, training and dedication were not enough. That is why his complaint – 'we met no other French painter' – reiterated 40 years later, echoed a genuine despair. Lhote's remorseless scholarship merely exchanged one dull discipline for another. He had hoped that he would meet someone, a great teacher or fellow painter, who could help him throw off the chains of academic rigour and set imagination and creativity free. Lhote was not that man. His inflexible teaching methods constricted what they should have liberated. Yet Paris itself, city of painters, worked its own sympathetic magic on a young man who began to realise that what he was looking for was inside his own head.

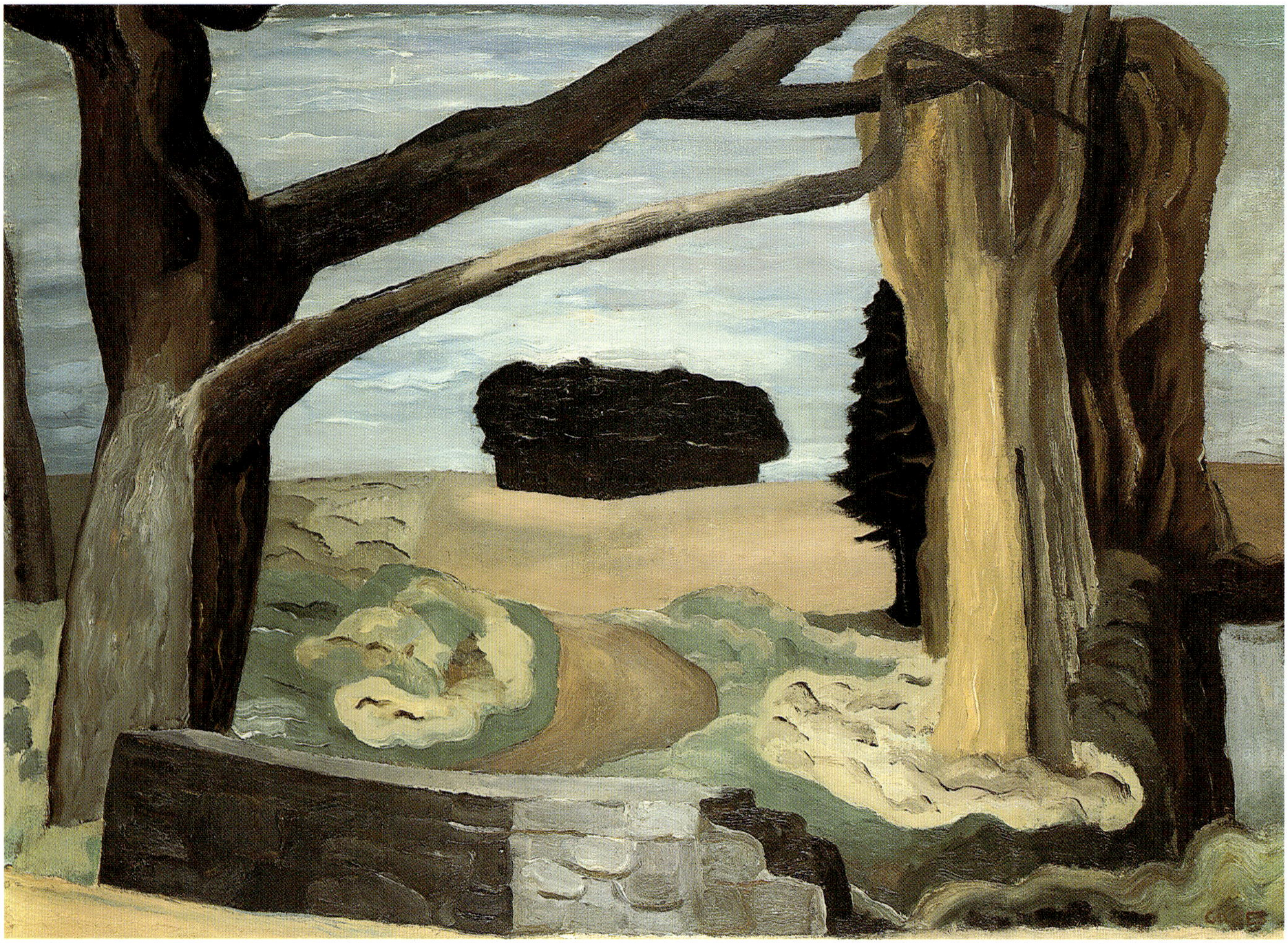

Trees and Coppice 1928 oil on canvas 89 × 124 cm

Up to that time he had seen few modern paintings, and pictorial reproduction in books and magazines, usually in monochrome, did the originals scant justice. The galleries of Paris – from the great state palaces of art to the plush salons of major European dealers – paraded the likes of Degas, Renoir, Pissarro, Gauguin, van Gogh, Picasso and Cézanne before his eyes. He also saw – probably for the first time – canvases by Bonnard, Vuillard, Braque and Derain, painters whose creative impetus and daring excited and stimulated him. What he learned from them and saw on the easels of young painters along the *rive gauche* turned keys in locks. They loosened his bonds and helped him to open a door on to his own vision of the world. Within a short time, and for the rest of his life, he borrowed from these French painters and any other source that galvanised his imagination and fortified his personal sense of freedom. It was as if he had taken Tennyson's *Ulysses* as his model:

I am a part of all that I have met;
Yet all experience is an arch wherethro'
Gleams that untravell'd world, whose margin fades
For ever and for ever when I move.

So, despite everything, despite the pedantic drudgery of Lhote's academy, he left Paris in the spring of 1924 with something stirred in his blood, an awakening of new sense and sensibility, and, despite his disappointments, a heightened awareness of art's problems but even firmer determination to overcome them. As Elder Dickson put it, 'the problem which exercised his mind, if only subconsciously, was how to reconcile the claims of visual perception and imaginative vision, technical skill and creative insight.'

Reporting back dutifully to ECA, Lhote said of his young Scottish charges:

> It gives me great pleasure to give you this information, because it is flattering to them and to their previous teachers. They have been following my courses with great application and subtle intelligence. They are both very gifted . . .the sort of students one dreams about, uniting sensitivity with intelligent comprehension, without which there is no art.

Although Gillies maintained throughout his life that his six months at Lhote's *atelier* had been disappointing, there is ample evidence that he absorbed more from the French Cubist than he was prepared to admit or even capable of realising. Harvey Wood, in his monograph *W. MacTaggart*, wrote: 'Although Lhote's influence on him [Gillies] was immediate and, for a time, considerable, it was not lasting . . . Actually, my recollection is that Gillies came back from Paris more excited about Derain than about Lhote, whose insistence on what he called "les constantes" must have been irksome to a natural and instinctive painter.'

At the end of March he left Paris for Italy. Truman Capote said that seeing Venice was like 'eating a box of chocolates all at once.' Gillies said it reminded him of Princes Street on a wet day. But the classical austerity of Florence – its sunny piazzas and shaded gardens, its gloomy churches emblazoned with frescoes and old gold, a city which proudly wears its unique art history on its sleeve – turned out to be a memorable visual adventure. He rejoiced, of course, in the glories of the quattrocento, but found a rare feast for his eyes in the work of the great innovators, like Duccio and Giotto, and other founders of the Tuscan visual language which paved the way for the Renaissance revolution.

There is a celebratory air – as well as the distinct presence of Lhote at his elbow – about his painting of Florence. Taking poetic liberties with the ancient city's topography and marshalling its monuments like a medieval woodcut, he kept faith with the natural colours of the region – raw and burnt siena with umber in the shadows – to produce a romantic exercise in decorative Cubism.

It is intriguing to compare the Florence oil of 1924 with his watercolour of East Linton, painted four years later, and to relate both paintings to the more overt Cubism of his friend William Crozier (1897-1930), who also studied under Lhote after training at ECA. Crozier enjoyed his time with Lhote and acknowledged its influence. The Tuscan landscapes which Crozier painted in 1930 and his celebrated *Edinburgh (from Salisbury Crags)*, painted in 1927 and now in the Scottish National Gallery of Modern Art, show how much he had assimilated Lhote's idiosyncratic attitudes to structured composition.

When Gillies returned to Scotland in the spring of 1924, his head teeming with exotic images, his heart even more firmly set on his vocation, he had to bring himself down with a bump and confront the stark reality that student days were over. He would have to find a job. By June he had given the names of the men at ECA who might speak up for him . . .

> He is possessed of very great ability and I have every confidence in recommending him as a Teacher of Art. He is an excellent draughtsman, is a good painter and has an excellent knowledge of colour. Briefly, he is a very exceptional student. *David Alison.*
>
> I formed a high opinion of his work. He was very conscientious, earnest and reliable in all he undertook. He is particularly suited for the position of art teacher for, in addition to his undoubted skill in art and a wide appreciation of it, he possesses considerable teaching ability. He has an easy and confident manner before classes, is quick in perception and readily understands the needs of his pupils. In my association with him I have every reason to depend upon him both as a man and as a teacher. *Adam B. Thomson.*

With those testimonials trumpeting his praises it was not surprising that Mr W.G.Gillies was appointed, on a year's probation, to the full-time post of art teacher at Inverness Academy, from 1 September, 1925. He found lodgings with a Miss Fraser and settled down, with characteristic diligence and enthusiasm, to do the job for which all the years of study had primarily trained him; the idea of becoming an established professional painter belonged to the fantasies of hope rather than expectation.

On the one hand, he was free now of all academic constraints and could paint to please only himself, to satisfy no other criterion but his own sense of achievement. On the other hand, such were the daily demands of the classrooom and his eagerness to fulfil his teaching obligations, that his painting time was restricted to those few weekends when he was not planning new work for his scholars, and during school holidays. By this time he had a small car – the first of many – and enjoyed nothing more than driving into the Highland landscape. He managed a few watercolours of which *Inverness*, painted early in 1925 and assembling a collage of local images in the Lhote manner, is a pleasing example.

A niece of Miss Fraser, his Inverness landlady, now owns two small oils of Anstruther harbour which Miss Fraser bought from him when he was 'a considerate and pleasant house guest.' Although early works, she feels they are representative of his style and 'typical Gillies' in their use of colour. She remembers her aunt telling her how Gillies brought his mother to his Inverness lodgings for short holidays, and how Mrs Gillies and Miss Fraser were taken by him for picnic drives in the country.

This demanding period in his life, which allowed him more time for reflective taking of stock than the execution of ideas, came to a happy and fortuitous end just before his probationary year at Inverness was due to finish. He was invited to return to his old college and take up a part-time lectureship in painting. He was going home – to Edinburgh and Haddington and the family who had made so many sacrifices for him, and to his old college, which would become another home and another family to him for the next 40 years.

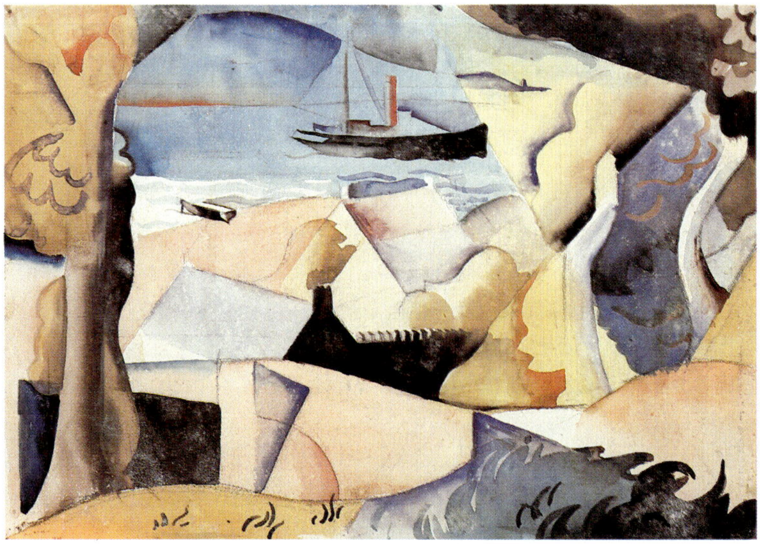

Inverness 1925 watercolour on paper 25 × 36 cm RSA

Chapter 4

David Alison had been Head of Drawing and Painting at ECA for eight years when he invited Gillies back to the college to join his teaching team. Trained at Glasgow School of Art, then at RSA Life Schools in Edinburgh, Alison's reputation as a painter had been well enough established by 1912 for him to become a founder member of The Society of Eight, which included the 'Glasgow Boys' James Patterson, John Lavery and Harrington Mann. The flamboyantly gifted F.C.B. Cadell had helped to initiate the society.

Backed up enthusiastically by the college's second Principal, the vivid watercolourist and mural painter Gerald Moira, and sensing that art education – the teaching of artists and the training of art teachers – deserved to play a significant role in post-war society, Alison set about building what Jack Firth describes as 'one of the most formidable teaching teams in Britain in a time of great fruitfulness.' He had inherited a gifted nucleus – from the veteran Henry Lintott to Gillies' three mentors Thomson, Sutherland and Moodie, all practitioners, all stylish draughtsmen. To them he added David Foggie, a disciple of Degas and Sickert and an inspirational teacher of drawing. In 1920 Penelope Beaton returned to her old college to spend a legendary professional lifetime discerning and nurturing young talent. Gillies often acknowledged how much he had learned from life classes conducted by Walter Grieve, a commercial art adviser and distinguished Academician. To these strengths Alison added the specialist gifts and knowledge of experts in illustration, printmaking, animal studies, and Celtic art, and – over the period that led up to the Second World War – a procession of outstanding part-time tutors, from MacTaggart to Geissler, Maxwell to Westwater, and even Peploe for a short time in the 30s.

Paradoxically, in the face of all this enlightenment, hidebound tradition continued to stultify and frustrate, protest that nothing of merit had been painted since the end of the nineteenth-century, and at times give the impression that the college was the last bastion of Philistinism.

For instance, Harvey Wood, in his MacTaggart monograph, measured the distance which separated David Foggie's view of painting and MacTaggart's. The young MacTaggart, excited by the revolution in France, declared that nothing in art would be the same again after the achievement and example of Cézanne. Foggie, an avid classicist whose only concession to Modernism was to admire Degas as a draughtsman and delicate colourist, poured scorn on Cézanne and his followers: 'Cézanne? The fellow can't draw.'

While admiring Alison's unswerving dedication to the academic craft of painting, Harvey Wood had a broader view of culture and knew that what was happening to painting in France was only part of a volcanic upheaval in all the arts. As an inquisitive student he tried to keep pace with the developments in music and drama.

'I used to find the fifteen-minute intervals of rest between poses a bit of a waste of time, and once found myself challenged by Alison at the door of the life-painting class. I had a book under my arm, and Alison's beard bristled as he challenged me about it. "What's the idea of the book, Wood?" I told him that I would be able to give him a better idea of it when I had read a little more of it; that it was a book of plays; and that I proposed, if he had no objection, to read it while the model was resting. He growled unhappily, then allowed me to pass, but not without saying, like a severe but wise father, "Ye'll find as ye grow older, Wood, that an Artist Has No Time For Books."'

Ten years later Alison was still sticking to his guns when a group of students returned from a study-trip to the London galleries and reported back to him. Jack Firth recalls Alison asking,

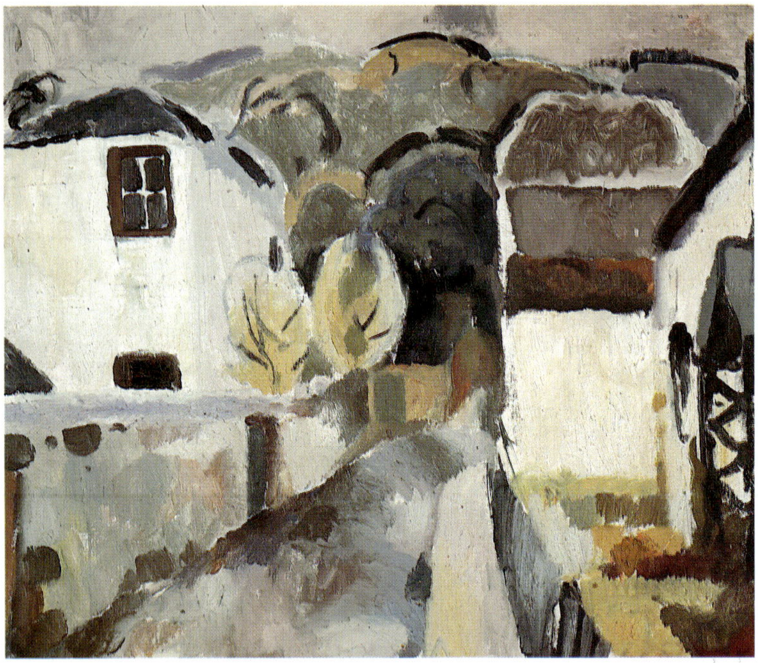

Duddingston 1929 oil on canvas 70 × 81 cm RSA

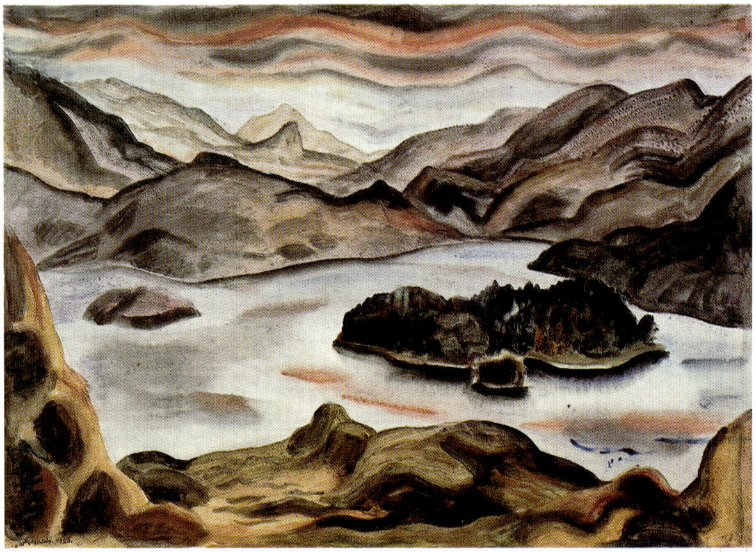

Loch Morar 1928 watercolour on paper 42 × 61 RSA

'Well, how'd ye get on? Whit paintings did ye see, eh?' Someone mentioned Titian's *Bacchus and Ariadne* in the National Gallery. Alison was delighted. 'Och, aye, Titian . . . Guid heid painter.'

However, the breadth and depth of ECA's catholic attitude to art education can be gauged by summoning the name Charlie Howieson to the staff roll of honour. You will not find Mr Howieson in any membership list of Scotland's artistic societies. Yet he presided over the School of Housepainting and Decorating, which used to be located in the College, and this fierce wee martinet played a key role in Alison's emphasis on the need for craftsmanship in art. No-one who learned to prime a canvas or panel under his instruction forgot his disciplines or ever saw their paint flake. Jack Firth believes that Howieson regarded art students 'as effete, and an interruption to the imparting of wisdom to his painting apprentices on day-release, but he was a very good, if abrasive, teacher.' Firth also remembers Max Doerner's *Materials of the Artist* being dinned into him by Peter Westwater, 'but we were none the worse for that, either.'

In 1926 Scotland's capital was beginning to burst at the seams. Speculative builders fanned out into green fields and sprouted a brick suburbia. Trams clattered through cobbled streets and when an East Coast haar mingled with the sulphurous soot of the city's chimneys 'Auld Reekie' lived up to its ancient soubriquet. Some of the slum conditions surrounding the art college, standing with its back to the Castle Rock and confronting the Braid Hills, were as shameful as anything in Europe. Militant Protestantism provoked ugly anti-Papist riots. Yet the optimism and gaiety of that happy-go-lucky decade prevailed. The phenomenon of the cinema was soon to find its voice and peddle the fantasies of the Hollywood dream factory, but that year Jean Renoir made the most of the magic black-and-white flicker with *Nana* and Ramon Navarro hurtled into history in *Ben Hur*. In dance halls you could buy a partner for the afternoon – and longer by financial arrangement. The new British Broadcasting Corporation had just received its Royal Charter; its transmission of classical and popular music, poetry and the drama of the spoken word was already changing the cultural tastes of the nation. Elsewhere, Chagall painted *Lovers' Bouquet*, Augustus John finished his portrait of Lady Ottoline Morrell, A.A. Milne wrote *Winnie the Pooh*, T.E. Lawrence his *Seven Pillars of Wisdom*. and Sean O'Casey's new play *The Plough and the Stars* caused a riot in Dublin. Meanwhile, up a stair in Soho, John Logie Baird demonstrated his miracle of television for the first time.

Gillies was back with friends, secure in an ambience he loved, settled again with his family, and doing the only thing in the world he ever wanted to do – draw, paint, and teach others to do both. From the beginning, he seems to have been sure of himself as a teacher, believing in carrots rather than sticks, an enthusiastic nudger and coaxer, and an exponent of that system of kindly encouragement which praises the merit of the particular in order to expose flaws in the general. It was a method he perfected over the years. Like Wordsworth he urged:

> Come forth into the light of things,
> Let Nature be your teacher.

And this canny innovator was already the living contradiction of Shaw's maxim for revolutionaries, 'He who can, does. He who cannot, teaches.' Like many other artists, Gillies actually enjoyed teaching, valued the contact with people younger than himself, and found that the constant expectation of analysis and criticism sharpened his perceptions and honed his own disciplines. He did not become embroiled in the arguments that raged among

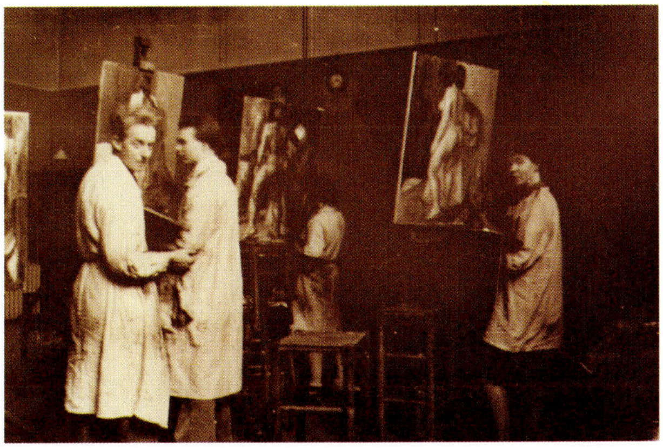

Early Teaching Days – A Life Class Taught by the Artist
(Photo: RSA Archives)

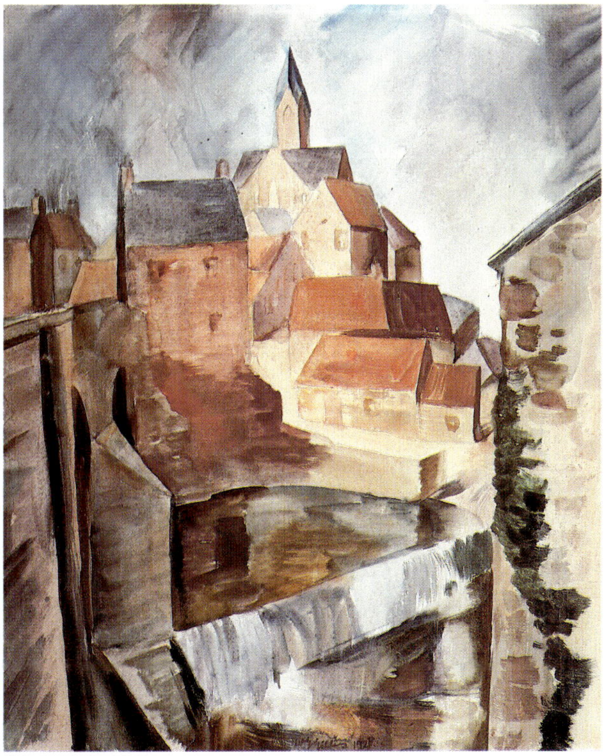

East Linton 1928 watercolour on paper 50 × 40 cm RSA

staff and students about art and life. He kept what he would have called 'a calm souch' – a quiet counsel – preferring to observe, listen, absorb, think.

All round him – on street corners, in newspapers, at his elbow every day – social, political and artistic stirrings had begun to awaken Scotland from a long slumber. The Saltire was being unfurled in the name of nationalism. Socialism marched the streets to put an end to poverty and exploitation. A Scottish Renaissance movement led by Hugh MacDiarmid sought to drive Scotland's literature out of the kailyaird. While the rest of the world danced the Charleston, Scots began to take their first faltering steps on the road towards a new national identity. Gillies felt no need to march or wave banners to proclaim his Scottishness or demonstrate his allegiance to these causes. He felt as deeply Scottish as the French peasant feels he is French, and never more so than when he was rubbing the earth of his country through his fingers or sketching, like a caress, the contour of a Lowland hillside. 'I've not yet painted a good picture abroad,' he said much later in life, more as evidence of his love of Scotland than any antipathy to foreign parts. He knew he could paint what he saw of his land and its character, was still trying to learn how to paint what he felt about it, and wanted to join the new Makars in singing his own songs in its praise.

If his painting output during the remainder of the 20s was not as prodigious as in the four decades that followed, it was hardly surprising. He was still taking stock of himself as an artist, still trying to get Lhote's Cubism out of his system. By the time he commuted back and forth from Haddington, coped with the anxieties of his new job, then settled into his new, head-of-the-household relationship with his mother and sisters, what he put down on paper and canvas was as much as he could manage.

Mrs Gillies was a remarkable woman by any standards. She would qualify as an archetype of the traditional Scottish mother – self-effacing and self-denying, kindly, properly proud,

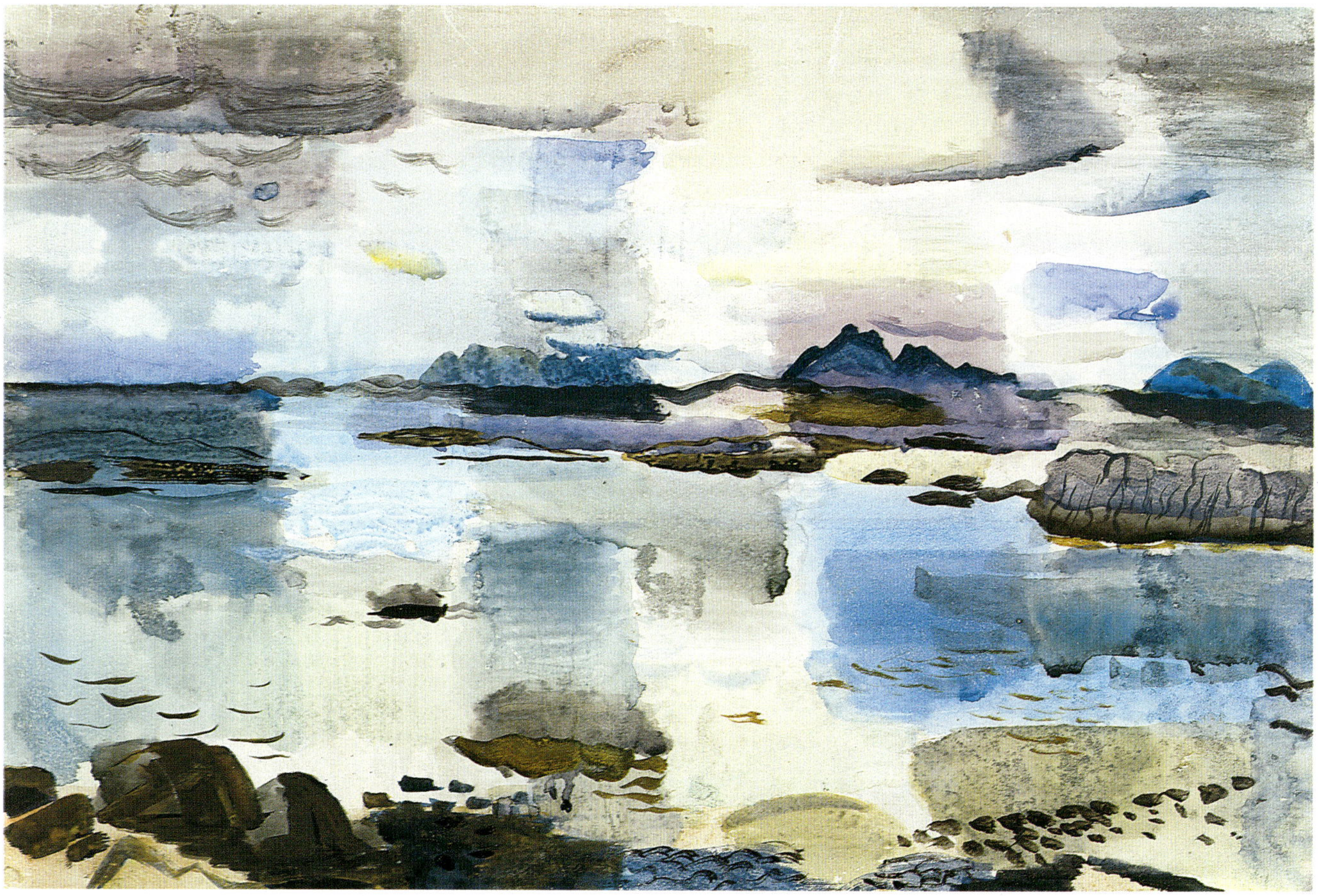

Skye Hills from near Morar 1931 watercolour on paper 38 × 56 cm SNGMA

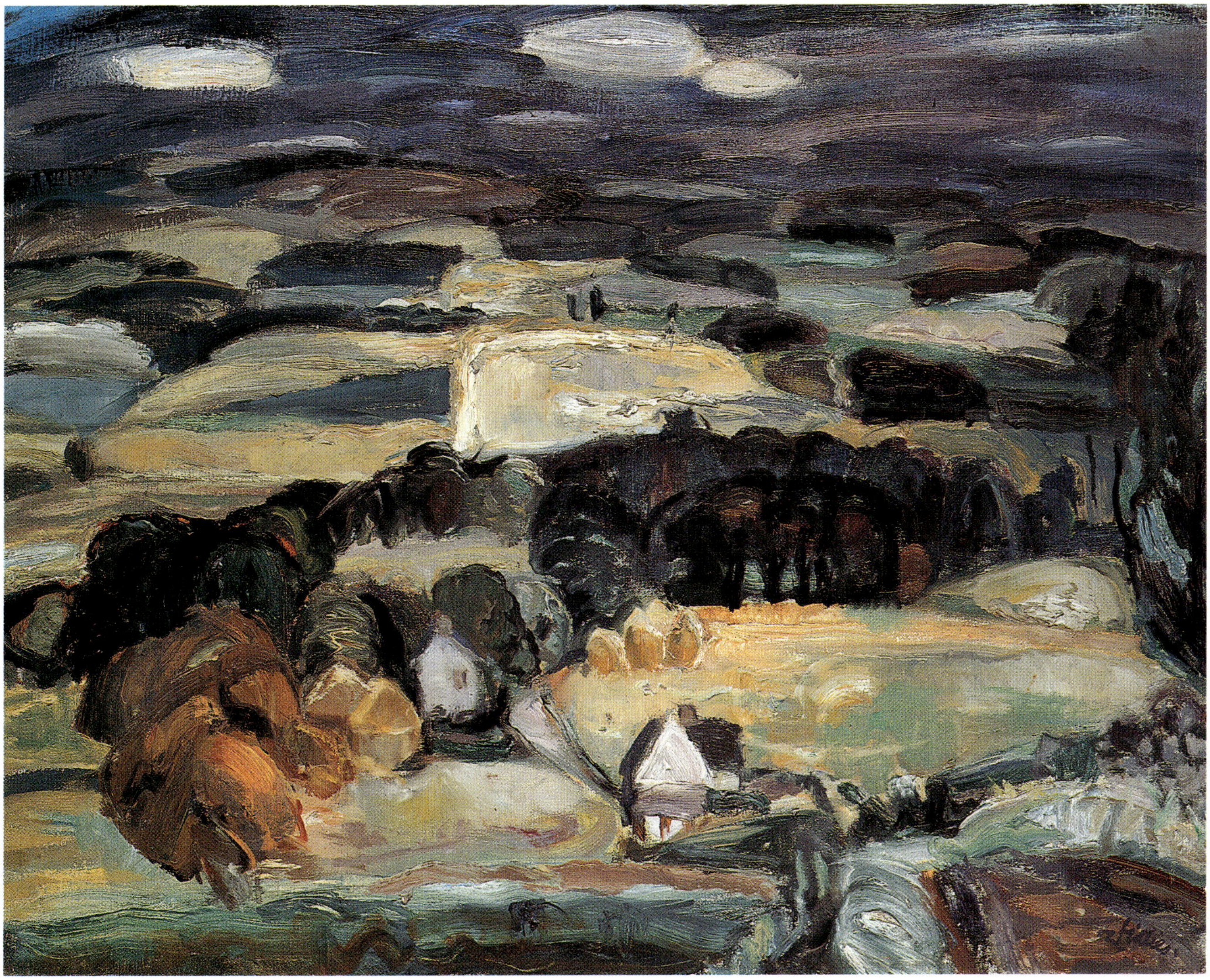

Borders Landscape 1932 oil on canvas 61 × 75 cm EDC

fiercely independent, dutiful and respectable – were it not for qualities which made her exceptional. A strange and affecting grace lay behind her mental and physical liveliness. This serenity – the capacity to live happily with oneself – as well as her sense of order and responsibility, her mischievous sense of humour, her thrift, energy and industry were all virtues she shared with her son. They enjoyed a trusting, intuitively considerate adult relationship which not only survived but blossomed over 40 happy years. When I met her, only a few years before she died, her extreme age neither concealed nor diminished her essential vivacity. Jenny, his older sister, was every inch her mother's helper and companion. Emma had artistic aspirations. After the family moved from Haddington to Edinburgh in 1928 she studied pottery at ECA for three years. Gillies' portrait of his sisters, dated circa 1925, was probably painted very soon after he returned from Inverness, perhaps as an intimate celebration of his homecoming. He neither shirks nor exploits sentiment. It is an affectionate study: Emma (in her mid-twenties) on the left, Jenny (nearer 30) on the right, two demure young women, conventionally pretty yet sensitive and sisterly – particularly in the dark penetration of their eyes. Retained all his life in his private collection, it is a picture which, over and above profound filial resonances, must have given him great pleasure.

The move to Edinburgh – to a bungalow in Willowbrae Road – was a matter of convenience. Gillies' part-time post had been made permanent, Emma wanted to give up the shop and study in the city, and Jenny was now working for a firm of Edinburgh solicitors. An ex-Army hut at the bottom of the garden served him as a makeshift studio.

The semblance of a social life opened out to him. He had the capacity to make friends easily, just so long as friendship made few demands on him. He enjoyed the company of other painters and they found him a convivial, humourous and loyal companion, unaffected and curiously wise for his years, but readier to go on a picnic into the countryside with them or share a cup of tea and a bun than racket round the town on drinking sprees.

By this time he had become deeply entangled in what was to become a lifelong love affair with the still new-fangled internal combustion engine. In 1935 the street where I lived as a boy on the other side of Edinburgh boasted only two motor cars in its half-mile of bungalows, so Gillies' 1928 jalopy, of unrecollected marque or vintage, was probably the only vehicle parked in Willowbrae Road. Motor cars – and later, more thrillingly, a succession of motor cycles – satisfied some compulsive urge in him and were his only material extravagance.

Apart from getting him to work three days a week and taking the family for runs in the country the car became the regular camping waggon for Gillies and his friends. There is no obvious location for *Trees and Coppice*, painted in 1928, but the elements of this broody, Derain-inspired collage of images were probably sketched in the countryside on one of the many weekends or half-term holidays spent in the open air, then worked up in oil in the studio hut. It is an uneasy picture, brash as a piece of stage scenery, curiously composed and coarse in its brushwork. He seems to be making a conscious effort to wrest himself from the harsh planes and splintered forms of Cubism. The first sense of escape, as spectacular as anything Houdini might have staged to a roll of drums, is accomplished with dashing flair in *Loch Morar*, a delightfully free and rhythmic watercolour painted the same year. As if to celebrate his taste of freedom – and perhaps pay homage to Utrillo or Vlaminck in the passing – his village scene *Duddingston* (1929) has spontaneity, sonority and affectionate warmth beyond bleak blues and greys. It would be some years yet before Gillies could banish all trace of Lhote's sterile indoctrination in Paris, but *Duddingston* signals optimism and is early evidence of the man's painterly aplomb and capacity to cast spells.

The Times didn't exactly thunder its praises when Gillies' work was seen for the first time in London.

> As is usual with English – and still more Scottish – painters who sit at the feet of the Frenchmen, his difficulty is to tame his colour sufficiently for the formal scheme. Every now and then it 'erupts.'

The reviewer credited him, however, with 'intelligently adapting Continental principles of design to the native impulse.'

Whatever the London critic meant by 'the native impulse' – and modern Scots might be more likely to read into it a typically patronising metropolitan attitude – Gillies probably accepted it as a complimentary and accurate description of the force that drove him to paint. By the end of the decade a cheerful friendship with John Maxwell (1905-1962) which began at ECA – when Maxwell's first year overlapped with Gillies' last – had developed into a mutually happy and rewarding bond between brother artists. Johnnie Maxwell, an iconoclast and visionary with extrovert personality, came from Dalbeattie in Kircudbrightshire. In 1929 Maxwell took Gillies on their first painting trip together to his home in this low-lying landscape, shelving down to the Solway Firth and offering up its broad flanks to fretful skies. This, too, was Gillies country, criss-crossed by drystane dykes and hearty fields, punctuated by copsy knolls and upstart steadings and roads that flew like arrows to the sea. *Near Kirkcudbright*, a bright watercolour accented by pencil, marked the end of a decade, the start of his mature life as a painter and, before very long, his reputation as the *enfant terrible* of Scottish painting.

Chapter 5

The first major event to change Gillies' life in the 30s came with the death of his friend and fellow product of the Lhote academy, William Crozier. A haemophiliac, Crozier fell in his studio and bled to death, aged 33. He had shared the painting space at 45 Frederick Street, Edinburgh, with William MacTaggart, and his tragic demise offered Gillies the opportunity to quit the garden hut and work in congenial professional surroundings alongside his fellow-founder member of the 1922 Group.

In 1930, when Gillies moved in, 45 Frederick Street was a lively artistic oasis in the centre of Edinburgh's douce and respectable New Town. Two women artists, Agnes Falconer and Lily McDougall, worked in adjacent studios and their friendship and informed criticism encouraged many young painters. They were particularly fond of Willie Gillies. Falconer trained at ECA, painted landscapes and flowers, and became a popular lecturer to organised parties of children at the National Gallery of Scotland. McDougall had an extraordinary pedigree at a time when 'lady painters' were supposed to be only gifted amateurs. Born in Glasgow in 1875, she trained at Edinburgh, The Hague, Antwerp and Paris, exhibited her flower paintings and still-lifes at the RSA from 1900 on, and was a founder member of the Scottish Society of Women Artists, an early feminist cause which was instigated by her father, Robert McDougall.

Lily McDougall's house at Eskbank, beyond Dalkeith to the south of Edinburgh, looked out over the road to Temple, the Midlothian hamlet where Gillies lived for the last 30 years of his life. When she wanted Willie to call in and see her she hung a special tablecloth in an upstairs oriel window so that he would see it on his way home. She had her first London solo show at the age of 72. The Scottish Gallery mounted her last exhibition in 1955, when she was 80.

The social highlight of every week for Gillies and Maxwell was their Sunday supper soirées at the Morningside home of Dr Frederick Porter and his wife Annie, a sister of S.J. Peploe. A general practitioner and enthusiastic 'Sunday painter,' Porter collected pictures and books and ranged his erudite mind over most of the arts. Maxwell enlivened their discussions with his infectious enthusiasm for music and poetry. Gillies talked only of painting and its problems, listened intently to everything else, and shrugged off jokes about the unreliability of the motor car which he 'somehow contrived to keep running' and teases about his appetite for food and wine.

The close personal relationship between Gillies and Maxwell took some of its strength from the attraction of opposites. Different temperaments, different curiosities, different enthusiasms induced a warm compatability that not only survived but seemed to thrive on their diverging attitudes to painting, work rate, subject matter, style and technique. Gillies, who admitted that it took him half a day to compose a formal letter and had only a rum-te-tum acquaintance with a few tunes, stood in awe of Maxwell's articulate literacy, his passion for poetry, his emotional and mathematical response to music. But Maxwell envied Gillies' amazing facility and energy and admired the way these forces were being yoked together to serve a creative intelligence which could adequately express itself only in paint.

Maxwell had also studied in Paris, but under Lèger and Ozenfat at the Academie Moderne, and had been drawn into the world of French Symbolist art through the work and teachings of Odilon Redon and the vibrant canvases of Chagall. These influences acted like a drug on his creative imagination and stimulated him towards deserting the landscape of the real world

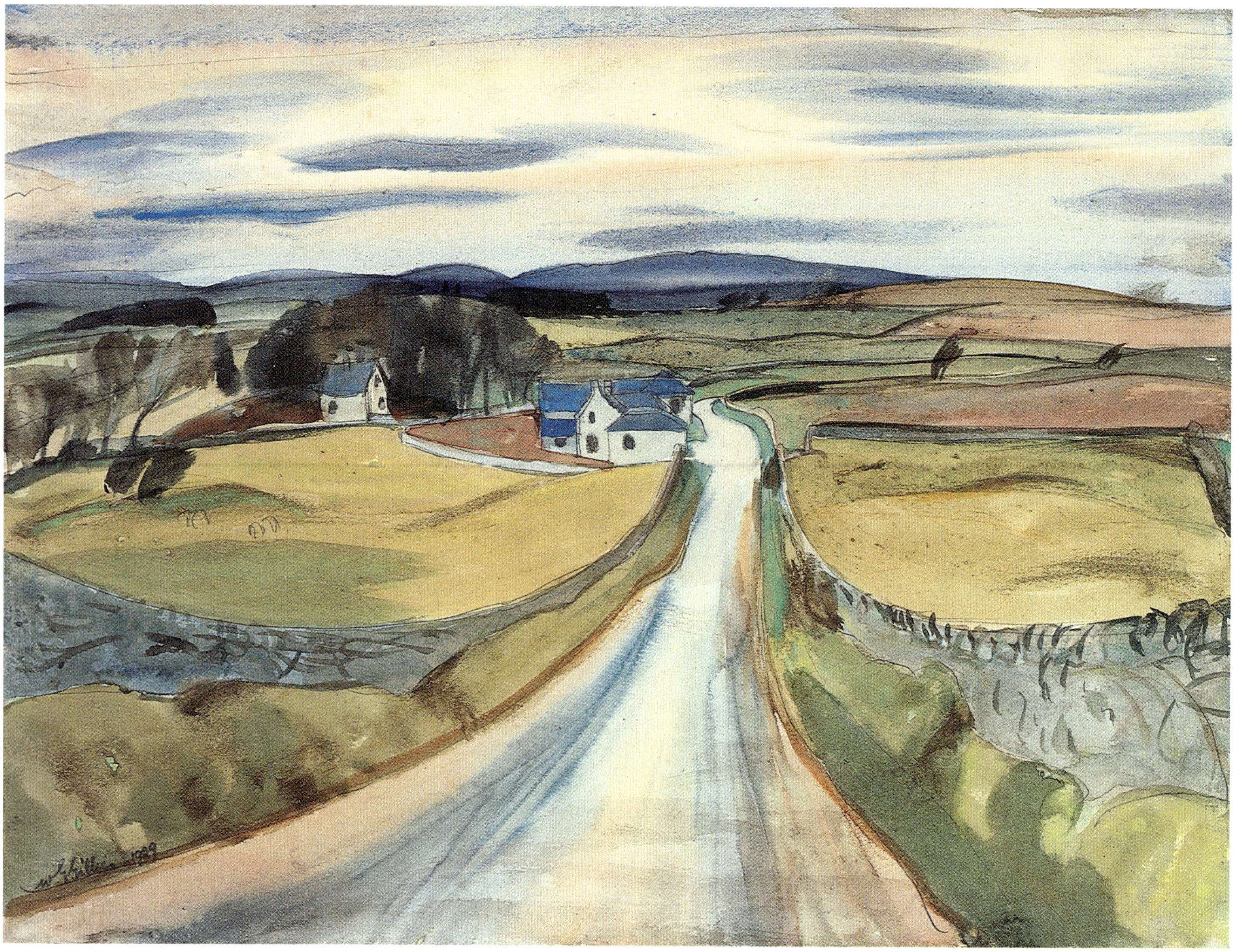

Near Kirkcudbright 1929 watercolour and pencil on paper 27 × 35 cm SNGMA

and inventing his own – a world with its own mythology and flora and fauna, its own runes and tunes and rhythms, the product of a poetic vision which remains unparalleled in Scottish painting.

Meanwhile, Gillies seemingly content with what caught his eye, recorded what he saw, more or less, and remained faithful enough to the original for the casual observer to accept it as a likeness. But, consciously or not, he was following the great dictum of Redon, one of Maxwell's masters, to put 'the logic of the visible world at the service of the invisible.' Gillies made few attempts to explain how he tried to match what he saw against the responses of his own mind. It is doubtful, given his lack of pretension and distrust of words, if he could have done. Redon, in many senses, said it for him:

> My most fruitful way of working, the most important in my development, has been to make a direct copy from nature, carefully reproducing objects with all that is most minute, special and random about them. After trying to make an exact drawing of a pebble, leaf, human hand or any other living or inorganic object I begin to feel a mental seething; I need to create, to let my imagination run riot.

As time went on and they developed their independent, intensely personal styles, Maxwell and Gillies also learned how to move away from romantic realism towards a more ambiguous, suggestive mode of expression – what Redon called 'living within the realm of the equivocal, the realm of two- and three-fold appearance, or the shadow of appearance.'

A controversial event of 1931, the first British exhibition of work by the Norwegian precursor of Expressionism, the tortured genius Edvard Munch, amazed the populace and shook Gillies to the marrow of his bones. Here was 'the shadow of experience' cast long and painfully. The SSA invited the exhibition as part of its policy to stimulate the development of Scottish painting by featuring in its annual show the work of significant foreign artists. More than a dozen Munch landscapes were brought to Edinburgh by a Norwegian critic and writer on fine art, Fanny Aavatsmark, who later married William MacTaggart.

Elder Dickson quoted Gillies as saying that he had never seen so much emotion compressed and contained in paintings. He returned to the exhibition many times to be astounded again, thrown off balance, his senses confused and baffled.

> He was quite unprepared for this startling confrontation . . . Everything he had seen before now seemed tame and spineless . . . Here was painting which seemed to spring from the very roots of human passion and experience . . . Its form and colour were tense and explosive. It was also disturbing, combining poignant tenderness with agonising anxiety and fear.

There was another jolt the following year. The 1922 Group had held its last show in 1928. Gillies missed its easy camaraderie and its democratic freedom from the lottery of

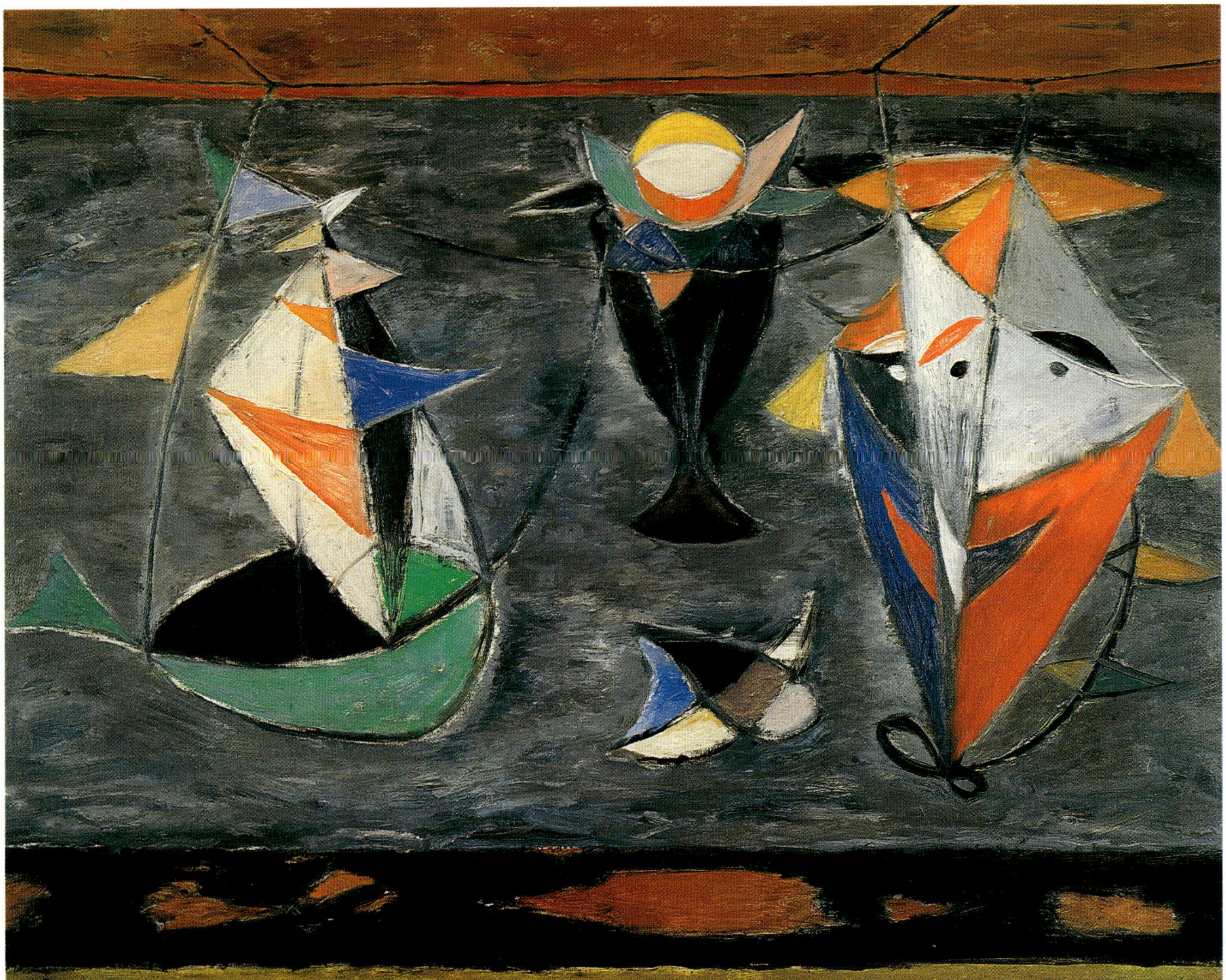

Still-life with Toy Boat and Kite c.1935/36 oil on canvas 76 × 94 cm RSA

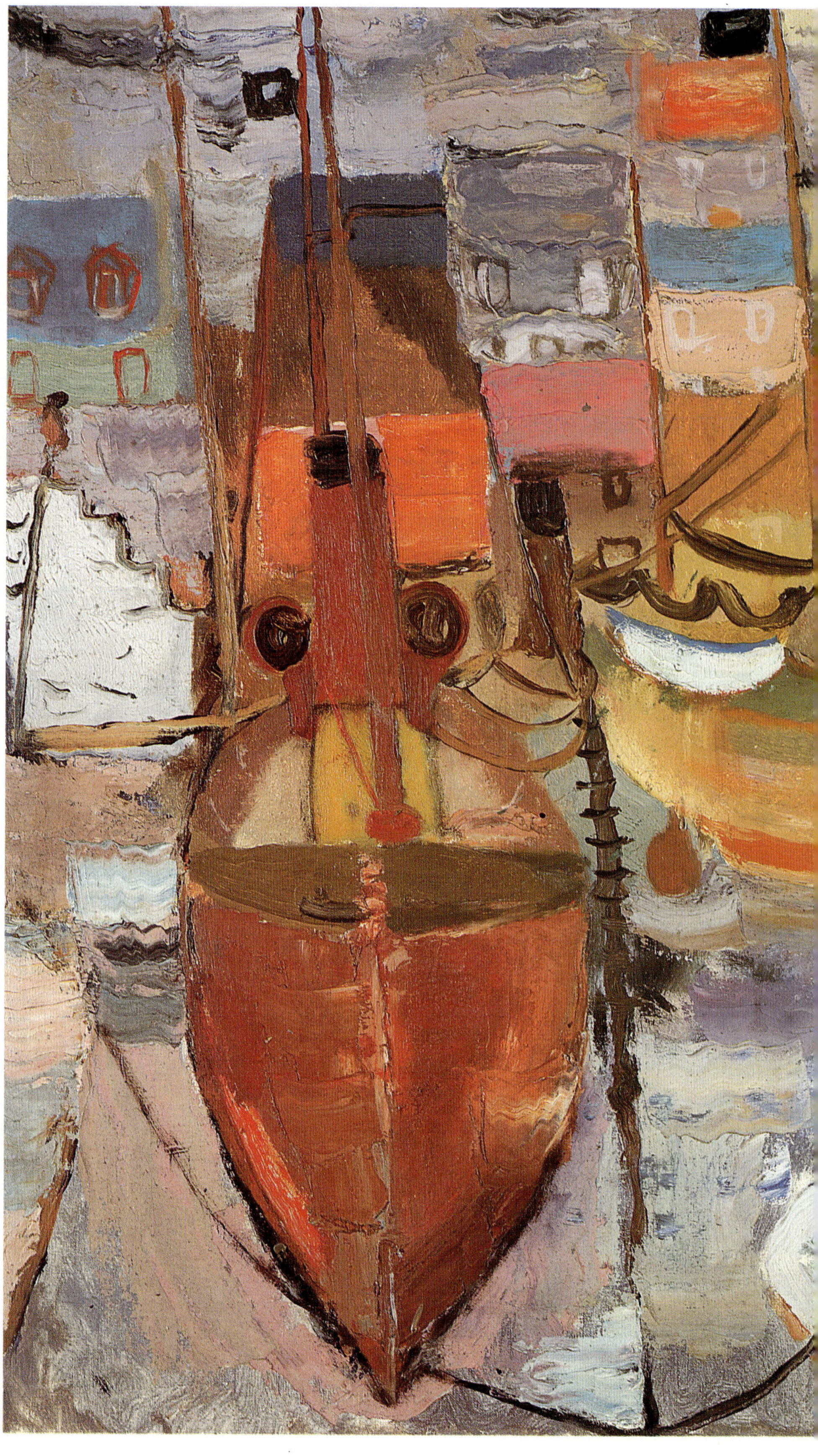

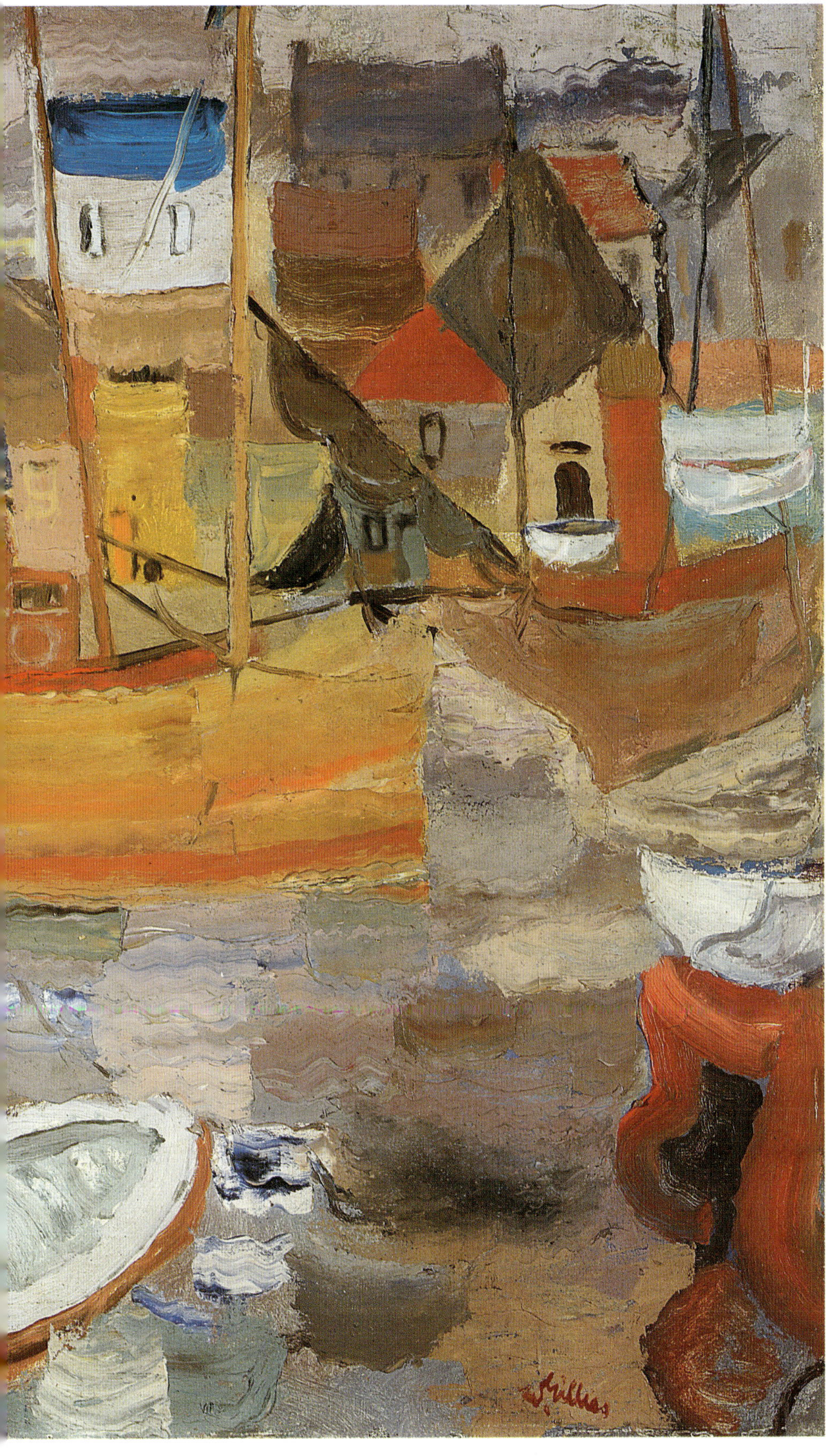

The Harbour c.1938 oil on canvas 77 × 92 cm SNGMA

submitting pictures to the committees who sat in judgment for RSA and SSA exhibitions. Nothing that had been said in the interval prepared him, however, for one of the most pleasant surprises of his life. In 1932, while still only 33, he was invited to join Sir James Guthrie, Sir John Lavery, Cadell, Alison, Lintott, John Duncan and MacTaggart as a member of the exclusive and celebrated Society of Eight. New members of the club could be elected only as the result of a resignation or death. The news came as a happy shock to Gillies. It was apparently an astonishment to others. 'Why on earth did you elect that fellow?' someone asked Cadell. 'Well,' replied Gillies' proposer for membership, 'seven of us thought he was the right man.' Peploe was Gillies' other sponsor.

The Society's annual exhibitions – lit by gas in Scottish winters – had earned a reputation for the highest professional standards and a liberal, progressive outlook. Each member could submit upwards of a dozen paintings – 20 was not uncommon – and took it in turns to hang their work on the most favourable wall of the New Gallery. When it was wound up in 1938 the Society had enhanced Scottish artistic life for 26 years and reflected the best in Scottish painting, from 'Glasgow Boys' Lavery, Mann, Paterson, Guthrie and MacGregor to the 'Colourists' Cadell and Peploe and the next generation, MacTaggart and Gillies.

The shock of the Munch exhibition showed up in some of the paintings that began to flow from Gillies' brushes. Its effect on his manipulation of paint and palette was dynamic. It was almost as if he heard harmony and counterpoint and the threnody of the minor key for the first time. He made no attempt to plumb the profound depths

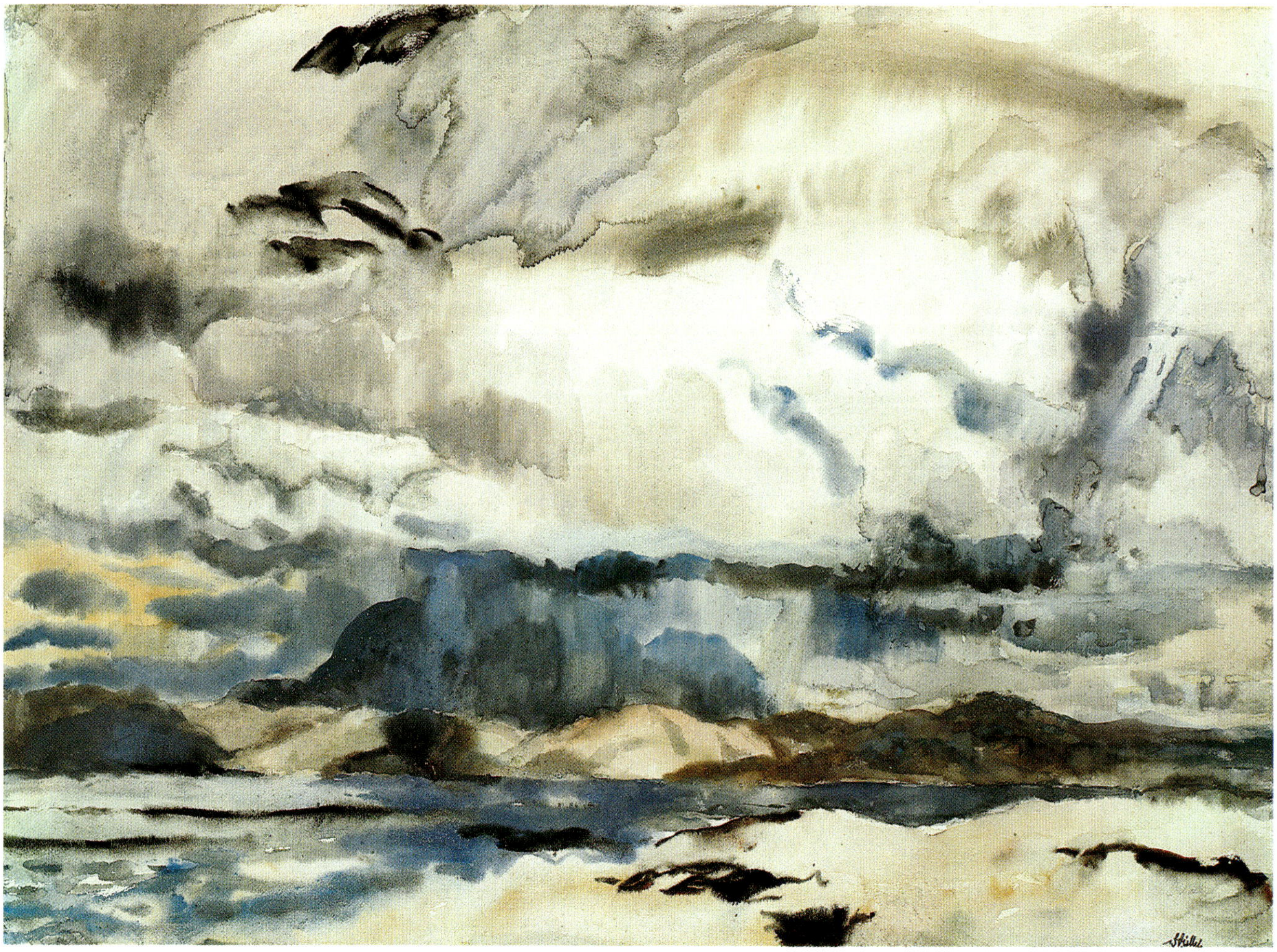

Threatening Storm 1936 watercolour on paper 52 × 63 cm A Fletcher

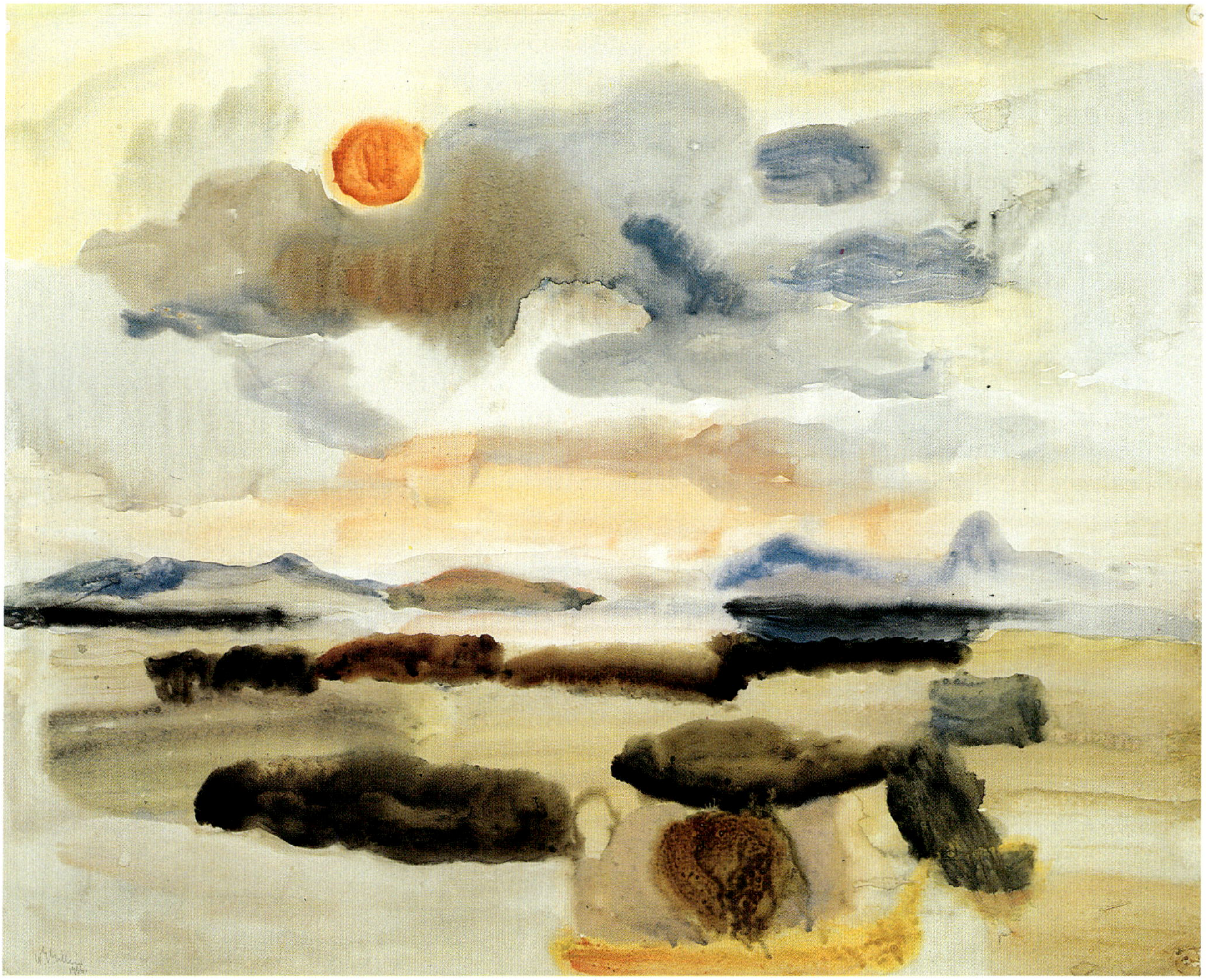

Highland Landscape with Suilven 1936 watercolour on paper 52 × 63 cm A Fletcher

of Munch's anguish – the calm order of his own life gave him no cause to – but he had at last found a way to put the visible at the service of the invisible and express the emotions, many of them rejoicing and optimistic, of his 'seething' mind. A few expressionist portraits were inevitable. Street scenes around Edinburgh and a sequence of passionate landscapes kept up the impetus. Two superb watercolours *Skye Hills from near Morar*, in the SNGMA, and *Wester Ross*, in the collection of John Houston and Elizabeth Blackadder, have echoes of Munch and reveal the masterly conviction and spontaneity that Gillies had achieved in his handling of this most fugitive medium. At Morar, as is so often the case, we are left in no doubt that it has rained, will soon rain, or is already raining.

The brushwork in *Borders Landscape* is brisk and summary and lyrical. Anyone who has shared a Moorfoot or Lammermuir summit with sheep, and felt the world falling away to an indeterminate horizon over a patched quilt of coppices and dyked fields, will appreciate the exhilarating effect of his high viewpoint.

Teaching three days and evenings a week left him little opportunity and even less energy for painting, but he had whipped himself up into such a frenzy that he crammed what he could into every spare moment. Trapped in stuffy studios, surrounded by the dusty casts of classical sculpture, he fretted for the the clean air of the countryside and, like a child out of school, ran to it as often as possible. Camping trips took him as far west as he could go on the mainland into the Ardnamurchan wilderness, south again and again to the Solway Firth, and along the necklace of fishing villages that studded the eastern coastline from the Moray Firth to Berwickshire.

Legends grew out of these excursions with Maxwell, Geissler, Moodie, other friends and sometimes the family. Most of the tales speak of Gillies' incredible industry – exemplified in the photograph of 'the Calidon show.' The flamboyant point of the signposted snapshot is that all of the watercolours were probably painted in a morning. Maxwell, good-natured as ever, realised that his painting subjects were no longer out there in the wilds, he could not have kept up anyway, so settled for good companionship and peace at any price. 'Sometimes I would find a thistle, or something like that,' he said, 'and I would draw that until he came back.' The trips continued, like raiding parties, for at least another 20 years. The Gillies onslaught never faltered. Robert Henderson Blyth joined the band on a tented trip with Gillies to Banffshire in 1950. It was his turn to have breakfast ready by eight o'clock. When he got up to start cooking Gillies had disappeared in his car. But at eight on the dot Gillies reappeared, bearing several well-developed watercolours.

The carefree spirit of these painting trips sings out in postcards sent to the Gillies home.

> This is the view from our doorstep [*wrote Maxwell on the back of a photograph of the Cuillins*] Last nite it was really amazing with the Cuillins sailing on a raspberry jam sea like an immense blue & pink cake. I have the beginnings of beard like a wisp of rather rough hay which I'm afraid is only refuge for the persecuted insect life. Bill's is not quite at that stage yet, though it might harbour the smaller species, but mine is almost ready for daddy-long-legs or imperial airways as we call them. Johnnie.

John Maxwell's 1933 oil in the SNGMA *View from a Tent* reveals a Highland house and a scatter of small boats set against mountain scenery. The pleasing scene is framed by the flaps of the tent. It provokes two very different responses. The casual viewer will find it a cunningly composed and assertive example of Maxwell's early landscape painting – a survivor, in fact, because he destroyed so much of his work in bouts of severe self-criticism. But the joke among his fellows, who knew it was the result of a bivouac with Gillies, persists. Johnnie, they say, was too tired on a damp morning to follow Willie on yet another foray into the heather, so sat where he was and painted what he could see from inside the tent.

The SSA's choice of foreign guest artist in 1934 was Paul Klee, with work by Picasso and Derain also on show. Gillies and Maxwell influenced the invitation to Klee. On the face of it, it might seem that the Swiss artist's preoccupation with fantasy appealed most directly to Maxwell – although it is surely not fanciful to feel that Gillies' *Still-life with Toy Boat and Kite*, painted in 1935 or 1936, was inspired by Klee. Gillies dallied with abstraction for a time – few developments in art failed to arouse his curiosity – but, having borrowed what he wanted from them, went his own way. Abstraction 'threw too much overboard,' he told a friend.

It is very likely, however, that Gillies took heart from Klee's famous Bauhaus metaphor of the artist as a tree: the pattern of natural growth in the roots is the artist's source of forms and ideas; this pattern is mirrored, as the artist develops, in the growth of the branches and leaves; but the final flowering – the work of art – is transformed by the richness of the artist's imaginative instincts.

Even if art theory, as expressed in books and magazines and the endless debates of his colleagues had only a limited influence on his judgment, Gillies the teacher had to keep abreast of advances and innovations. Particularly when, in 1934, his teaching post at ECA was made full-time and he became a member of the permanent staff.

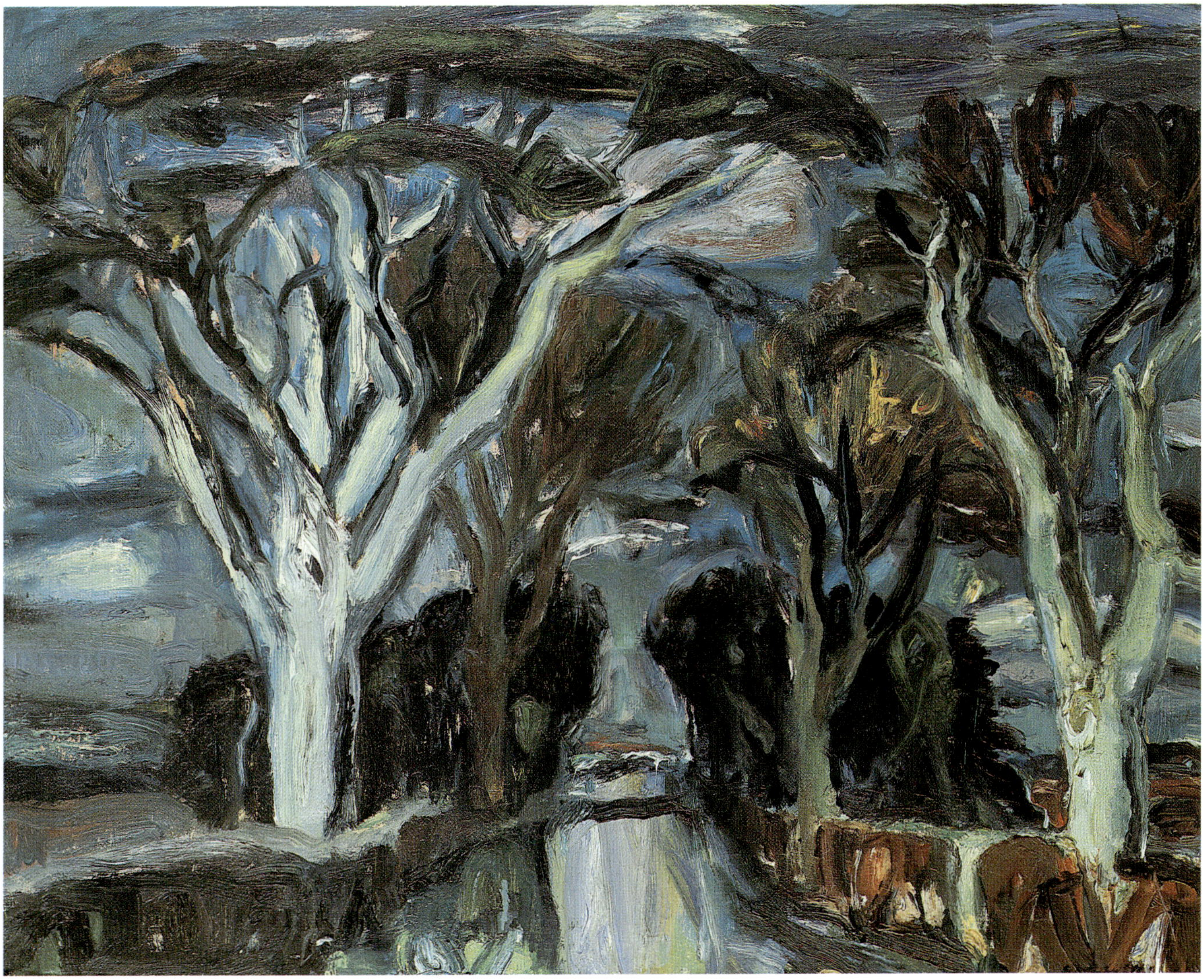

Woods near Humbie 1936 oil on canvas 64 × 72 cm A Fletcher

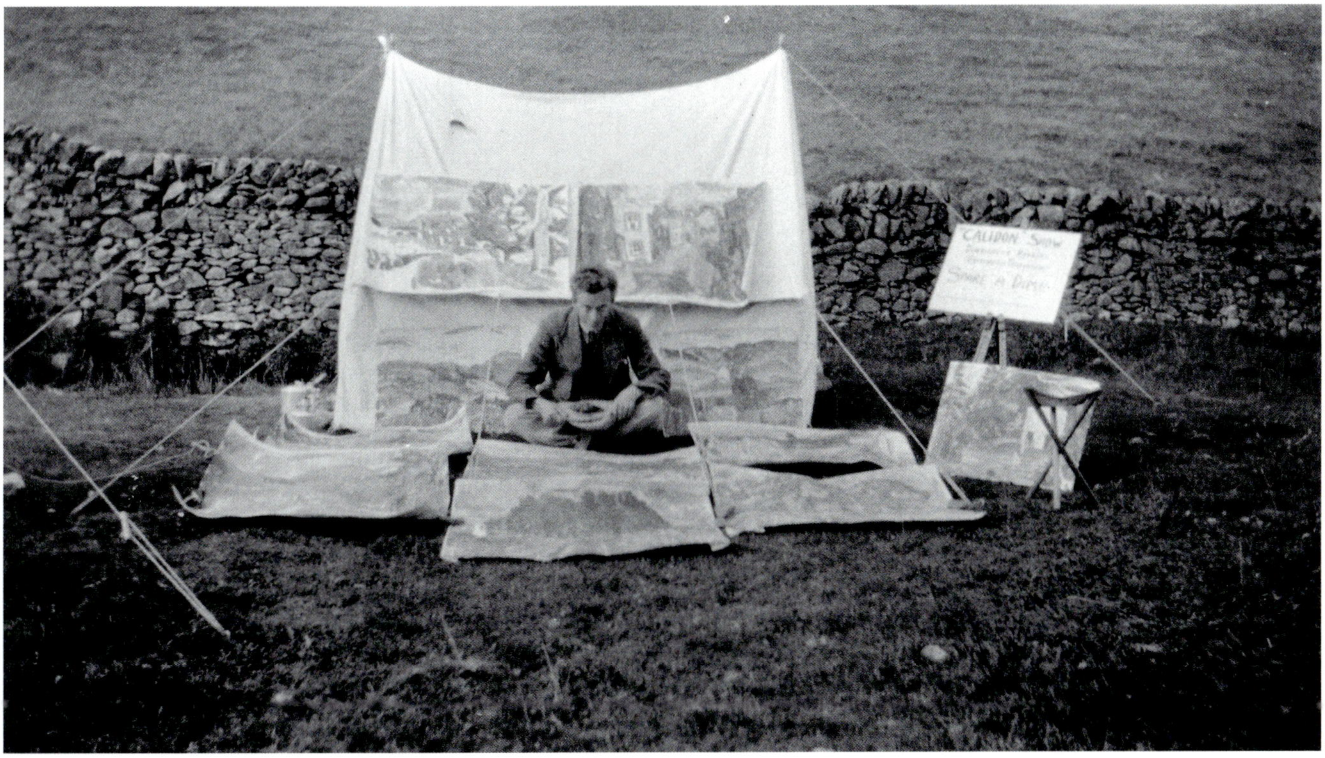

A Day's Painting – Highlands, c.1931 (Photo: RSA Archives)

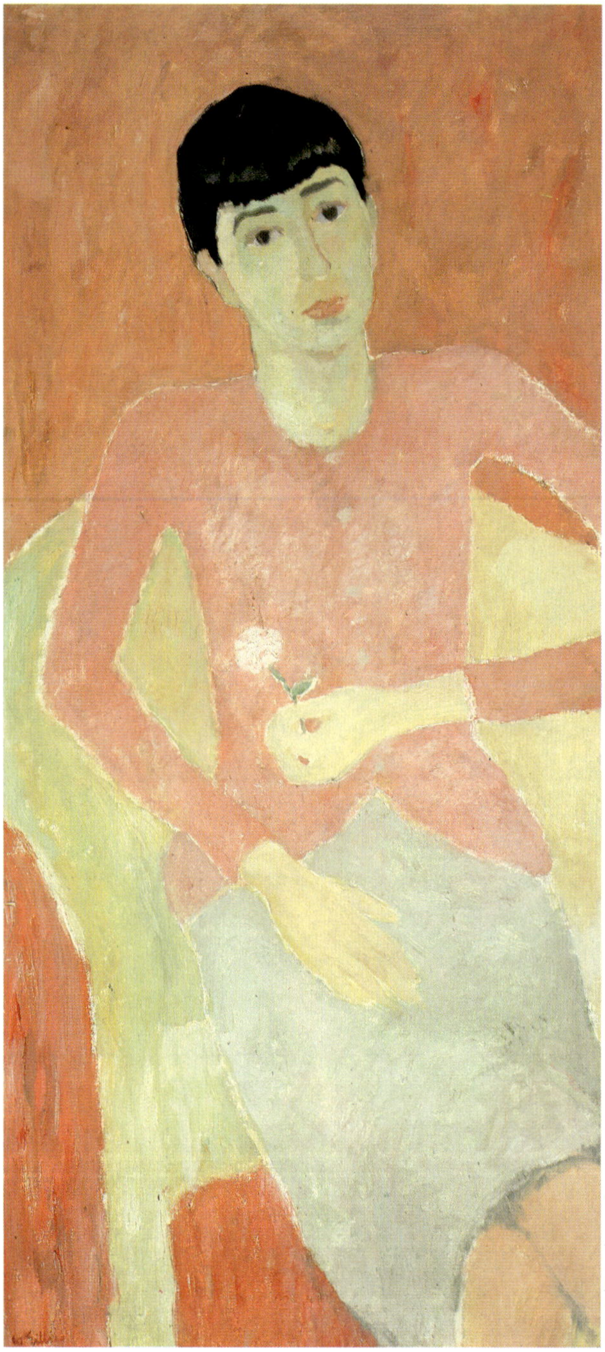

Portrait of Margery Porter c.1934/5 oil on canvas 121 × 57 cm RSA

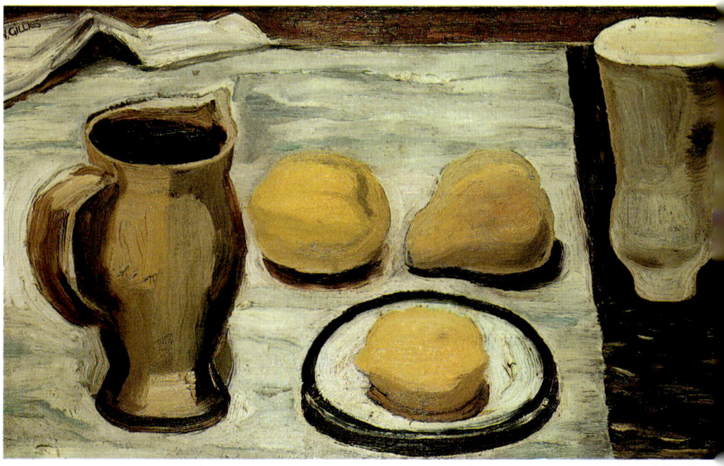

Two Pots, Saucer and Fruit 1933 oil on canvas 31 × 51 cm RSA

Chapter 6

Actors are often accused of carrying their best reviews in their wallets and reading them at dark times to buck up their spirits. By the time he was established as the doyen of Scottish painters Gillies might have employed his reviews of the 1930s for different purposes. The young Turks of the 1950s, who treated Gillies, the head of their college, with respect and affection, tended to dismiss his work as the cosy extension of Edinburgh's *belle peinture* tradition: tame, accomplished – of course – but safe as houses and as far removed from the violent extremes of De Kooning and Jackson Pollock as the Fauves had been from Raphael in the days when Gillies was a student. One newspaper cutting from 1934 would have astounded them.

> Mr Gillies has beaten his own previous record in the bizarre and puzzling . . . We take it that Mr Gillies really means to do what he is doing. That is to say, his work is not merely an attempt to be ultra-modern or a leg-pull . . . These somewhat nightmarish designs and colourings are like the poetry of the very advanced literateurs – they exist in statement and a certain amount of shape, but their meaning is known only to their maker – if, sometimes, to him . . . It is very much doubted if the future of painting lies in such works as these. Mr Gillies has shown that he can do more conventional work and do it well . . . At this year's Society of Eight exhibition extremes have met; small as it is, it is undoubtedly a conspectus of Scottish art today and yesterday, but, we hope and believe, not of tomorrow.

If that demolition by George Rowntree Harvey bothered Gillies in any way, *The Listener's* reviewer of the same exhibition showed commendable foresight in his appraisal of an *enfant terrible* who was making a bold début.

> The most recent recruit is W.G.Gillies, and the inclusion of his work in this year's exhibition, which has just opened, is likely to provoke a public, already insulted and enraged by the current exhibition of the Society of Scottish Artists, to further expressions of horror. But there can be no doubt that the public that now accepts Peploe and Cadell will some day accept Gillies – as true a son of his generation as they are of theirs – and we can only commend the courage of the Society [of Eight] in including him in their number.

Two Pots, Saucer and Fruit from about this time is a good example of a process which had developed into an essential discipline in Gillies' approach to all painting. It involved systematic planning, fixing the idea for a picture, stripping content to essentials, laying form bare, judging the relativity of tonal harmonies and, like an acrobat, bringing off a balancing act. This simple arrangement of objects, reminiscent of Morandi, is, like most still-lifes, a picture painted under the artist's magisterial control, a scheme set up in advance, but flexible enough to allow for intuitive improvisation.

He tried very hard to make that code of discipline serve him in less certain circumstances – to make a secure base from which he could catch the fleeting glance of a portrait or that moment of breathless tension when the wind suddenly drops in a landscape. He was always conscious of a gulf between his still-lifes and landscapes, something that transcended technicalities, almost as if they could be the work of another hand and eye. This had less to

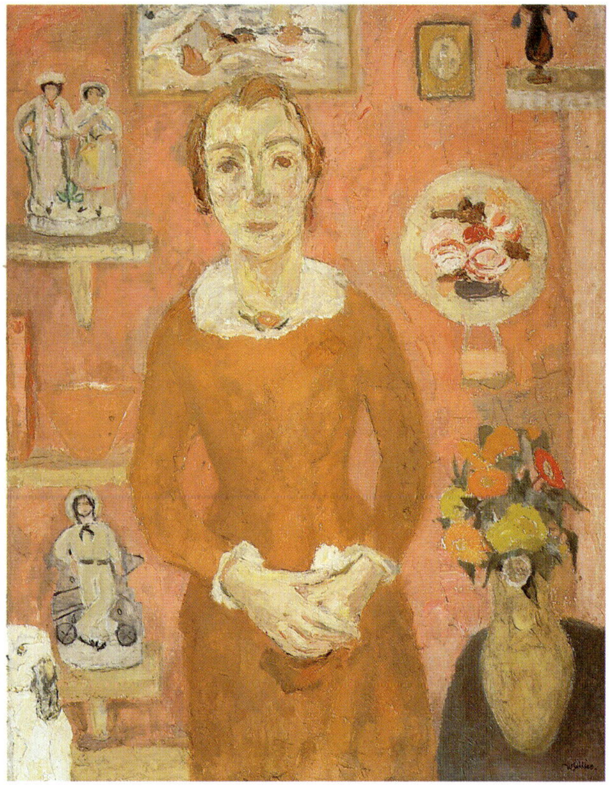

Portrait of Jenny (the artist's sister, Janet) 1936 oil on canvas 116 × 90 cm Sir Robin Philipson

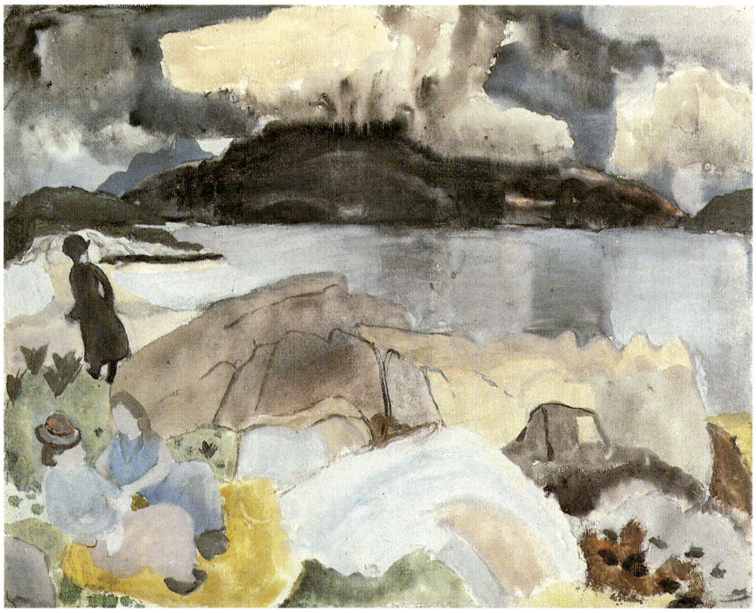

In Ardnamurchan 1936 watercolour and bodycolour on paper 51 × 63 cm SNGMA

do with the degree of physical control he could exercise than his emotional response to the subject.

In the studio – like a window-dresser or stage manager – he set up ceramics, textiles, fruit and what was to become a bizarre collection of ornaments and jumble sale bric-a-brac as if they were medieval icons or votive offerings. As often as not he followed a carefully considered design scheme; at other times he would juggle shapes and textures until that important constituent of art – happenstance – revealed an arrangement that caught his fancy or stimulated a new challenge. Then the happy accident was bent to his will.

Out of doors, offering himself up to something he recognised as sublime in nature, he succumbed and responded, but like a sailor engulfed in a storm, held on for dear life to his seamanship and charts. 'The navigator doesn't travel from A to B,' said that great helmsman Tristan Jones. 'The world passes underneath him. He doesn't arrive at his destination, he fetches it to him.'

Apart from adjusting the path of a road or re-routing a line of telegraph poles to strengthen a composition Gillies seldom altered what he had chosen to see. The elevation of the superb draughtsman to consummate artist came through his physical manipulation of paint and colour to register his emotions. Long before Marshall McLuhan propounded his communication theories Gillies understood that the medium was the message – and the massage, too, if that was his intention.

Just when it seemed as if the wind had never blown fairer for him, tragedy struck the close-knit Gillies family in 1935. His young sister Emma, always frail and delicate, was rushed to hospital and died soon afterwards. With her naturally cheerful disposition she had managed to put a bright face on several years of recurring illness. From all accounts she had talent as a potter and might have gone on to use her craft skills and college training to make her own way in the arts.

Nothing had prepared the family for such a shock. Gillies was devastated. Many subtle bonds united the family, and each was special in its way, but between Emma and Willie there were empathies of spirit and character, kindred sensitivity and susceptibility, which enriched their profound affection for each other. He painted Emma six times in the 30s, but the first of these portraits, completed in 1931, remains one of his most exquisite accomplishments. A study of classical force and simplicity, combining the dramatic intensity of its composition with airy modelling of the features, it conveys the gravitas as well as the serenity of the sitter. It may be whimsical now to read into the portrait some premonition of the tragedy which would befall this lovely young woman, but were one to know nothing of her fate or the nature of the artist's love for her, as a painting it would always express a mysterious melancholy shared between the artist and his subject. There is no doubt that Gillies meant his portrait of Emma to pay homage to their relationship. Over the many years she did not share with him, in many still lifes and interiors, he made tender small testaments to her memory.

Portrait of Margery Porter, the daughter of his Sunday-night Morningside friends, is the first of three painted in the early 30s. A carefree Expressionist gesture, it signals a complete breakaway from the last strictures of academia. Brave in its dash and severely cropped composition, deliberately naive in its unrelieved planes and chalky colour, the black cap of the young woman's cropped hair and bright button eyes give her a startled but engaging intensity.

These great decorators Matisse, Bonnard and Vuillard – he had begun to admire all three, and Braque had also started to cast his spell – could all be summoned as potent influences on *Portrait of Jenny*, painted intermittently between 1936-7. It is, however, a Gillies masterwork, stamped with his own authority as a painter, caressed by his sensitivity, compelling in its intimacy. Like his portrait of Emma it speaks without embarrassment or sentimentality of his deep feeling for his elder sister. A homelier person than Emma,

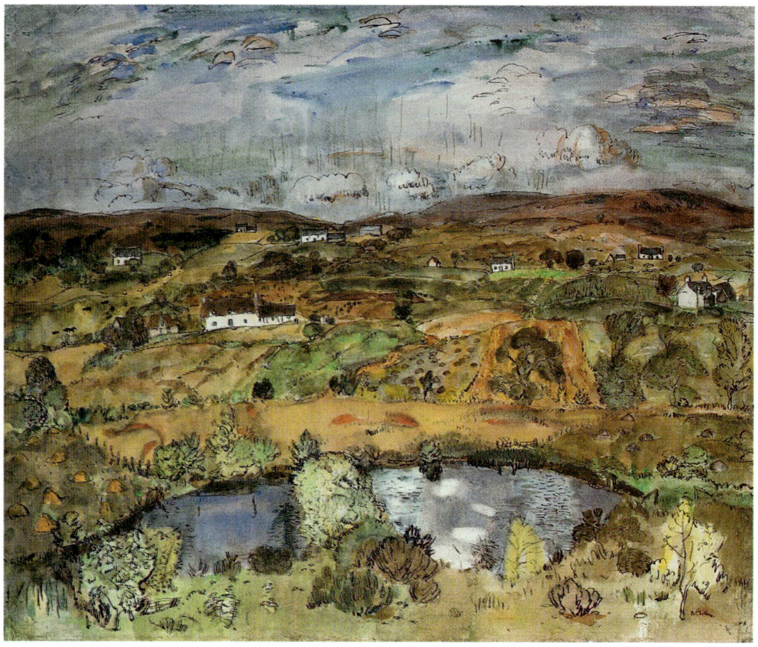

Crofts, Bonar Bridge c.1938 watercolour and ink on paper 67 × 79 cm SNGMA

plainer and more practical, Jenny stands straight-on to us, slightly to one side, and not quite foursquare. It is as if diffidence tilts her body to one side – an innate reticence that cannot, however, conceal the focussed frankness of her eyes or the repose of her cupped hands; hands that have washed socks and dishes and stoked fires; his socks and dishes and fires. Her whole person seems caught in equipoise, some shy inner strength keeping vulnerability at bay.

As a painting it sings like a candlelit altarpiece. The palette conjures warmth and peace and the cosiness of a jolly home. Its rich ochres and dusky pinks, deep lilacs and rusty browns bind together in muted harmony. Texture bites deep and lively, the paint knifed on to the canvas. The frothy white of cuff and ruff frames hands and face and emphasises the ovoid scheme of the composition – head; arms and hands; descending trunk; and the tonic form reciprocated in the vase alongside. Then the outer frame of apparently random objects – from 'kiss me quick' vulgarity to folksy embroidery – telling us something about the subject's simple tastes and sense of fun. David Alison's yardstick was 'a guid heid.' *Portrait of Jenny* is not that. Gillies himself, as Jimmy Mowat reminded me, reserved his finest accolade for a 'handsome' painting. *Portrait of Jenny* is certainly that, and Gillies probably thought so. But its quality goes well beyond that modest estimate. More than half a century after it was painted this portrait still proclaims its unique character and haunting immediacy.

As if Emma's death – with its inevitable intimations of mortality – had concentrated his mind and spurred him to even greater effort, the second half of a decade that was brewing up another world war produced some of his most intense and exquisite work. A family holiday in the West Highlands introduced rare human figures to one of his landscapes. Mrs Gillies, Jenny and Aunt Margaret act as tiny foils to the brooding grandeur of *In Ardnamurchan*, a watercolour executed with the daunting facility of a magician. That (in those days) almost secret peninsula enthralled him with its rocky coves, awesome seascapes of the Inner Hebrides, and a primitive way of life that had changed little since Culloden. Further north, in the great wilderness of Sutherland, he waved his wand again and with breathtaking economy produced watercolour images of landscape – *Threatening Storm* and *Highlands With Suilven* are among the finest – which would distinguish him in any company.

It would be easy to read some of Munch's foreboding into the fretful impasto of *Woods Near Humbie*, but anyone who has driven through East Lothian at dusk or with headlights undipped in the dark will know why Gillies made such stark sentinels of these trees. Across the Forth estuary, in the East Neuk of Fife, he emblazoned the harbour of *St Monance* with loose gestural fluency, using big-brushed wet technique with a riot of colour that would not have dismayed Dufy. *The Harbour*, painted in oils a few years later, is tighter and more consciously ordered, and probably inspired by the same setting. In the SNGMA's *Scottish Art Since 1900* exhibition of 1989 *The Harbour* and Maxwell's *Harbour With Three Ships* were hung, imaginatively, side by side – as if we were sitting at their elbows at the same viewpoint – revealing at a glance the striking differences and similarities in the vision and technique of two of Scotland's most persuasive painters.

The two friends made a rare trip abroad in 1938, to the picturesque fishing port St Valèry-en-Caux, near Dieppe. Only the tricolours at the stern of two boats in Gillies' pencil sketch of the harbour – and perhaps the formal architecture of the quayside buildings – signals that he is in France and not among the herring gulls on Scotland's seaboard. Years later Jimmy Mowat, who as a trusted friend had the run of Gillies' studio, came across an unfamilar harbour sketch. 'I haven't seen this before,' he was able to say with encyclopaedic authority. 'It's not mine, it's Johnnie Maxwell's.' Mowat, anxious to add at least one Maxwell to his collection, asked if he could have it. 'Certainly,' said Gillies, explained that it was not signed, then wrote on the back of the sketch: 'This is the only drawing that Johnnie Maxwell did when he was with Bill Logan and me in St Valèry-en-Caux. He did it on borrowed paper!' Gillies brought back only a few paintings from France, but one blustery day at the harbour encouraged him to dash off, without a hint of preliminary drawing, the lively and liquid – almost to the point of being juicy – watercolour *St Valèry-en-Caux. Crofts, Bonar Bridge*, painted the same year with meticulous inked detail, seems almost mimsy by comparison, but is an early example of Gillies' clever use of the pen with watercolour – neither the drawing before the painting nor additional topographical information. Jack Firth describes this calligraphy which Gillies developed with such mastery as 'complementary to the loose washes and a kind of linear foil to the main melody of the chromatic chords.' *St Valèry-en-Caux* and *Crofts, Bonar Bridge*, better than any words, illustrate the range and intensity of his emotional response to a subject and his ability to express it in paint and, perhaps less obviously, in his drawing.

Family Group – Willowbrae 1937
oil on canvas 126 × 173 cm RSA

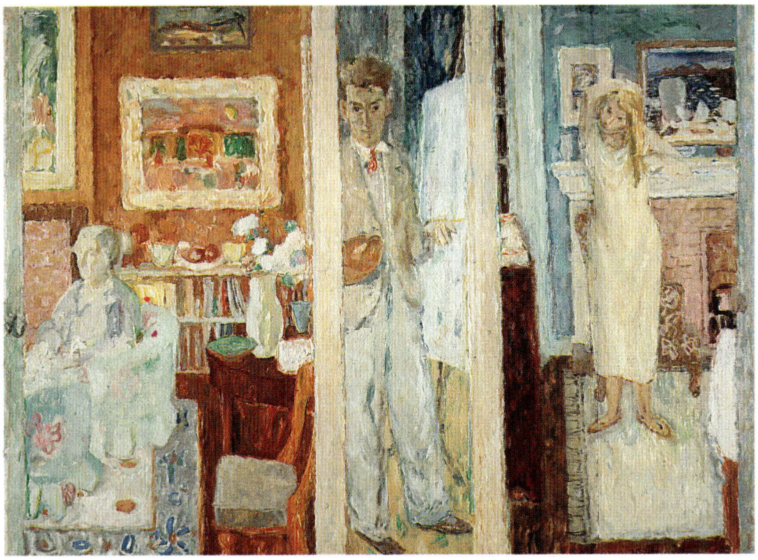

George Scott-Moncrieff, in his elegant fashion, paid particular attention to Gillies' drawing in a foreword to the catalogue of National Trust exhibition in 1953:

> What might seem the most casual curve or loop, a scribble or a scratch across a picture, is in fact aptly expressive of what the artist wishes to convey. What might seem a mere scribble of lines, an unthinking doodle, carries in it, clear and simple, the whole tangle of a hedgerow. A harsh stutter of exclamation marks brings unerringly the vision of a sparse stubble-field; a cluster of black curves stabs the sky with homing rooks. Gillies has sharpened our eyes, added to our happiness with the world about us, giving us new ways of seeing familiar things; the curves of cows against hillsides, the wooden gate with broken hinges, the smear of nets on the harbour wall, the shapely, sensuous boles of beech trees. In his work abstraction retains, and therefore explains, the forms of reality.

In 1937 Gillies was elected a professional member of the SSA and that year painted one of his most striking and innovative canvases, *Family Group*. This daringly contrived triple portrait, set in two rooms connected by the hallway at Willowbrae Road, has the artist standing by his easel at centre; through an open door on his right his mother sits contentedly in what she no doubt called the parlour; through another door to his left, in what is probably her bedroom, his sister Jenny stands, adjusting her hair. This is a family at peace with themselves and each other. It is generally agreed that *Family Group* has Bonnard as its inspiration, but – as ever – Gillies borrows only to pay back in his own new-minted coin. Framing each person in the household in their own relaxed and informal space he stresses their individuality, yet through the device of the open doors connects them as a family and celebrates their unity. The harmony of the tripartite composition is accentuated by its tonal concord. Each item of decoration is an emblem of studied pleasure. This, says the artist looking us straight in the eye, is a happy house.

Within a couple of years, with war on the way, the family flitted from Willowbrae Road and made the last move of their lives.

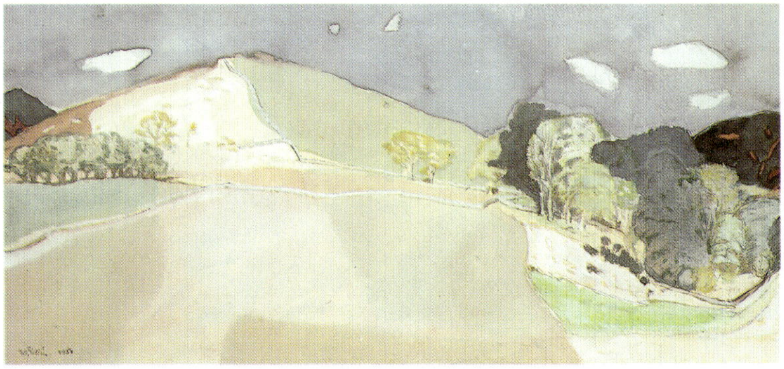

Outside Broughton 1951 watercolour and pencil on paper 23 × 35 cm

Chapter 7

Emma's death had maybe unsettled the family more than they knew. Or perhaps, in the marrow of their bones, these country folk the Gillieses had always felt too far away from the land in a tarmacked Edinburgh suburb. It might even have been the portent of Luftwaffe bombers that tipped the balance, but when a cottage in the tiny Midlothian village of Temple came up for sale in 1939 they felt as a family that they would be happier and more contented on the bosky banks of the South Esk at the base of the Moorfoots, with Edinburgh 15 miles behind their backs. It was going home, to Gillies country, and a chance to begin a new life in old remembered ways.

He was 41, his mother 76, Jenny 43. Temple, like Haddington, sits in fertile countryside fringed by open moor. Sheep scutter about the hills, the river cuts through deep chasms, trees offer shelter in deep groves. The village is a gaggle of curiously tall cottages on each side of a road to nowhere in particular. A friendly place with fewer than 100 inhabitants, and most of them in those days born in the parish. It got its name from the roofless medieval church which had been the chief Scottish seat of the Knights Templar before that powerful military order was suppressed in 1312. The village kirkyard boasts a gravestone, erected in 1847, which bears the entire last will and testament of a local cleric. Temple's only other claim to fame, is made modestly on a stone set in the front wall of his cottage, saying: 'Sir William Gillies 1898–1973 lived and worked here.'

The cottage offered the family comfortable living accommodation and Gillies a studio and garden. These were valuable bonuses. But if he had written a list of painting subjects which would appeal to him – gently undulating hill country dotted with bonny hamlets, drystane dykes, steep screes, tracts of trees and water, moody skies, and the quaint hugger-mugger of a village street – surely he would have hoped for too much to find them all in one place. Yet there they were on his doorstep.

As if he were conducting some solemn rite, adorning a tabernacle with familiar relics and secular totems, and fusing the symbols of his inner world with nature's promises in the garden beyond, one of his first paintings at Temple, *The Blue Window*, seems to be a very personal act of consecration and dedication. This intensely intimate and reverential interior – it is decorative still-life extended to an extra dimension – carries the assertion of a statement of intent. Inspired by Temple's visual riches, comforted by the family's immediate adjustment to their new environment, it is as if he suddenly feels secure and confident of the way ahead.

This assurance speaks even more eloquently from his *Self-Portrait*, painted in 1941. 'This above all,' advised Polonious, 'to thine own self be true.' How many painters, using the self-portrait as a convenient modelling device, painting their own image only as an exercise, resist the temptations of flattery? Here the artist, with the hands and clothes of an artisan, gives himself no airs and graces. It is as if he has just entered the room, after a diffident knock on the door, and pauses before saying, 'Excuse me, I'm Bill Gillies. I'm a painter.' Or consider another scenario:

> *The artist has been trying to paint what he sees himself to be; he turns away from the canvas to check his image in the mirror; looking back at him, leaning in to him, is the painted portrait and not his flesh and blood; and he knows it to be honest and right.*

As a portrait it has that hint of a reverberating Cocteau dream. As a painting its balance and poise make it seem weightless. It floats, defying gravity, contradicting its down-to-earth solidity.

Soon after moving to Temple he had been appointed to the post of First Assistant in the School of Drawing and Painting at ECA – an increase in salary, of course, and more responsibility, but recognition of his gifts and abilities as a teacher. More significantly from an artistic standpoint, his peers at the RSA elected him an Associate [ARSA].

Despite the war and its depressive effect on people's lives – or perhaps even because of it – painting in Scotland continued to develop and flourish. *The Glasgow Herald*, reviewing work in three galleries in 1942, thought new Scottish painting had energy but, occasionally, impetuosity,

> 'with some vigorous effects of colour often laid on with the palette knife, which in the hands of some results in over-emphasis. The cult of the knife in place of the brush may be due to the example of W.G. Gillies, an artist who, in his present phase, obtains purity of colour by this means.'

The critic went on to voice a reservation that now seems irresponsibly out of touch: 'Gillies' loose style is not for the observer looking for facts clearly stated . . .' The writer could have been referring to the magnificent table-top collage of textiles and bric-a-brac which Gillies titled – mischievously, I suspect – *The Red Squirrel*. The majolica sailor – sporting the saucy challenge *Ready and Willing* and a survivor from the ornamentation of Jenny's portrait – is a more dominant image than the rodent camouflaging himself against the background. Commenting on *Still-life with Breton Pot* the Glasgow critic felt it was 'a good example of his colour' after saying, yet again, that 'his looseness in construction, intentional or otherwise, hardly makes for enduring beauty.' The Breton pot endures in the SNGMA collection.

National newspapers paid scant attention – then as now – to Scottish art at the best of times, and even less under the enforced rationing of newsprint. But an exhibition of Scottish painting taken on tour of English cities by C.E.M.A. [forerunner of the Arts Council] excited Hubert Wellington, writing in *The Listener* in 1943 with its 'exhilarating sense of clear, fresh colour, of gay pattern, of carefree handling of paint in schemes based on blue and silver rather than on gold and tawny harmonies.' Wellington had been Principal of ECA from 1932 to 1942. After explaining how 'the Scottish art student usually leaps over London and is better acquainted with the galleries and studios of Paris,' and the effect of that Franco-Scottish alliance on the output of Edinburgh artists in particular, Wellington singled out Gillies as 'the most potent figure of his generation.'

> He is a draughtsman who can discover the essential rhythms in the most complicated tangle of trees and undergrowth. His early paintings were impressive designs built up in masses, but his colour has since gained brilliance and his handling become exceedingly free and varied.

Gillies had already absorbed most of what he wanted from Picasso and Matisse, and would go on doing so to his own personal glory, but now turned to post-Cubist Braque still-lifes and Bonnard's poetically intimate interiors, not for whatever is meant by 'inspiration,' but for confirmation of his own intuitive and rather lonely attitudes to studio painting. Braque's declared ambition, to produce 'a new sort of unity, a lyricism which issues wholly from the means employed,' had always sounded like something he should nail above his easel. Gillies chose to interpret lyricism as that harmonious effect by which forms and colours can be made to register their own appeal without any physical reference to the object. And the means employed would have to include his passionate flair for decoration and the occasional,

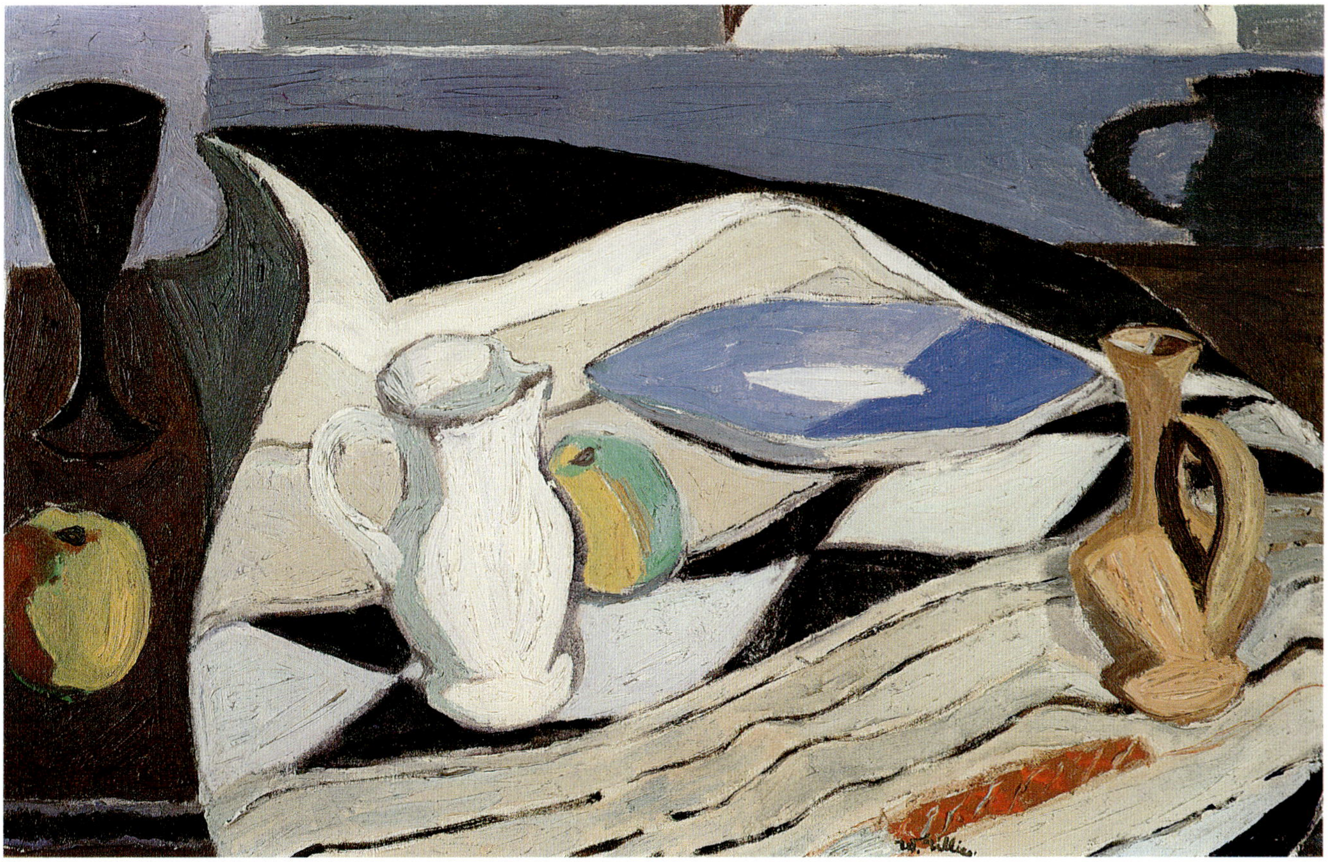

Still Life (Apples and Jugs) c1952 oil on canvas 51 × 76 cm

almost wanton, eccentricity of vivid colour. He was also excited by Braque's major 'pictorial obsession,' the elimination of perspective and manipulation of space, so that the objects in a painting were thrust forward and upward, inviting the viewer to enter that space and explore it, to touch it with their eyes.

Some physical factors dictated the tempo and texture of his painting life. Temple village had no electricity until the 1950s. Artificial lighting depended on wick-burning oil lanterns – tongues of flame smoking behind tall glass globes – or on pressurised Tilley lamps, which sent pumped-up paraffin vapour hissing through an incandescent gas mantle. The Tilley, an intense and efficient light source, white-hot at the centre and falling away to a buttery perimeter, roared and spat and threw long shadows. Objects set up in the arrangement of a still-life stood in stark contrast to each other. Colour sang with more raucous intensity. Even the constant hissing, changing pitch at every fresh pumping, can seem like a sinister obligato. Gillies overcame these handicaps when he had to, but learned to exploit the Tilley and turn its idiosyncrasies to dramatic advantage.

The blackout, the long drive to and from college five days a week, petrol rationing, the mixed blessings of Temple's isolation in a severe winter all contributed to a routine that settled into a regime designed to leave him as much painting time as possible. *Temple, Winter, Street* and *Winter, Temple, Back of Houses* are doorstep examples of his never wasting the chance to make a picture; the oil slabbed and expressive in its austerity; the inked watercolour leaping to life with its intense blues and terra-cottas and twiggy filigree. *Temple Village* snoozes through a more benign day, muted overall, but busy with colour in its textured walls, rubbled gables and pantiles.

A family trip north to Kirriemuir, his mother's ancestral home in Angus, produced a clutch of drawings, some of which – like *Kirriemuir, Houses on a Slope* – rival the fluid but

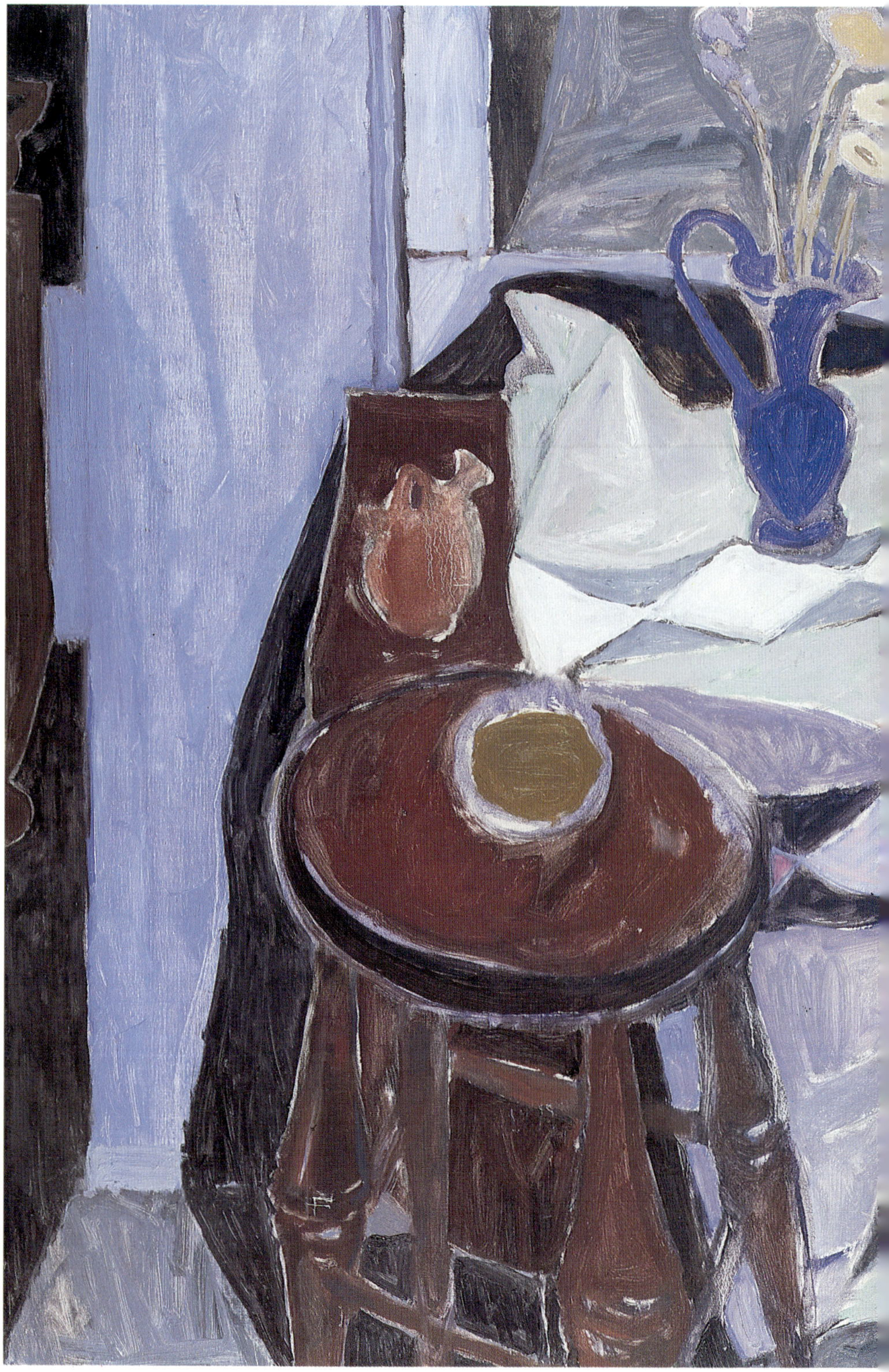

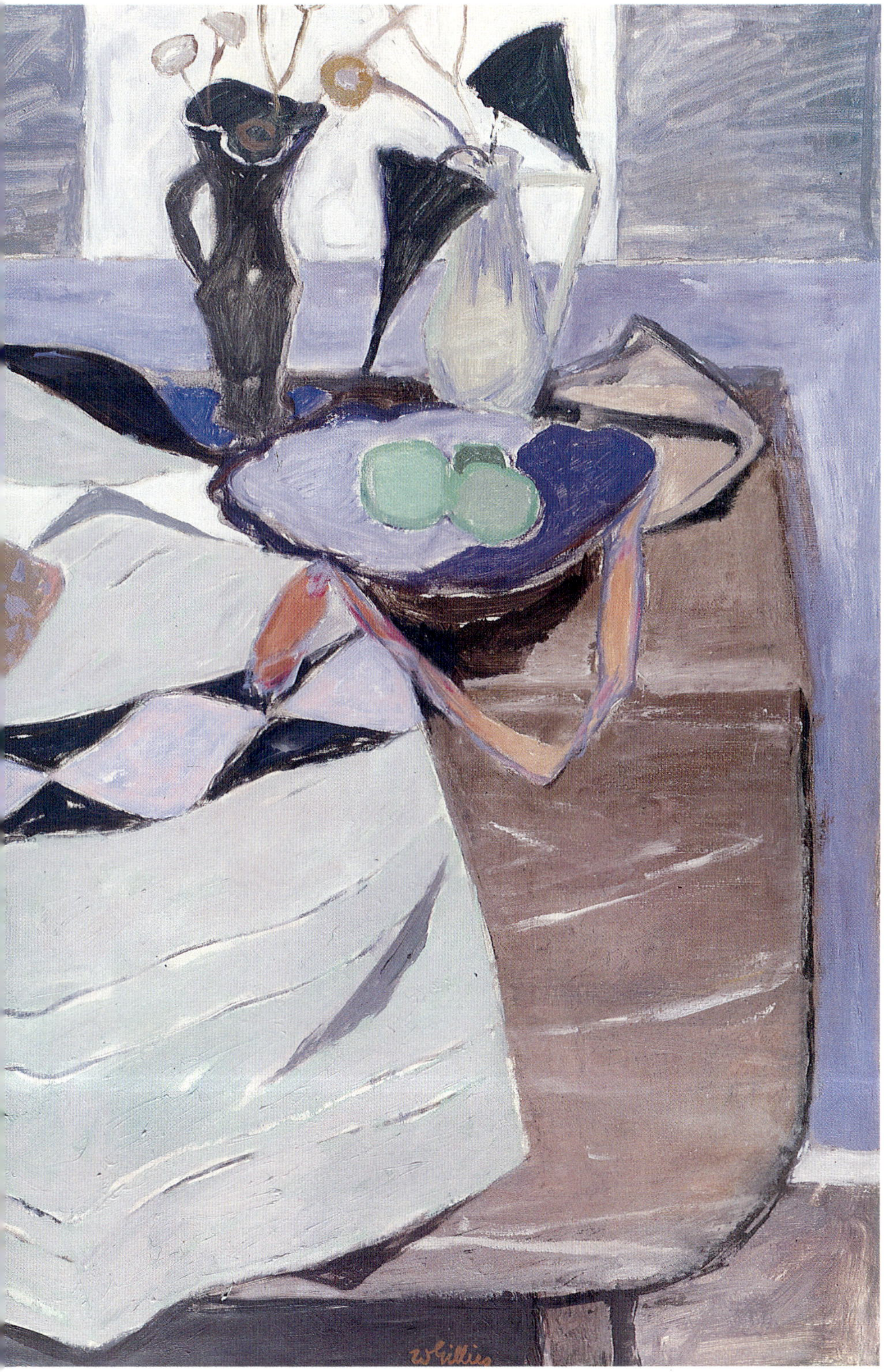

Still-life, Blue and Brown 1952 oil on canvas 99 × 137 cm GAGM

finicky spontaneity of van Gogh's sublime draughtsmanship in Provence. The East Neuk of Fife kept calling him back to its squawking harbours. Gillies reverted to his old student habit of carrying a sketchbook everywhere, and even though Temple and its immediate vicinity offered an embarrassment of subjects, he mounted a motorbike – there were times when he owned no fewer than three – and followed the fingerpost signs to Carrington and Garvald, Heriot and Gifford, down where the rivers ran and up into the gousty hills. He had learned to make the mood of a landscape part of its true record. 'The Gillies way of looking at landscape is full of natural truths,' says Jack Firth. 'His factuality is like Monet's at Giverny. When one is there it seems there is no other way the place could be painted.'

During long dark Scottish nights or the mirk of winter weekends the Tilley would be pumped up and the studio flooded with its noisy light. *Still-Life with Octagonal Table*, dramatically tipped up towards the spectator on its vertical plane so that it forms its own background, employs a distortion of perspective that would serve him for many years. Its success as a painting lies in Gillies' personal synthesis of 'simplification,' as advocated by Matisse, and Braque's theories about the manipulation of space. Each object is thrust at us, lustrous and exuberant, casting no shadows, framed by the octagon, and our eyes are led through the composition's simplified geometry from bottom to top by the trailing white cloth and the green fronds in the jug.

His restless physical energy was matched in intensity only by his insatiable curiosity. People remarked on his gait – seldom back on his heels, usually up on his toes and, as if walking were too slow for him, pecking at the ground in a stuttering run. His bright eyes missed nothing. He found pictures where, on the face of it, none existed. Yet all his furious activity, the focussing of his entire person on one dedicated purpose, generated none of the angst, no hypertension that anyone ever saw, none of the extremes of temperament or behaviour that have to be excused so often in the wake of a questing, creative spirit.

He must have known hurt, disappointment, a sense of failure or inadequacy. He knew, better than most men, that a work of art is never finished 'only abandoned.' It would belittle him as a human being and diminish him as an artist to believe otherwise. But such was his equilibrium, so secure the world he had made for himself and his family, so small his demands and expectations from life, so certain his artistic will, so down-to-earth his sanity that by the time the war ended and the world started to rebuild itself he had become, like one of his canvases, a very still life – ordered, rhythmic, purposeful, everything occupying its own space and allocation of time, a muted ground lit occasionally by bright flashes of fire.

In 1946 he was appointed Head of the Drawing and Painting School at ECA in succession to his old mentor David Alison. Gillies had made the place a substantial part of his life and given its students much of himself. The post, a coveted distinction, was just and fitting reward for a dedicated master who, without stinting his commitment or teaching responsibilities, had also become Scotland's most celebrated painter. And he took charge of the school at a critical time, when the college was about to accommodate its first batch of peacetime students, many of them ex-Service men and women – as it had done all these years ago when he came home from the trenches. The new head inherited one of the most spectacular painting studios in Europe – its huge glazed north wall frames a sensational view of Edinburgh Castle – but neither that privilege nor any trappings of authority changed the man's humane and pragmatic view of the world.

The following year he was elected Academician of the Royal Scottish Academy and in 1950 a member of the Royal Scottish Society of Painters in Watercolour – a medium with which Gillies achieved a virtuosity unsurpassed by any Scottish painter this century and not many anywhere else.

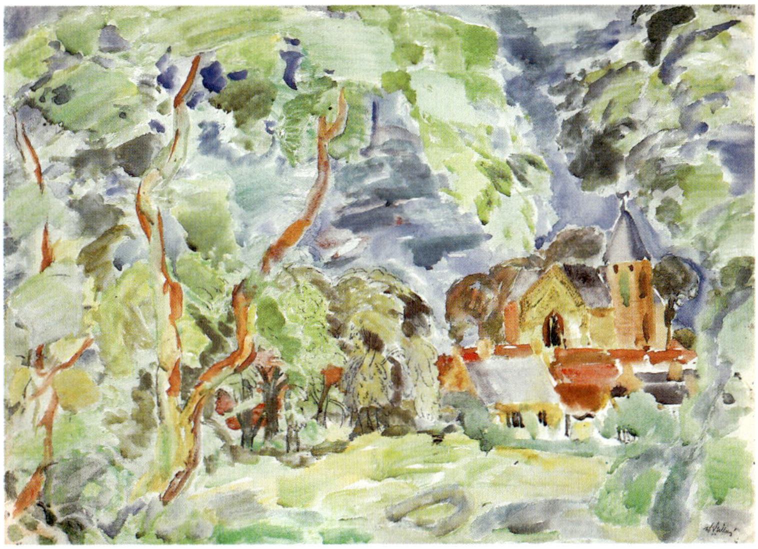

Carrington watercolour and ink on paper c.1938 57 × 79 cm

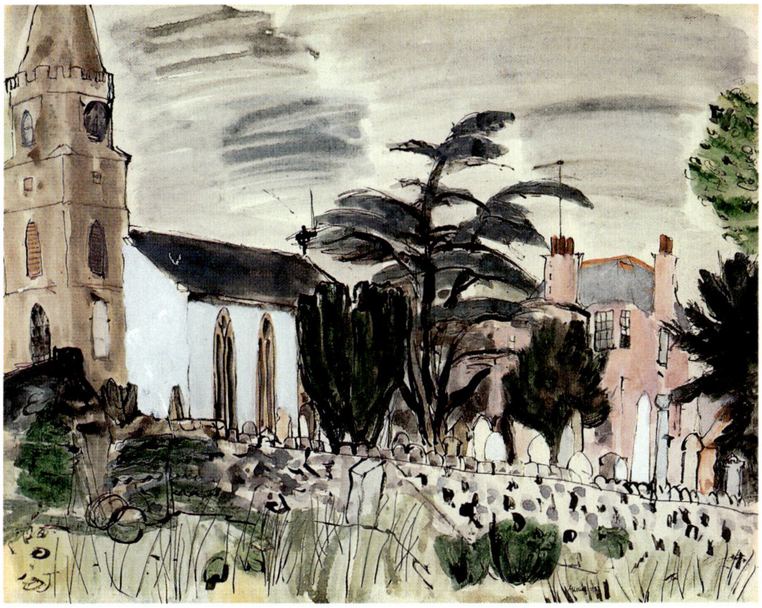

Old Churchyard, Gamrie 1950 ink on paper 45 × 58 cm

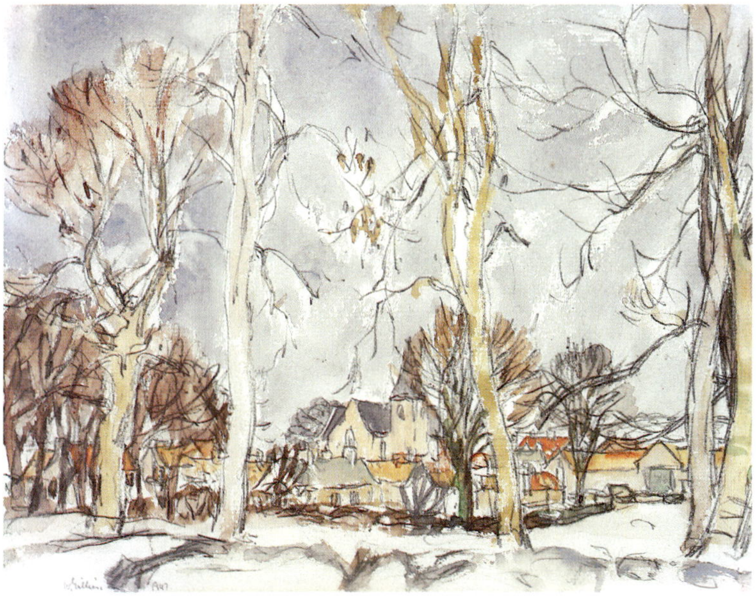

Winter, Carrington 1945 watercolour and pencil on paper 20 × 26 cm SNGMA

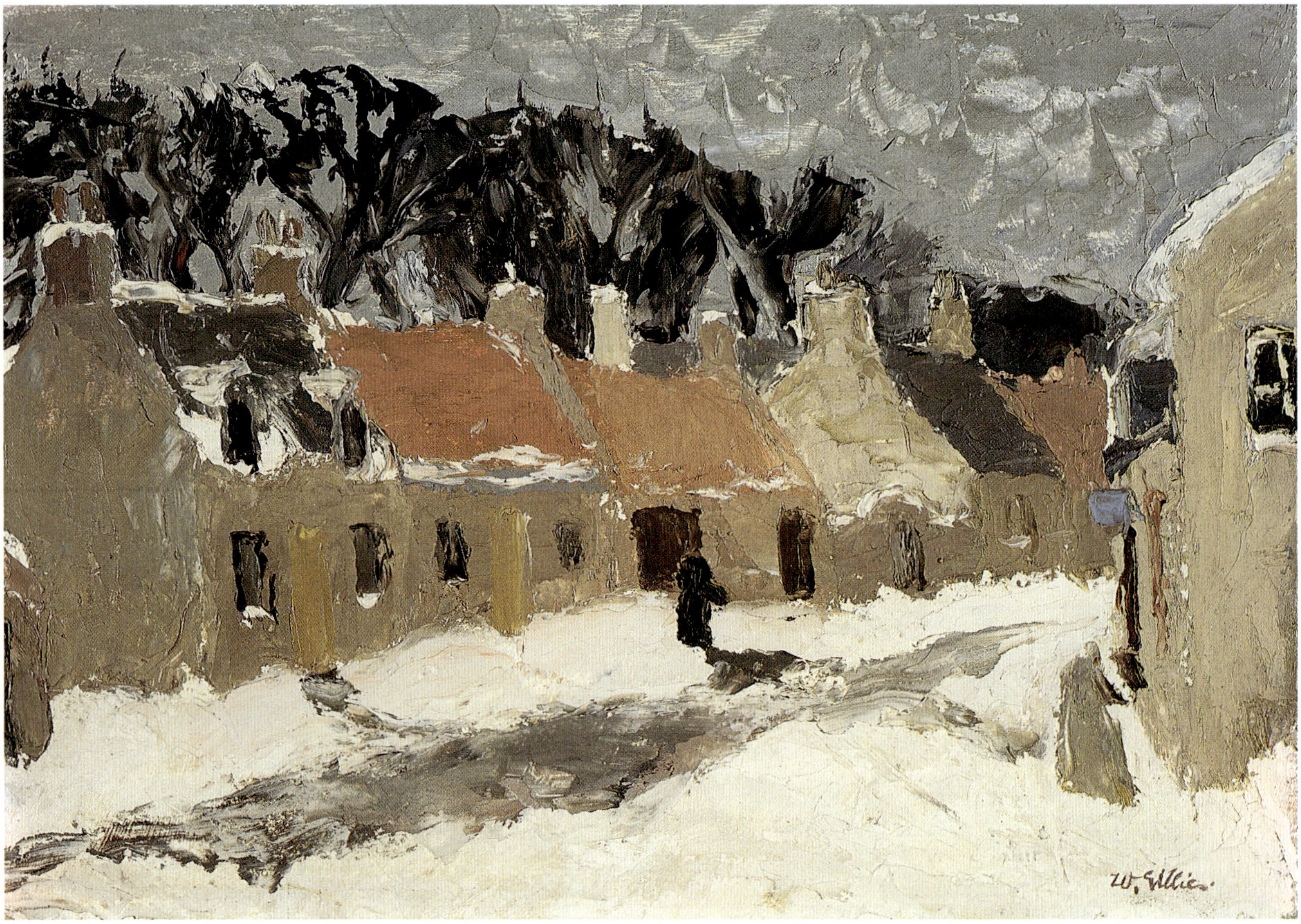

Temple, Winter, Street c.1945/8 oil on board 38 × 51 cm SNGMA

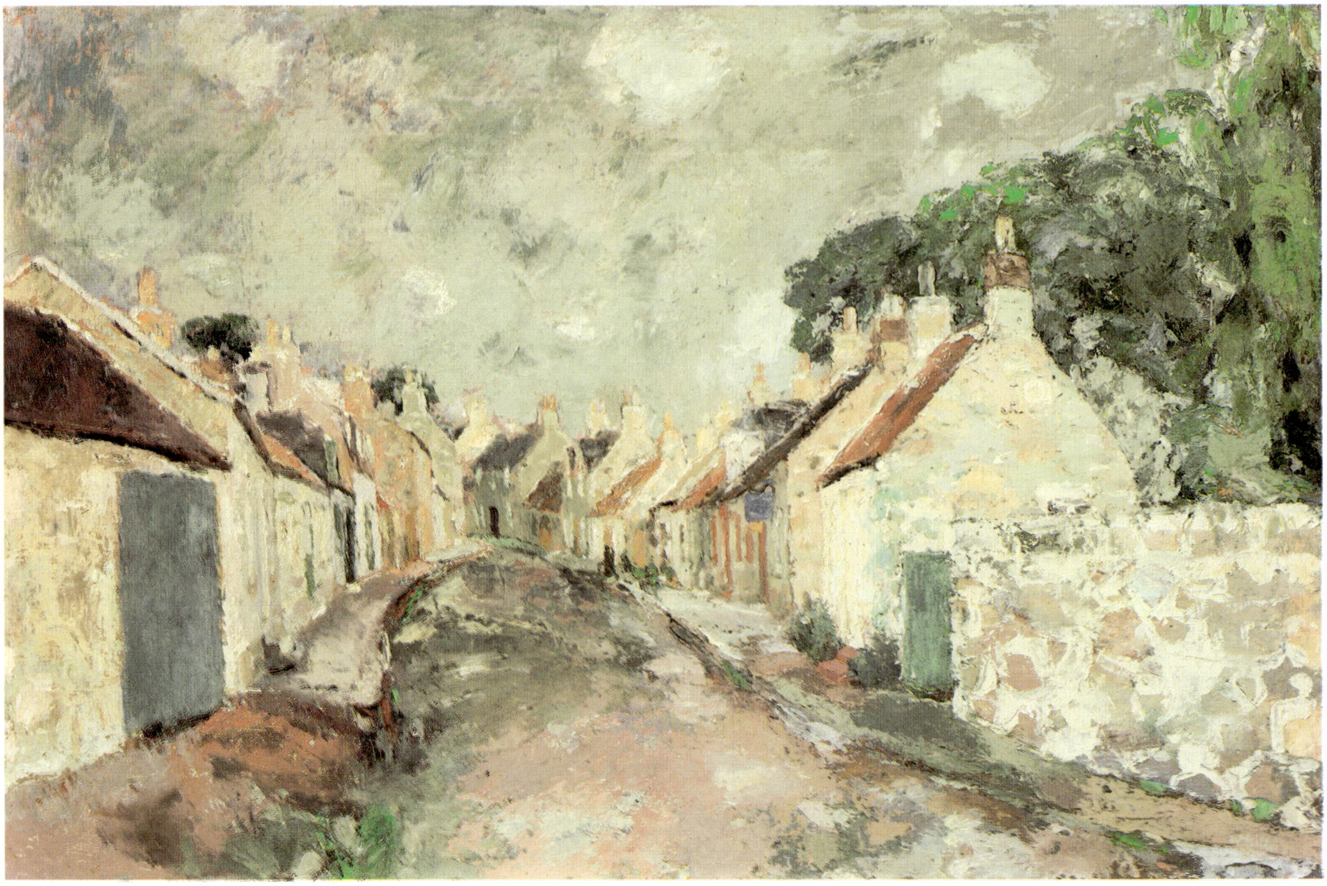

Temple Village c.1942 oil on canvas 60 × 91 cm SNGMA

Chapter 8

Now Bill, the lad from Temple Hill,
Would be all right if he'd sit still.
He'd build a house or fell an oak,
He canna stand lethargic folk.
He'll strip an engine to the core
And turn out pictures by the score.
Some say he owns the largest share
In I.C.I and Metro-Goldwyn-Mayer.
The snows may fall, the sun may shine,
Our Bill clocks in by ten-past-nine.
Gentle by nature, slow to wrath,
A golden wonder in his bath,
And Brussels sprouts around his head,
He delves and paints and sometimes goes to bed.

That affectionate skit, penned and delivered by his old teacher, college colleague and painting pal Donald Moodie at an ECA thrash, reveals more about Gillies and the way his friends saw him than its levity suggests. It speaks of his fidgety energy, physical strength, impatience with idlers, practicality, reliability, even temperament, and such a passion for gardening that he accumulated as much earth as paint under his fingernails. There is a sly dig, too, about his financial affluence – 'the largest share in I.C.I.' – provoked, no doubt, by the notoriously thrifty ways he inherited from his mother. The reference to M-G-M, however, should be taken in facetious conjunction with 'pictures by the score' – which there certainly were – and Dr Robert A. Lillie, an avid Edinburgh collector, had begun to buy a great many of them, over 500 as it turned out at the end of his long life. Dr Lillie bequeathed over 300 paintings to the Scottish nation, most of them by Gillies, and they form the backbone of his work in the SNGMA collection.

In a fascinating memoir of a visit to Dr Lillie's home, a suburban bungalow turned into a temple of modern art, Jack Firth recalls: 'I sat on a chair and he proceeded to bring out his treasures – all the Gillieses, or at least a large number of them. He had a trick of picking up a picture from the pile facing away from me and then, as he got to the easel, suddenly whipping it round like a conjuror's rabbit, and staring at me to see if I registered liking for it . . . they were Gillies at his most spontaneous, that effortless genius with which he could paint when he was at his most natural and unaffected . . . I do know that Dr Lillie had no paintings which showed Gillies in his more formal vein – Lillie had a dislike of conscious structuring and could get annoyed with Gillies when he thought he was being "too stark." On that first visit I started to learn things about Gillies' painting I hadn't realised before, and I have seldom talked with someone who, although not a painter himself, could see like one.'

In 1955 Sir John Rothenstein, director of the Tate Gallery, came to Edinburgh at Lillie's suggestion on the chance that he would purchase a Gillies. Two pictures were bought 'off the easel' at Temple, but when Rothenstein saw the oil *Esperston* at Lillie's home it was sold to the Tate. 'Not without a pang,' as Lillie later confided to Firth, 'but for Mr Gillies' reputation. It's a good picture.'

Apart from his generous patronage, Lillie became a good friend to Gillies and his womenfolk. They went on picnics together, 'took tea,' exchanged small gifts and enjoyed quiet social outings. Lillie struck up a touching relationship with Jenny and exchanged letters and postcards. Jenny expressed the family's appreciation of his support in an early note: 'Both Mother and I are so pleased that you have been so interested in William [*his Sunday name, surely; he was Willie to his family and early acquaintances; Bill to most of his adult friends*] and his pictures. You have brought his work to the fore, in a way no one else would have done, and I am glad all this is enjoyed by Mother . . . [*Dr Lillie had tried to encourage Gillies to visit a one-man show of his work, culled from the Lillie collection, at Aberdeen*] . . . If he doesn't want to see his own works, he would enjoy seeing the fine pictures of other artists in the galleries . . . We will try and get him to move. Thanks for giving timetables of trains . . . He doesn't like to meet people, as you will know by now, and keeps in the shade.'

Dr Lillie did Gillies and Scotland a great service by helping to 'put Gillies on the map' – as he intended. It is only fair to say, however, that even without the help of his most generous patron Gillies would have secured his own reputation. Burrell's remarkable collection of over a hundred Crawhalls must have seemed some sort of Scottish record before Lillie came along, but the Lillie bequest to the National Galleries of Scotland, including it should be said many other fine works by twentieth-century Scots, was an endowment of rare significance.

The RSA show of 1951 attracted the attention of Eric Newton in *The Sunday Times*.

> The paintings that remain in mind for their fearlessness and their fine discipline are the big still-lifes by William MacTaggart and W.G. Gillies. They are far more than tasteful. Both these artists realise that a simple arrangement of commonplace objects on a table can be a starting point for a voyage into uncharted regions of adventurous colour and formal design.

Interior, Temple from that same period treats his home as table-top, tilting the floor towards us and arranging his mother and sister, their furniture and bits and bobs of family life, as if they were objects in a still-life or actors frozen for a moment in the setting for a play. His division of the canvas into lively rectangles, the strength of his vertical supports, the cunning placing of the human figures in shafts of daylight so that the eye is drawn irresistibly across the painting's diagonal depth, and the softening of its hard geometry by ribbons and flounces of fabrics combine to create a masterly composition. T. Elder Dickson thought 'a strange sense of drama and imminent action haunts the picture space' and said the painting is 'fraught with exquisitely balanced anxieties and affections.' I find the drama elusive. Gillies played down his theatrical gift of imminence, but understood it as an emotional persuader. Even his landscapes can presage a thunderclap, a blatter of rain, or blinding blaze of sunshine. But this interior, the last of his family groups, seems – like his great self-portrait – another variation on the theme 'here we are,' and the curtain has just risen on a scene of order and tranquillity, a domestic idyll. Jenny's only anxiety is likely to concern a cake in the oven or whether her jam will set. Mrs Gillies concentrates on the washing-up. The unseen artist declares his affections in an ambiance that almost purrs with satisfaction.

As his reputation grew, the fearlessness that Newton spoke about began to be demonstrated more widely. His lyrical *The Studio Table*, one of his most persuasive still-lifes – all its warm elements suspended in exquisite spatial and tonal harmony – put him alongside many other important British artists in a Festival of Britain exhibition,

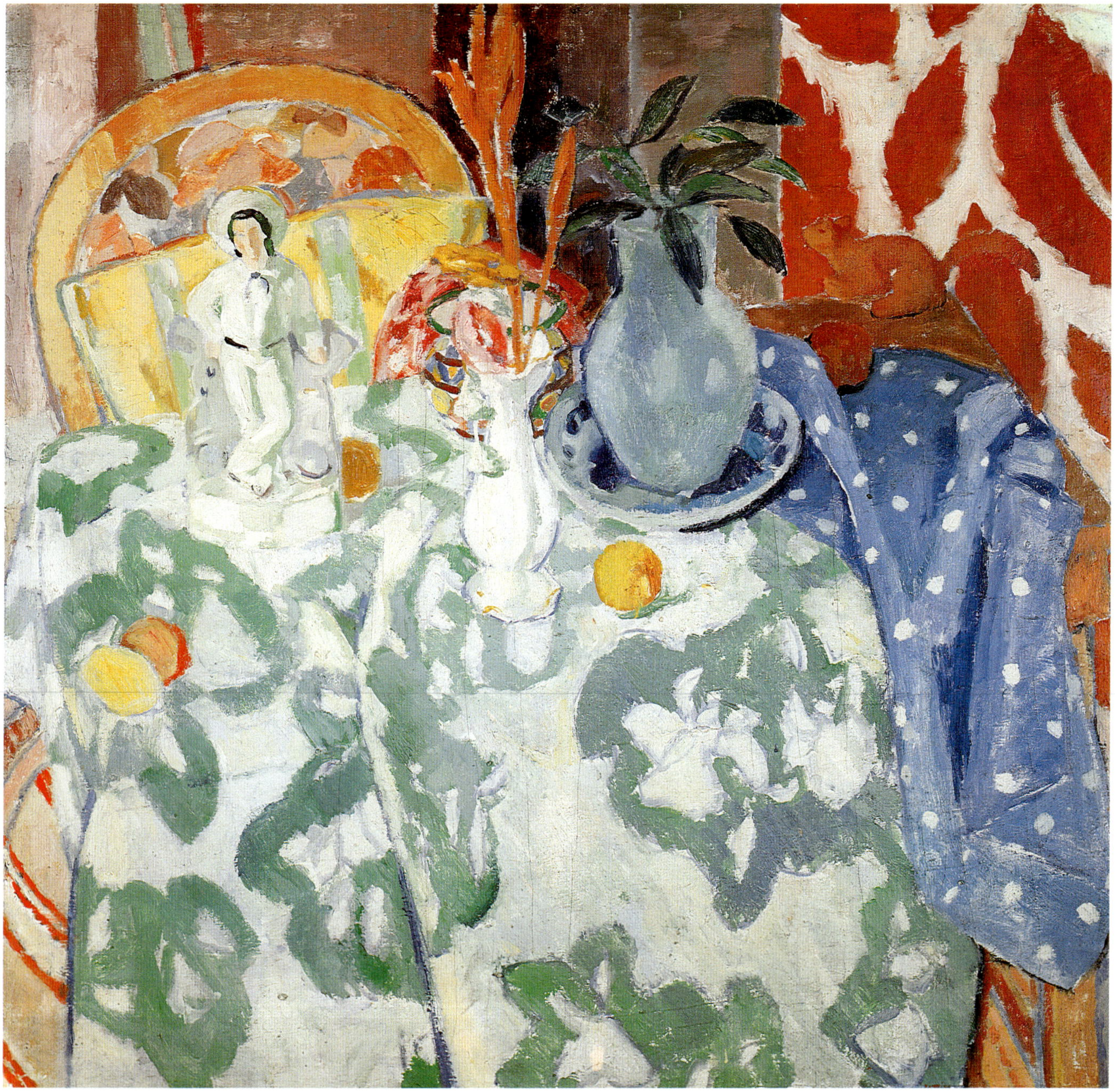

The Red Squirrel 1941 oil on canvas 112 × 114 cm RSA

Sixty Paintings For Fifty One, organised by the Arts Council. That celebratory year also saw his work in *Britain in Watercolours*, at the RWS Galleries, London, and the Arts Council included him in *British Painting 1925-50*. Throughout the 50s, at home and abroad, the so-called Edinburgh School – Gillies, Maxwell, MacTaggart, and Anne Redpath – began to be grouped together in critics' minds as an identifiable extension of the ECA *belle peinture* tradition, but earned national recognition as distinctive individualists.

Glasgow's fine municipal collection at Kelvingrove includes *Still-life, Blue and Brown*, a superb example of the intense Tilley lamp period, commanding in its austerity, alive and dancing with contrapuntal shapes and forms, eschewing the artifice of contemplative painterly illusion in favour of dynamic design.

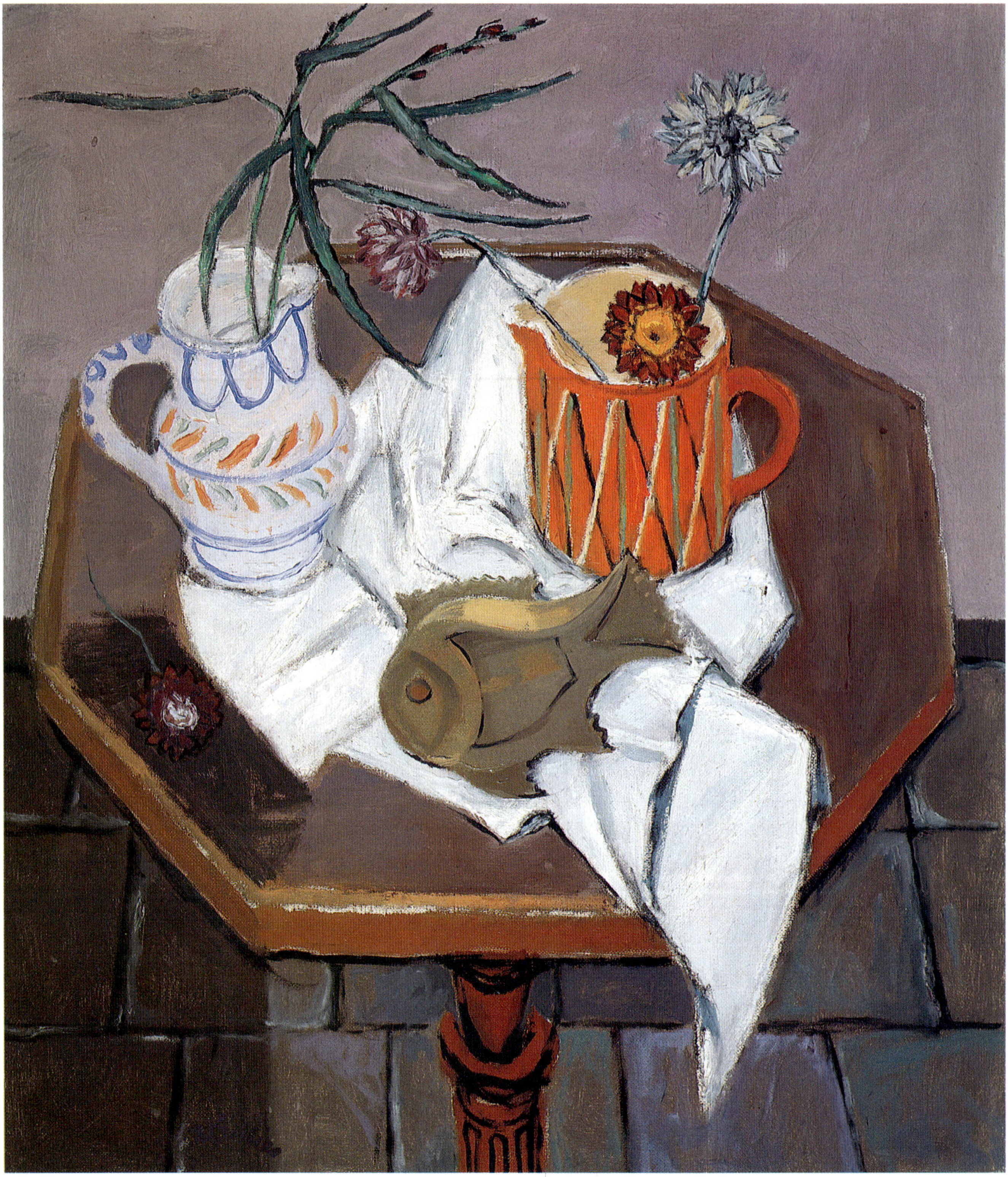

Still Life with Octagonal Table c.1958 70 × 50 cm

Since his first one-man show with The Scottish Gallery in 1949 Gillies had stayed faithful to Aitken Dott and they continued to show his work at their Castle Street gallery in Edinburgh until the end of his life. His old friend and colleague John Houston recalls how, in the early 50s, a small deputation of regular exhibitors at the gallery, including Redpath and Willie Wilson – another of Gillies' camping cronies – buttonholed Bill Macaulay, of Aitken Dott, and asked him to persuade Gillies to push up his prices. Since Gillies was the market leader, his prices determined everybody else's; young painters in particular suffered from there being no movement in the system. At that time his small watercolours were fixed at £14, including the frame – precisely what Houston paid for his first Gillies, and got it reframed to seal the bargain. Medium-sized watercolours cost between £20 and £25. When the 1973 RSA exhibition opened, the day before Gillies died, two watercolours were priced at only £50 each. I saw a fine example from the 50s in a Glasgow gallery in the spring of 1991, priced at just under £5000.

A happy event for the two great chums of the Edinburgh School, Gillies and Maxwell, was the Arts Council of Great Britain exhibition of their paintings, drawings and watercolours at the New Burlington Galleries in 1954 – a rare chance for London to see a substantial body of work by two of Scotland's finest artistic ambassadors, two weavers of magical spells. As David McClure says in his sensitive book on Maxwell: 'Gillies could wring from his subject a kind of instant poetry – a lyrical truth . . . Maxwell finds his way by analogue and metaphor. Often his pictures seem to begin from an observed reality, but during the process of painting, this reality becomes transfigured by his own particular alchemy . . . In Gillies' work there are resemblances to things other than the overt subject matter, but they are never fanciful or metaphorical. Perhaps it is we ourselves who find these resemblances in Gillies' work. Maxwell finds them for us.'

Both succumbed to the 'strange witchery,' as Archibald Geikie called it, of Lowland landscape, which thrilled the minds of poets like Wordsworth and Scott. 'Art,' said Johnnie Maxwell – enlisting the help of Degas – 'is not a sport,' as Gillies shot out of the tent to catch another watercolour before the kettle boiled. In his later years Maxwell painted few 'pure' landscapes, preferring to make the natural world only part of his unique phantasmagoria. The psalmist's hills – 'from whence doth come mine aid' – were Gillies' hills. They pulled him away from the fireside and sent him racketing into the teeth of the wind on his motor bike to snatch a sketch of drifted snow on the Moorfoots. Or with deft sweeps of a flooded brush he would conjure the shifting shadows of clouds on a sunny meadow.

Sir Walter took the American essayist Washington Irving for a ramble into his beloved hills. 'Now,' said Scott, 'I have brought you, like the pilgrim in the Pilgrim's Progress, to the top of the Delectable Mountains, that I may show you all the goodly regions hereabouts.' Back in New York, Irving wrote:

> I gazed about me for a time with mute surprise. I may almost say with disappointment. I beheld a mere succession of grey waving hills, line beyond line, as far as my eye could reach, monotonous in their aspect, and so destitute of trees, that one could almost see a stout fly walking along their profile; and the far-famed Tweed appeared a naked stream, flowing between bare hills, without a tree or thicket on its banks; and yet such had been the magic web of poetry and romance thrown over the whole, that it had a greater charm for me than the richest scenery I had beheld in England. I could not help giving utterance to my thoughts. Scott hummed for a moment to himself, and looked grave; he had no idea of having his music complimented at the expense of his native hills. 'It may be pertinacity,' said he at length; 'but to my eye, these grey hills, and all this wild border country, have beauties peculiar to themselves. I like the very nakedness of the land; it has something bold, and stern, and solitary about it. When I have been for some time in the rich scenery about Edinburgh, which is like ornamented garden land, I begin to wish myself back again among my own honest grey hills; and if I did not see the heather, at least once a year, *I think I should die*!'

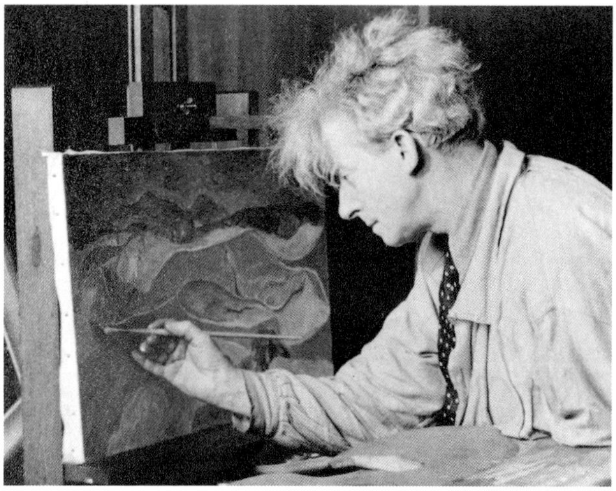

The Artist at Work (Photo: RSA Archives)

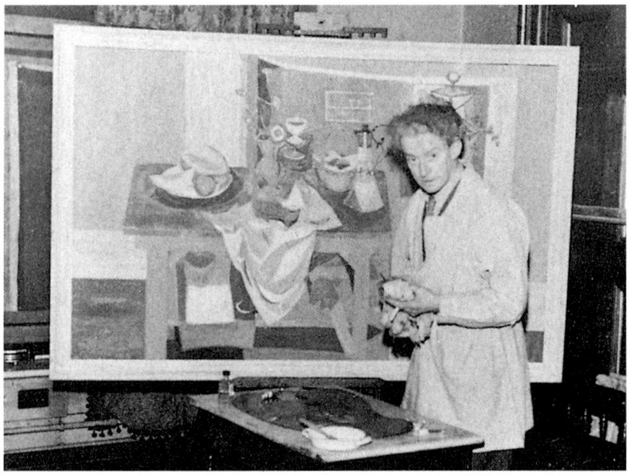

The Artist in Front of 'The Studio Table', 1951
(Photo: RSA Archives)

In *The Scenery of Scotland*, Archibald Geikie, the eminent Scottish geologist, graced his science with art in a riposte to Irving which might stand for all time as the definitive description of Gillies country:

> The casual traveller to this region usually finds at least three fundamental faults with it – featurelessness, treelessness, and monotony. To him it is a smooth bare sweep of bushless hills, rising ridge beyond ridge, interminable in their continuity of tame outline and oppressive in their sameness of colour . . .
>
> For my own part, I have never been able to understand the charge of want of feature. True, the hills do not mount into crests or peaks, nor are their sides abundantly gashed with ravines, or roughened with many crags and precipices. Yet, of feature, and most expressive feature, every one of them is full. Nowhere else in Scotland can the exquisite modelling of flowing curves in hill forms, due partly to the contours of underlying solid rock, and partly to the lines assumed by accumulating detritus, be so conspicuously seen. These characters are not obtrusive, indeed, but perhaps on that very ground they afford a keener pleasure to the eye that has been trained to detect them . . .
>
> The so-called monotony of these softly undulating hills constitutes, I do not doubt, one main element in the peculiar fascination which they have always exercised upon minds of a poetic cast. From the sky-line on either side, gentle but boldly drawn curves of bent-covered moorland sweep down into the grassy meadow on the floor of the valley. These are architectural forms of the hill-slopes, and remain distinct at all seasons of the year. But their beauty and impressiveness vary from month to month, almost from hour to hour. For the most part they are aglow with colour, now purple with heather-blooms, now bright-green with bracken, now yellow with golden bend, now deepening into orange and russet as the early frosts of autumn lay their fingers on the ferns. And these colours are suffused, as it were, over the slopes, like a thin enamel, that never conceals the modulations of their form. In winter, when the ground is covered with snow, the endless diversity and grace of the curves stand out in naked beauty and offer to the student of hill-forms an admirable lesson . . .
>
> The long sweeping lines of form and colour, which would be utterly lost under a covering of trees, plunge down into the flat meadows of the valley through which a clear stream is ever murmuring . . .

> The very barrenness of the landscape becomes itself a charm, allowing the soft gentle outlines of the hills to have full play upon the fancy. There is a tender grace in the landscape that is offended by the protrusion of no harsh feature, no abrupt crag or yawning ravine. Moreover a pleasing loneliness broods over it all, which, in the case of sterner scenery, becomes oppressive and almost insupportable. The silence is broken fitfully by the breeze as it bears back the murmur of the distant brook, or by the curlew screaming from the nearer hill. The very sounds of the valley – the plaintive cadence of the river, and the low sad sough of the wind along the slopes – combine to produce that tone of melancholy which seems so characteristic and so inseparable from these pastoral valleys.

I have quoted those nineteenth-century writers at such length because, in their own medium, they needed that amount of space to say what Gillies, in full flood and brimming over with his own witchery, said many hundreds of times with a few strokes of a brush – *March, Moorfoot; Outside Broughton; The Peebles Train* (twice); *Border Valley; Roadman's House, Lyne; Fields and River; Dusk; Summer, Moorfoot; Heriot Valley* are only a representative sample of his Scotland in all its moods and seasons. It has been estimated that he exhibited more than three thousand paintings in his lifetime and at least two thousand of these would have been landscapes. 'I have always enjoyed weather,' he said, lumping the bad in with the good, 'always seen landscape pictorially, and I've got immense satisfaction in recording swiftly in line and colour the fugitive, the subtle and the grand in nature.'

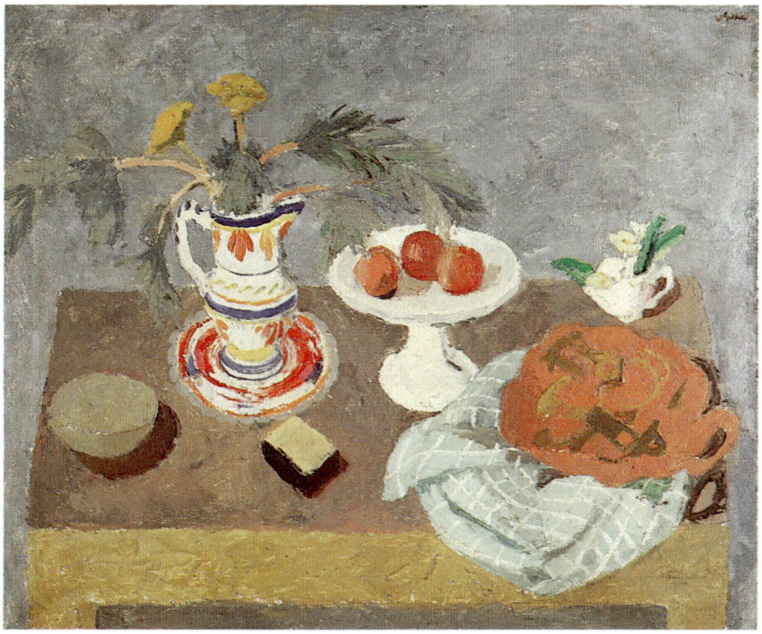

Still-life with Breton Pot 1942 oil on canvas 77 × 89 cm SNGMA

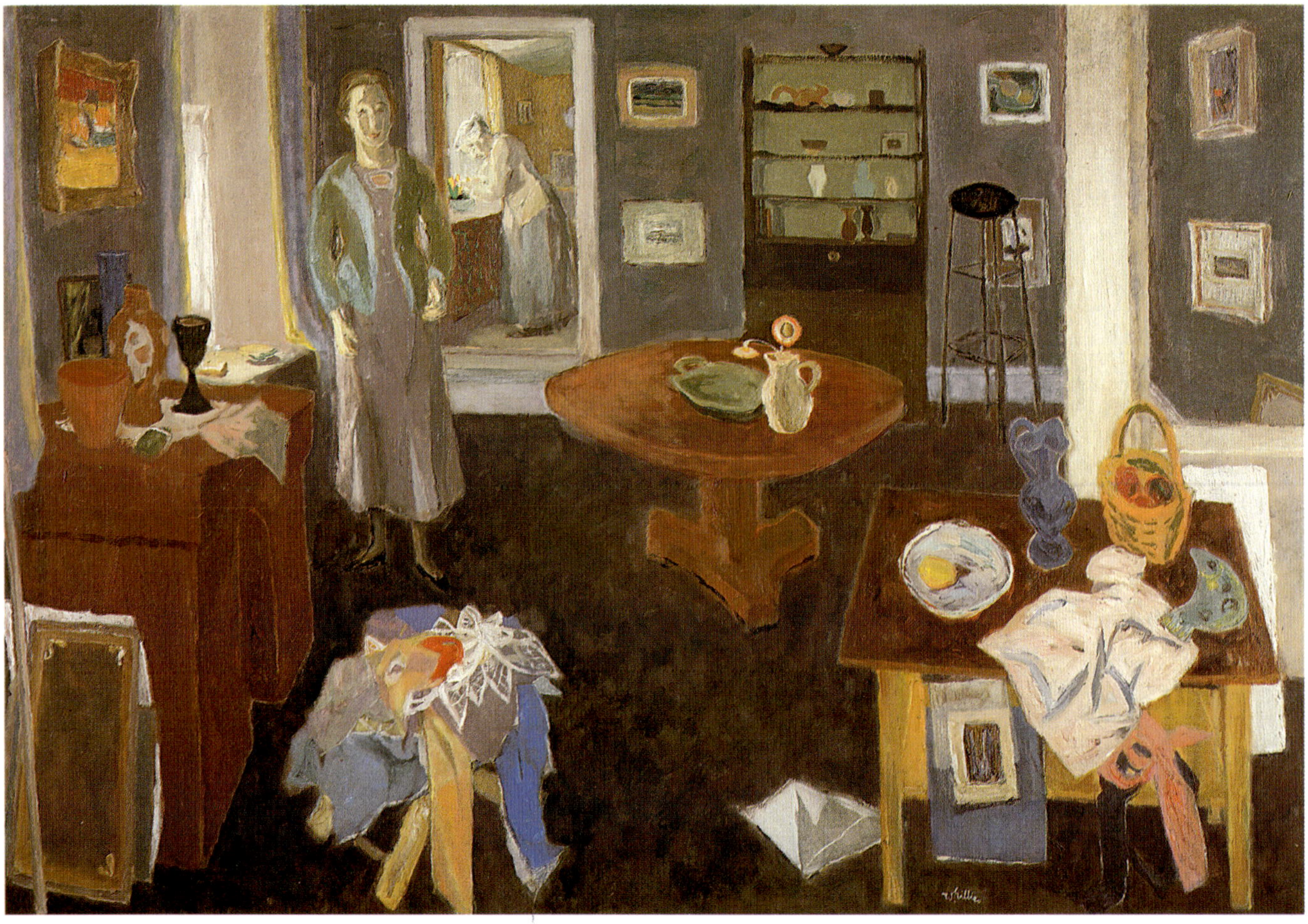

Interior, Temple 1951 oil on canvas 122 × 173 cm A Fletcher

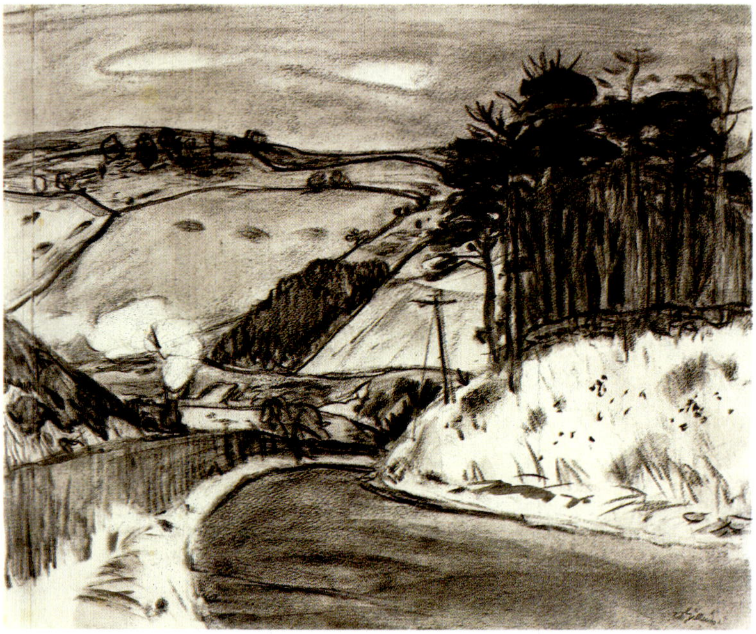

Border Valley c.1950 charcoal and ink on paper 35 × 42 cm SNGMA

Chapter 9

Time at Temple oozed rather than passed. The seasons and the years slipped away in a succession of jam and wine crops, summer picnics, winters round the Raeburn, and optimistic springs. Through the ever-open door of the Gillies cottage the old mother seemed as spry as her son, but Jenny's health had begun to fail her redoubtable spirit. Neither the telephone nor television seemed necessary or desirable, but electricity had dragged the village into the twentieth-century and silenced the roaring Tilley. Refugees from the city began to buy themselves peace and quiet. Mrs Gillies started to take a nightly glass of sherry 'to help her sleep.' Her son continued to cover the walls of some rooms with papers of assorted patterns, ostensibly because he 'couldn't make up his mind,' but probably because he had bought them as a job-lot in a sale. Only the fear of disrupting the household prevented him from making improvements to the cottage like those going on all over the village. Dormer windows sprouted where thatch had once been. Attics became extra bedrooms and playrooms for a new generation of children. Roses still grew round the doors, but parked cars clotted the village street. Gillies drove a pre-war Alvis Silver Eagle into Edinburgh and a favourite Norton motor bike into the hills.

He had been made a Commander of the Order of the British Empire in 1957. In 1960, after 14 years as Head of Drawing and Painting, he became Principal of ECA – a distinction, certainly, but in a vexed world peopled by planners and administrators, yoked to a daily round of time-tabling, wage-bargaining and bureaucracy which he found corrosive of spirit and erosive of painting-time. He had no real heart for it and told his neighbour Mary MacIver – who, with her husband Hector, had become good friends – that he was 'just a caretaker government,' an over-modest joke against himself. In fact, he was an extremely popular Principal and 'a bonny fechter' for the good cause of his college.

He had been teaching adults for 34 years, saw fathers and sons go through college, believed passionately in the ethos of art education, treated none of his posts as a sinecure, worked hard and enjoyed that part of teaching which, at its happiest, should feel like an extension of one's own youth. In his teaching time there had been convulsions in art and society. Abstract Expressionism and Pop Art had replaced Dada and Surrealism in the affections of the eager young, whose access to art school had been facilitated by grant-aid from a more egalitarian social system. Television and specialist magazines began to bring art out of its elitist closet. Surreptitiously, television was teaching the world a visual vocabulary. Improving design standards heightened perceptions of excellence. It seemed a century since David Alison taught the only way he knew how – by example, even if that meant taking up a student's brushes and, before his very eyes, over-painting the canvas. Gillies himself had been known to give a student outline a bit of bite here and there or smudge some emphasis into the paint with his fingers. These days were over.

Despite the thousands of students who passed through his classes a surprisingly small number remember being 'taught' by Gillies on a one-to-one basis. He was everywhere and nowhere. Offhand words of encouragement were cherished like testimonials. Outright commendation could sustain flagging spirits through a term of disasters. His pawky one-liners became college legends. Affectionate anecdotes were handed down through the decades. Students and staff learned to mimic his curiously flat accent and rising inflections – '*awfully* nice passage, that,' or '*quite* handsome.'

On 8 November, 1960 he sat down at Temple and wrote to Dr Lillie:

> Just a note to let you know that Jenny passed away, very peacefully, early this morning. She had been showing signs of improvement but yesterday went into a coma, from which she never really emerged. Mother is bearing up wonderfully well. She has been so constantly with Jenny that the full realisation of the loss may take some time. I'm sure, however, she is also feeling a sense of relief that she has been spared to nurse Jenny to the end . . .

He was 62, his mother an amazing 96. 'Time's wingèd chariot' was hurrying near and perhaps he could hear the thunder of hooves.

Despite its brave highlights of blue and pink and lemon *The Garden, Temple, Winter Moon* slumbers with an eerie spirituality, its somnolent greys and skeletal blacks haunted by an equivocal moon.

He neither brooded nor fretted. The immense sadness of Jenny's death coincided with a fresh determination in his painting to take simplification to its limits, to pare reality to its insubstantial bones, to detach himself even more from the evidence of his eyes and trust instead his perceptual responses. At times, in his big late still-lifes as well as his windowscapes and landscapes, he seems to be rehabilitating memory or playing back a dream.

One evening in 1962 the telephone rang in the kiosk outside the front door of a neighbour. The village call-box was the Gillies equivalent of a private line in a public place; he would often wait for calls by arrangement. The neighbour, who has since become the novelist Joan Lingard, picked up the phone and was asked to pass on to Gillies the sad news that John Maxwell had died. Hector McIver and Gillies drove to Dalbeattie for the funeral. McIver told his wife that it was the first time he had ever seen Gillies upset. 'The tears streamed down his face as the coffin was lowered into the grave.' A college appreciation, to which Gillies was one of the signatories, said:

> We cherish the memory of his gentleness, his gaiety, his magnanimity, his infectious humour, his tolerance and wisdom. We remember above all his transcendent gifts as an artist, his skill as a teacher, his wide knowledge and his passion for all that is purest in music and poetry. We remember his kindness and patience, the immensity of his spirit and the frailness of his body. We are grateful for the riches he disseminated and the strength he gave to our common purpose.

Few of the many honours Gillies received gave him as much pleasure as his election in 1963 as President of the RSW. No Scottish artist since Arthur Melville had used watercolour with such vision, flexibility and originality. His prodigious mastery of the medium and prolific output encouraged and inspired many artists to investigate that ancient and demanding painting craft and extend its aesthetic possibilities.

But 1963 also took his mother from him, in her hundredth year. For the first time in his life he was on his own. It is impossible to measure his loss and grief after 65 years of such a close and profound bond. Yet he must have rejoiced in the length of her healthy and happy life, in the vivacity of her spirit, and – most of all, perhaps – in her pride in his many achievements. 'This was, I think, a turning point in his life,' said Philip G. Napier, a good neighbour who wrote a warm memoir of Gillies in 1980. 'He had been the mainstay and support of his mother and sisters. Now he could devote all his time to his own pursuits.'

The neighbours rallied round. He bought himself a black labrador, called it Jet, and they were soon devoted to each other. A lady up the street cooked for him twice a week – the sort of simple meals he had been used to all his life. He split the food into portions and heated them up for his evening meals, washed and ironed his laundry,

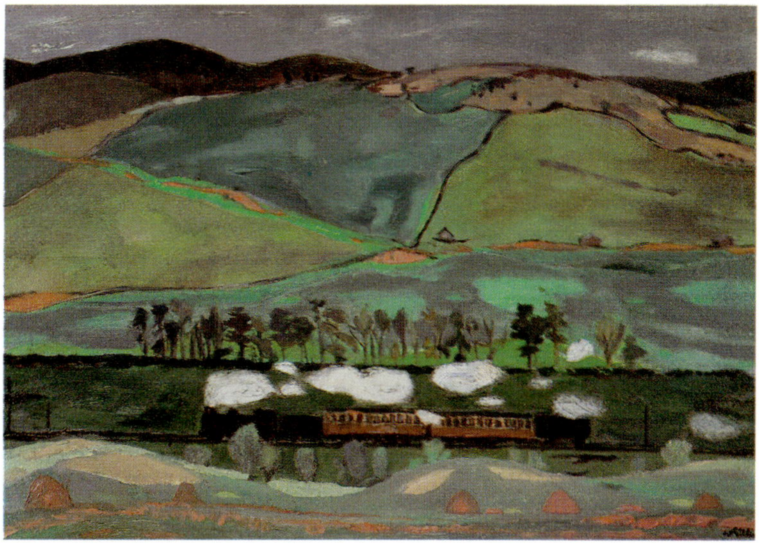

The Peebles Train c.1950 oil on canvas 49 × 71 cm

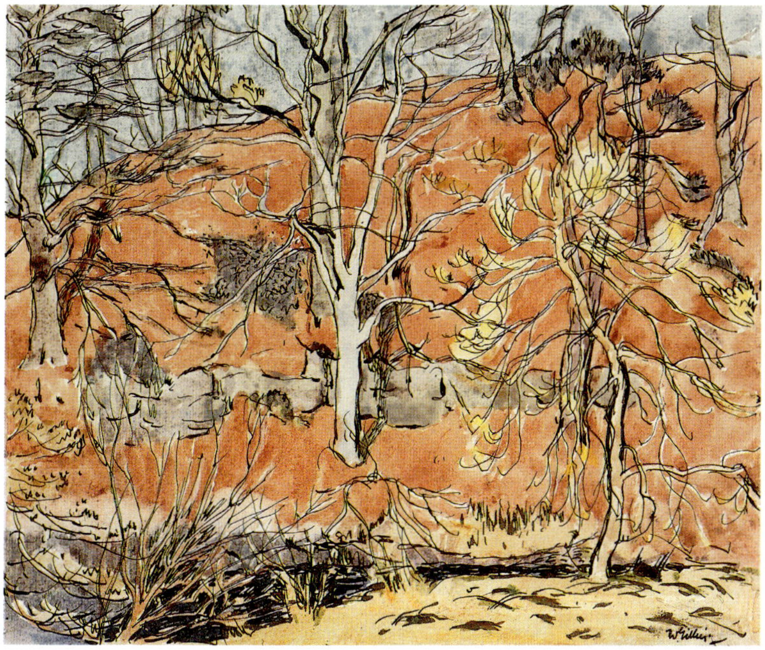

Trees c.1948 watercolour and ink on paper 27 × 32 cm Dr James Ritchie

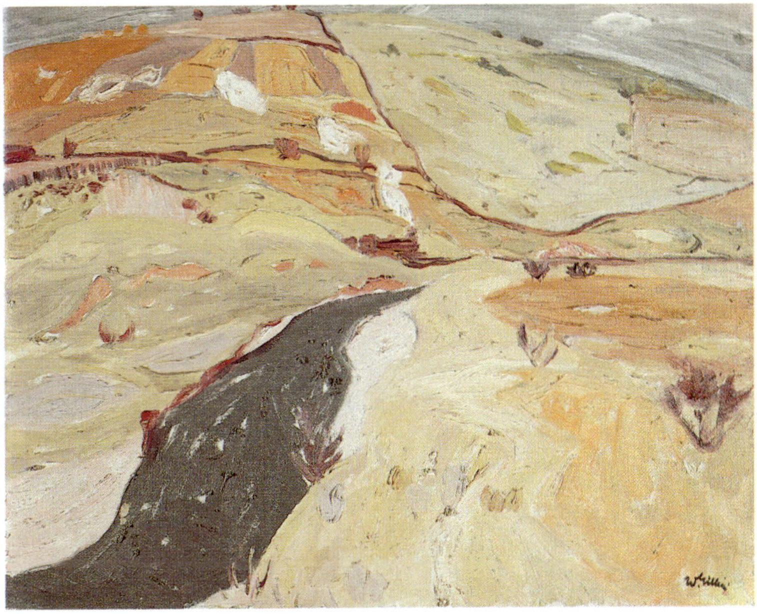

The Peebles Train c.1950 oil on canvas 46 × 57 cm SNGMA

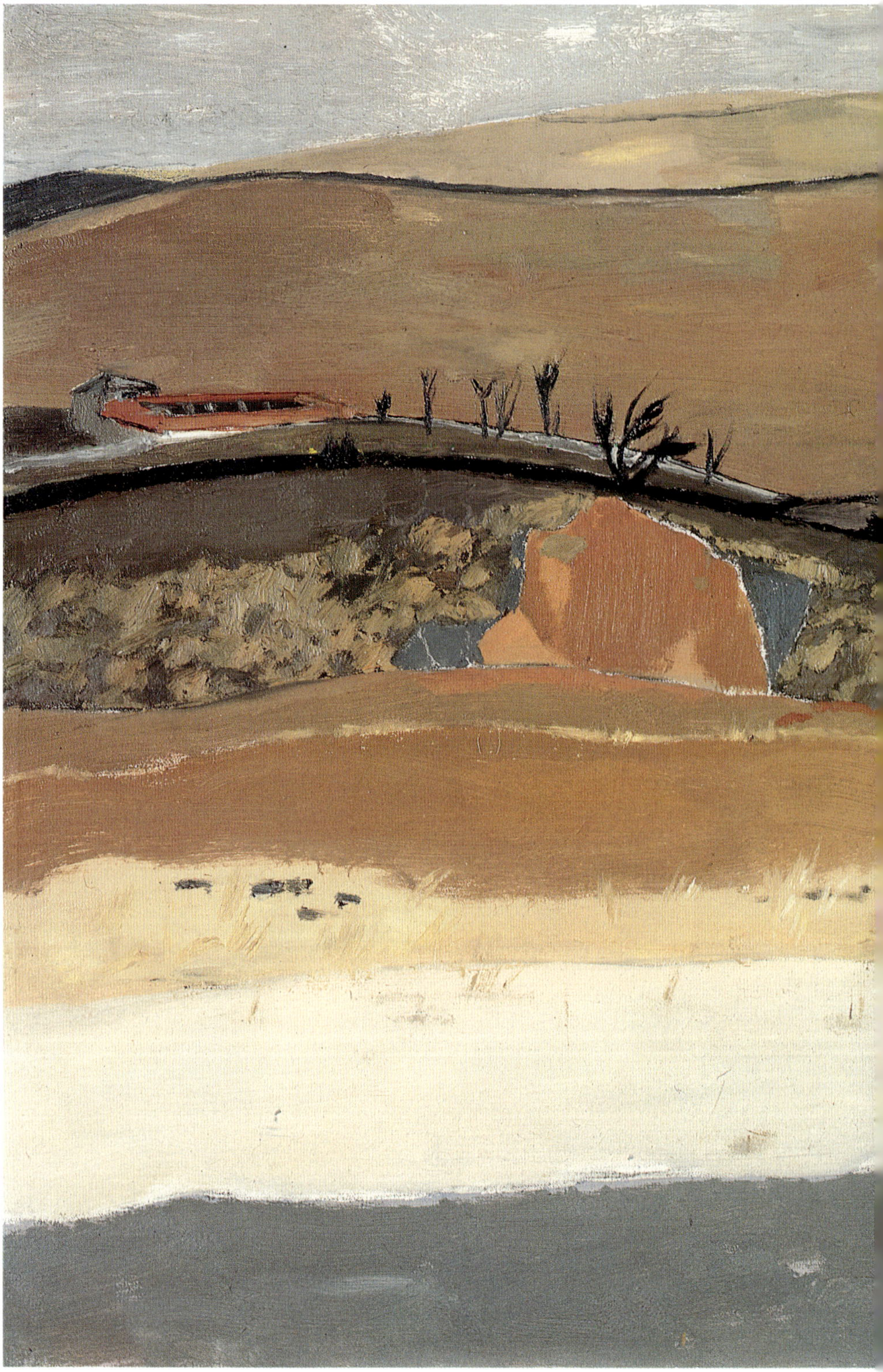

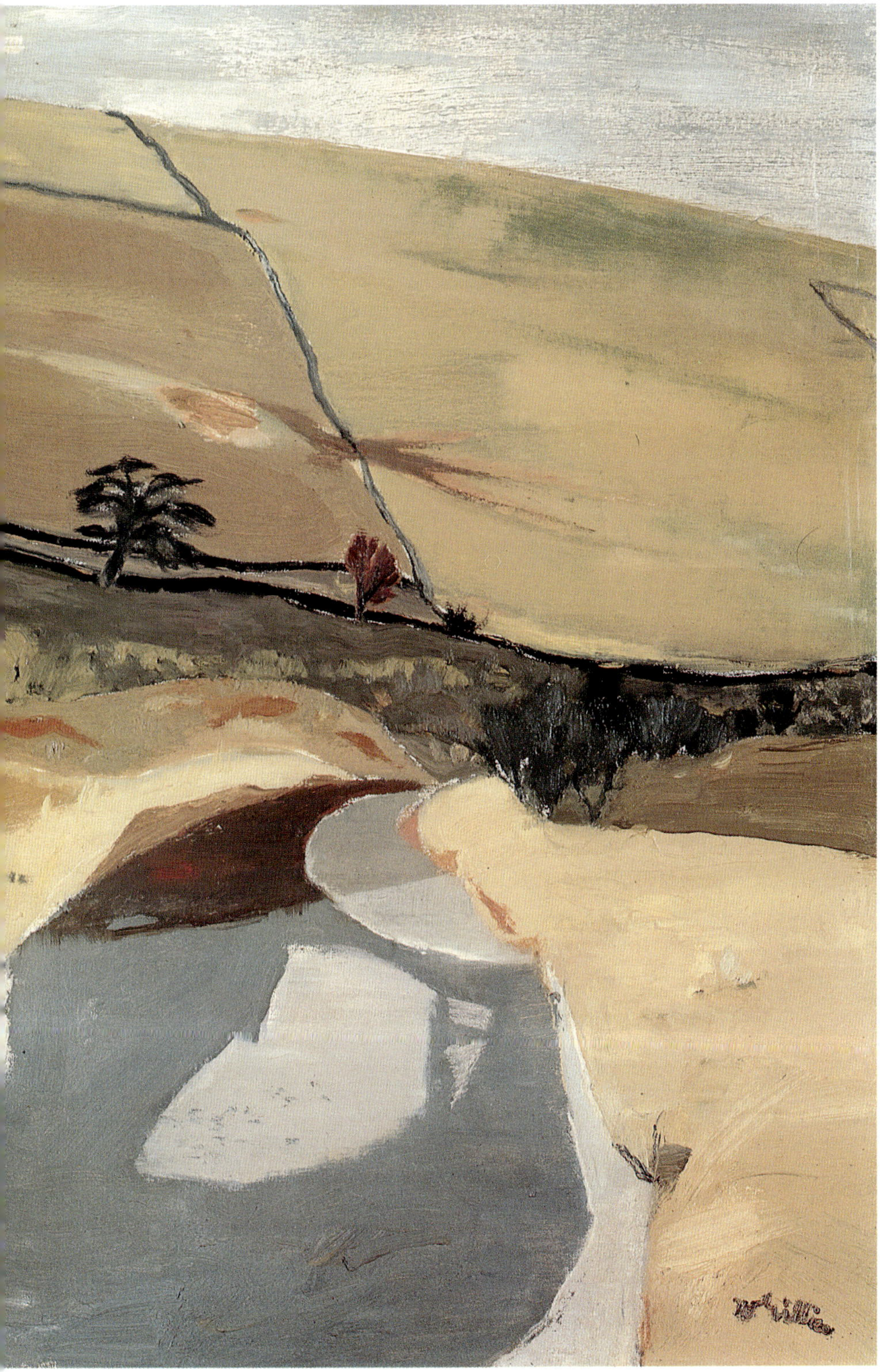

Fields and River c.1959 oil on canvas 63 × 86 cm SNGMA

darned his socks, and turned the worn collars and cuffs of shirts. William Jackson, who in 1991 severed his long connection with Aitken Dott to set up his own gallery in London, says that Gillies, from that time on generally refused to attend funerals of colleagues or contemporaries. 'Perhaps there had been too much sadness in his life for him to cope with, and he protected himself by declining social invitations.'

His intensely private home life opened out a bit. Edinburgh friends visited more often, especially at weekends. If neighbours knocked on his door without getting an answer they just walked in and Jet would lead them to his master in studio or garden. The McIvers made a fuss of him, especially at Christmas when he shared their festive dinners. Hector McIver, a larger-than-life Lewisman who is fondly remembered as a schoolteacher, broadcaster and Gaelic scholar, attracted his wide circle of friends in the artistic and literary world to Temple. Gillies met Sir Donald Wolfit and other celebrities in the McIver cottage where the drams flowed full and fast. On one occasion, when Chris Grieve [Hugh MacDiarmid] was staying the night, Gillies was invited to meet him. Mary McIver recalls how the men settled down to their whisky and 'even Bill, unusually for him, got very merry, and in the end, so abandoned did the three of them become that they decided to treat me to a display of a Highland Reel. Hector started to sing . . . As Burns says: "they reeled, they set, they crossed, they cleekit". As the merriment grew louder, I don't know why – nor could Bill remember either, next day – he suddenly took a comb out of his pocket and started to comb Chris's mane of hair down on his forehead, as he squared up to him. Thinking this was no less than a stroke of genius, the others whipped combs out of their breast pockets also, and for the rest of the dance, each and every one of them combed the hair down on the forehead of whoever happened to be prancing opposite to him.' Many years later Mary McIver made a lithograph of 'that rousing episode.'

She shared Gillies' interest in collecting china – 'I hadn't much money and Bill disliked spending much money; we rarely spent more than threepence on anything' – and his acquisitions ended up, often enough, in his still-lifes and interiors. He enjoyed telling her how some of the most spectacular trees and shrubs in his garden had cost him only sixpence at pre-war Woolworth's – 'the low price was part of the enjoyment' – and that he had 'found' a beautiful peony buried under weeds in the garden of a tumbledown cottage, rode his motor bike all the way home for a spade, and dug up the root.

Joan Lingard remembers his regular visits to a saleroom in Pathhead. 'He used to buy wardrobes, but I think he used them only to store his wine and jam.' His garage was so full of wine and motor bikes there was no room for his two cars which were parked in the street. His reason for having two cars, he said, was in case one broke down. The Alvis was his pride and joy – 'a fine-looking car to park in front of the college,' he said, 'I wouldn't want to disgrace the building' – but he had also owned an ancient Bentley. More than once both cars failed him at the same time. One day he went out with the intention of buying a colour television set. He returned with a shiny new Ford Granada.

He built himself a new studio with a long verandah, glazed against the weather, looking out over the garden. Then he went through the house systematically, creating a new kitchen out of a wide lobby, re-laying floors, building a new staircase, but doing nothing that detracted from the original character of the cottages. No job that needed doing by hand was beyond him. Not even severe imprecations by friends stopped him doing his own roof repairs.

He still resisted the idea of having television in the house; it was bound to lure him away from the easel in the evenings. But when Mary McIver bought colour television a small

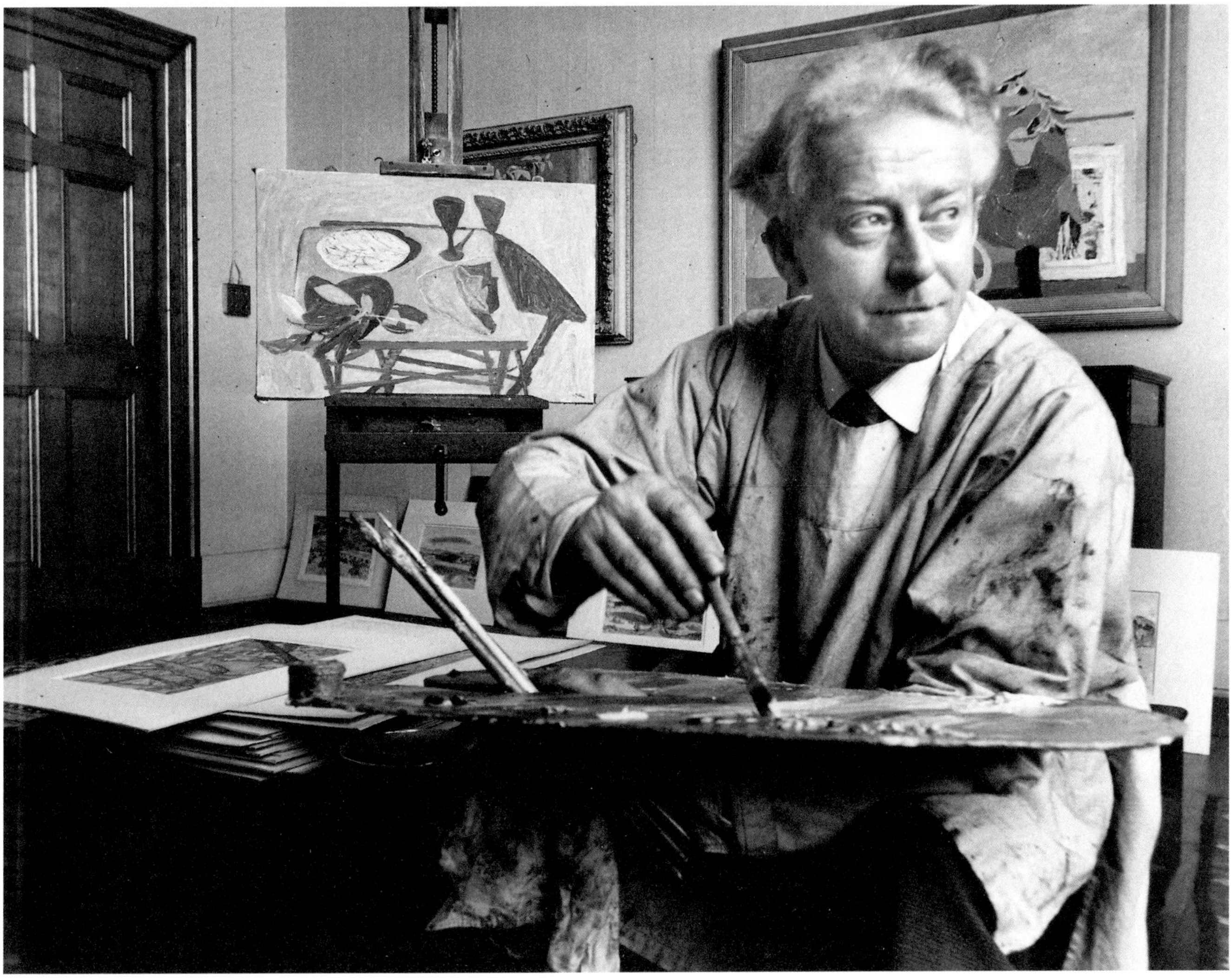

Artist in Studio (Scotsman Publications)

social ritual began. He would mark up in *Radio Times* programmes that interested him – art documentaries, features on china and antiques – and accept her invitation to come and see them. 'When I opened the door to him, he'd be standing there smiling in pleased anticipation, his mane of white hair, still hinting of the red I once remembered, brushed firmly back, his best suit on, and his hand held out, offering me as usual his present of After Eights which he'd probably just hurried down to the village shop to buy.' She always invited him to play some music on her record-player while she made tea. He always chose Strauss' *Der Rosenkavalier*. It seemed to mean something special to him but she respected his privacy too much to ask why.

Over the years London had seen his work on many occasions and he exhibited regularly at the Royal Academy. So far as metropolitan critics and commentators were concerned he was the doyen of Scottish painters in much the same way as Eric Linklater and MacDiarmid represented the Scottish novel and poetry. He was delighted when the Royal Academy elected him an Associate in 1964.

Two supremely confident paintings from 1965 pay homage to his masters while sustaining the impetus of his constant progression as an artist. The magnificent *Still-life with Black Fishes* is nothing short of deliberate emulation of Braque, but a salute rather than a parody, an invitation to acknowledge the similarities in order to recognise the differences. The allusive nod in Bonnard's direction in *Interior, Temple* – a *bonne-bouche* of pastel and watercolour

– celebrates the cosy order of his reconstructed home, its tokens of the life he has lived and a glimpse of the world beyond. It seems to echo a contented sigh and its resonance of colour is, as ever, his own.

His profoundly caring professional commitment to ECA, which had lasted half-a-century, came to a formal end in 1966 when he retired as Principal. Almost immediately the University of Edinburgh conferred upon him an honorary doctorate (D.Litt) and he was elected a Fellow of the Educational Institute of Scotland.

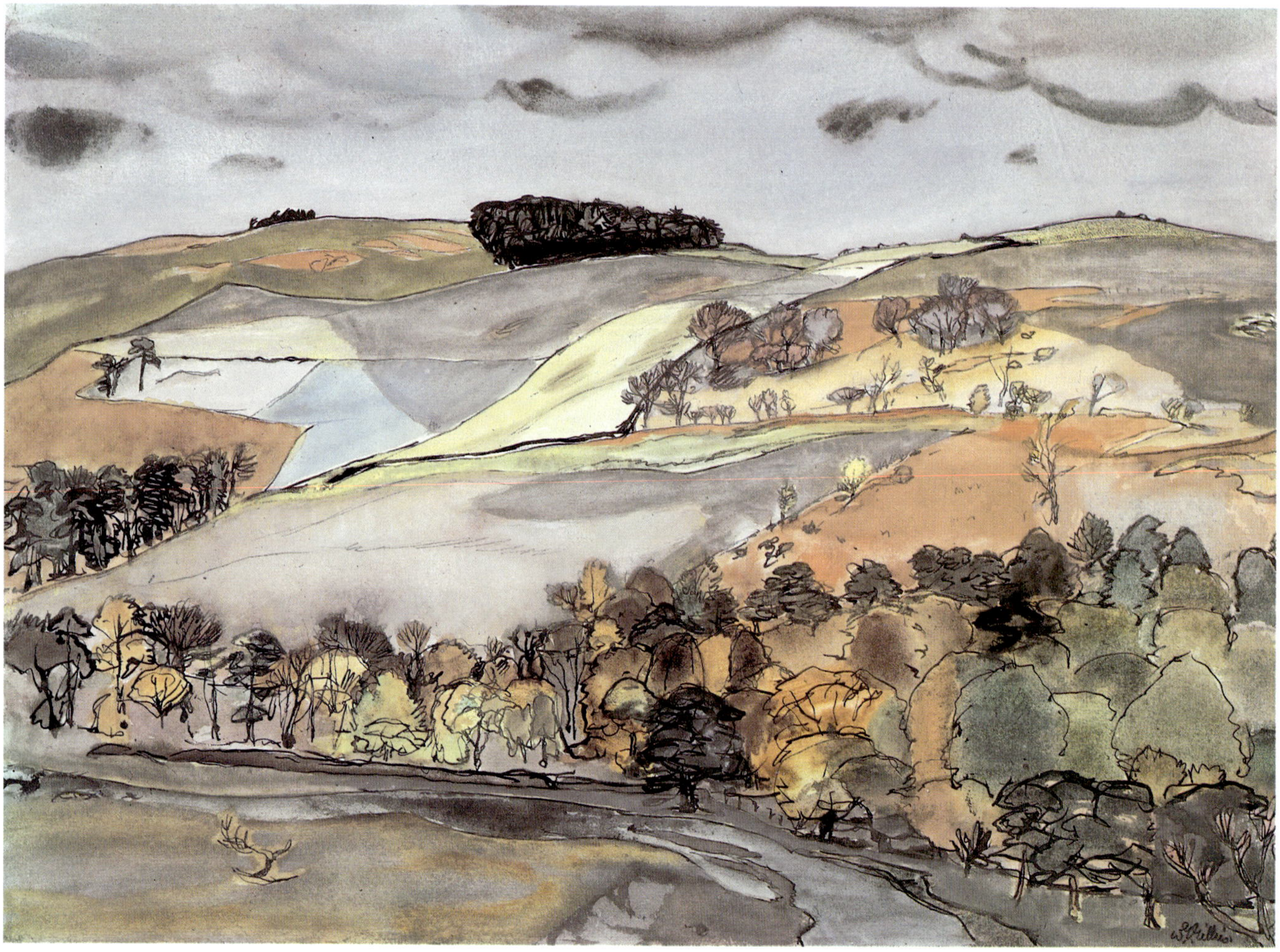

Heriot Valley 1963 watercolour and pencil on paper 39 × 52 cm AAG

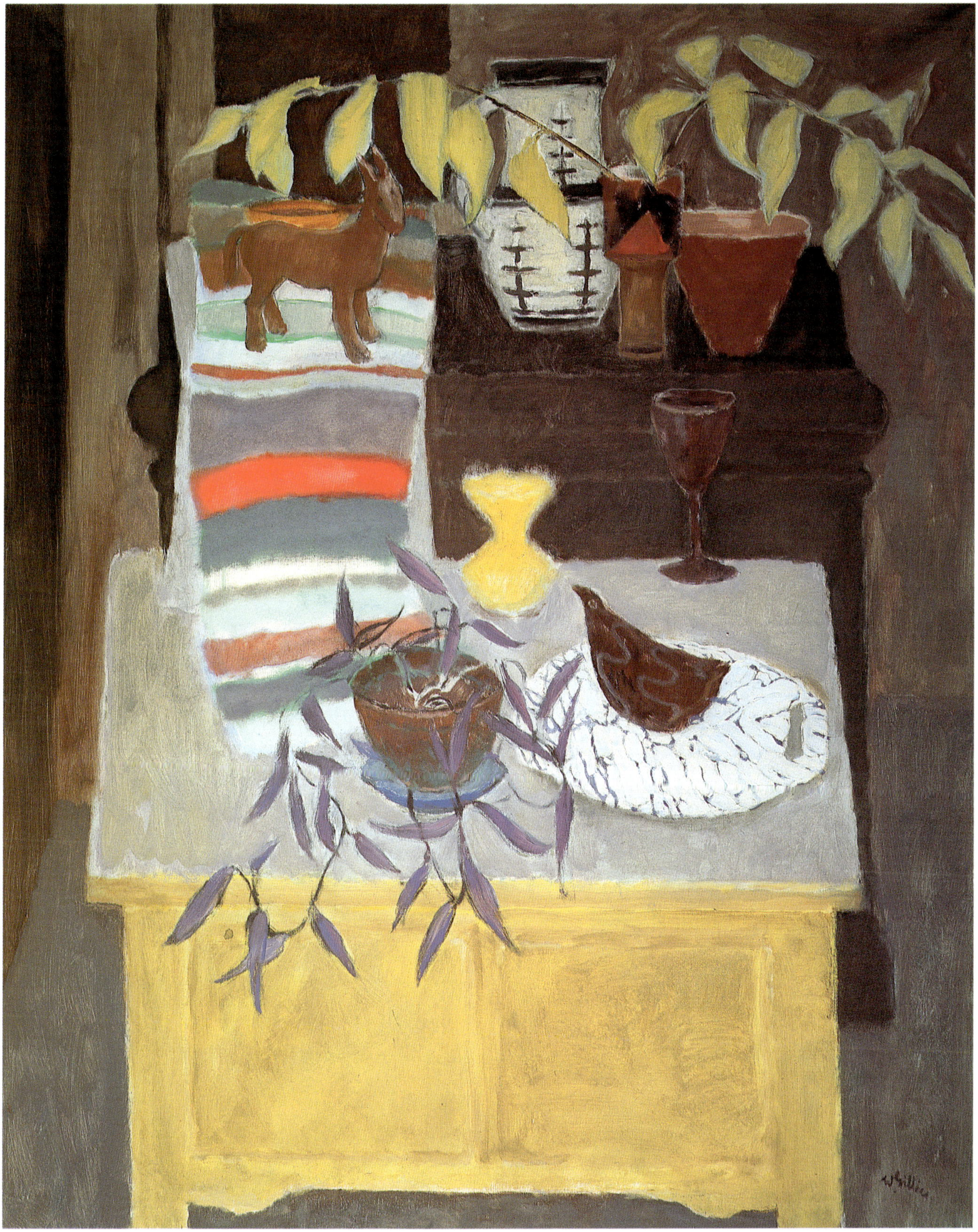

Interior with Still Life 1971 oil on canvas 127 × 102 cm

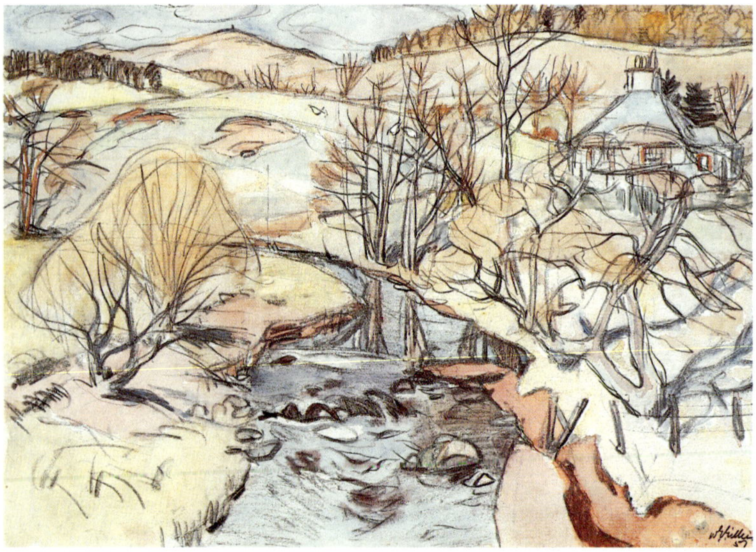

Roadman's House, Lyne 1957 watercolour and pencil on paper 26 × 85 cm SNGMA

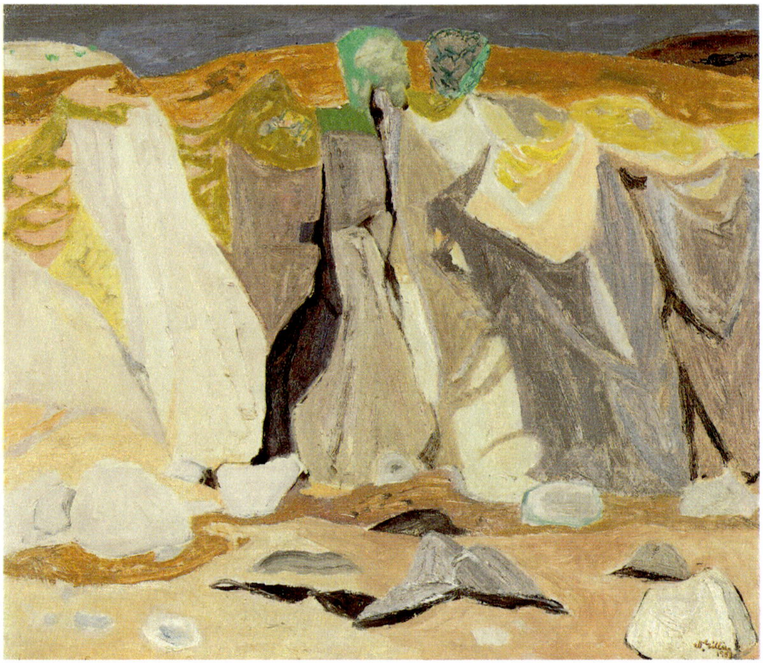

Cliffs, Dalbeattie 1953 oil on canvas 63 × 74 cm Royal Automobile Club

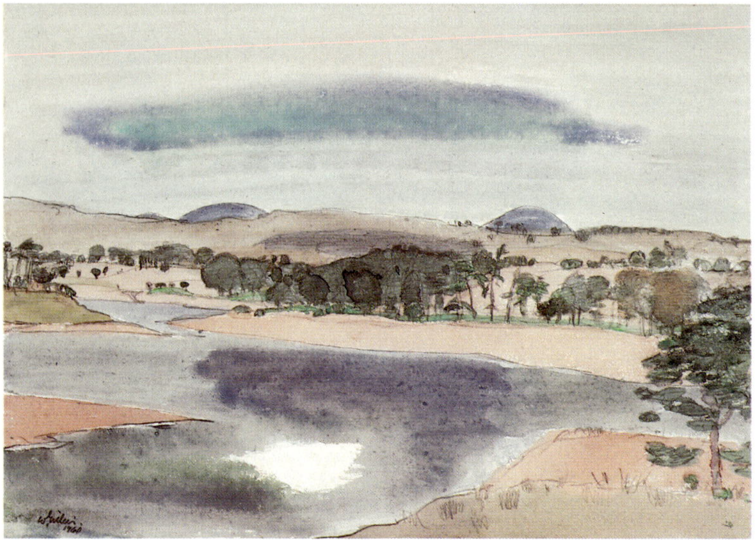

Summer, Moorfoot 1960 watercolour and pencil on paper 25 × 35 cm SNGMA

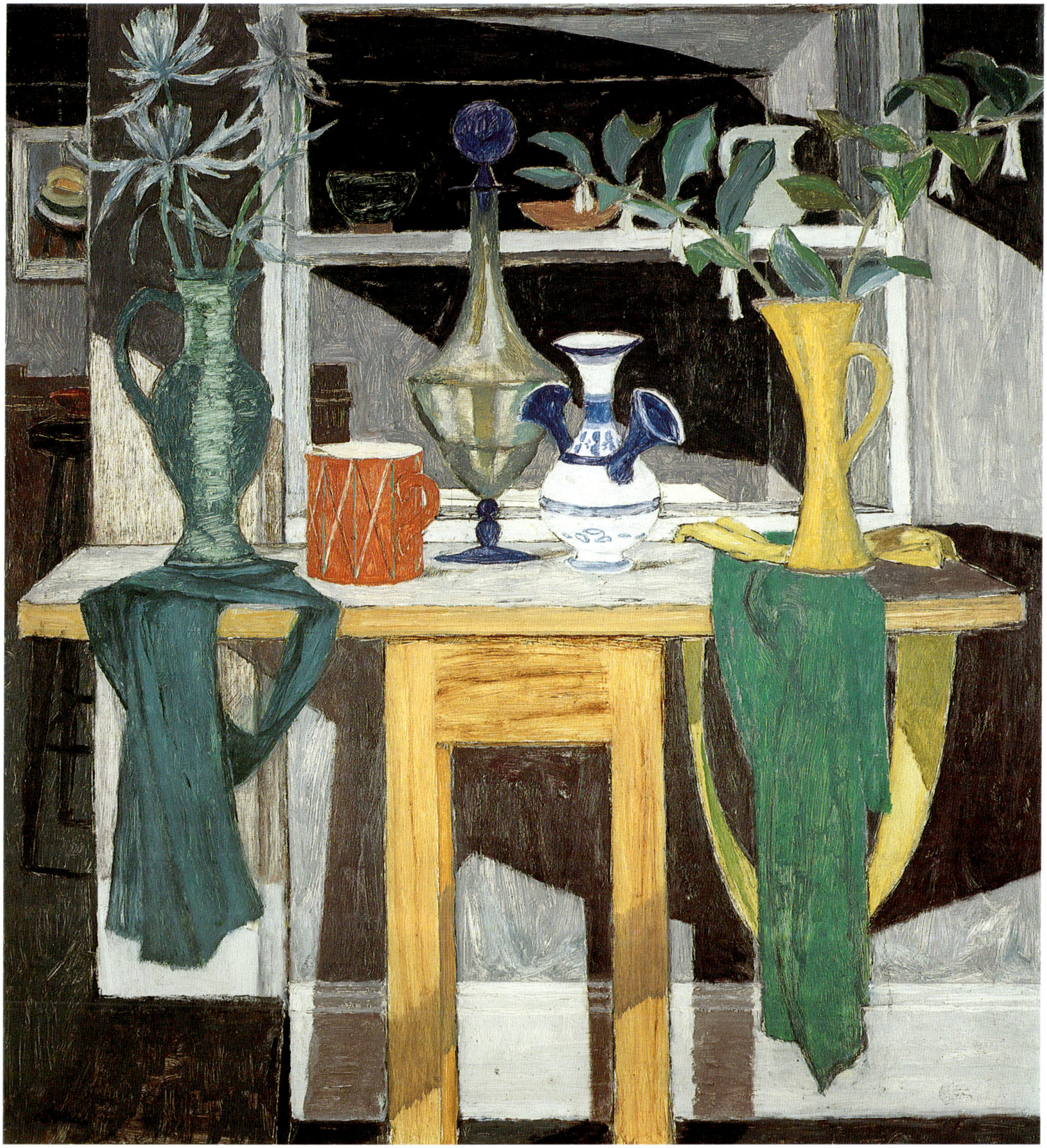

Shadowed Interior 1961 oil on canvas 108 × 98 cm EDC

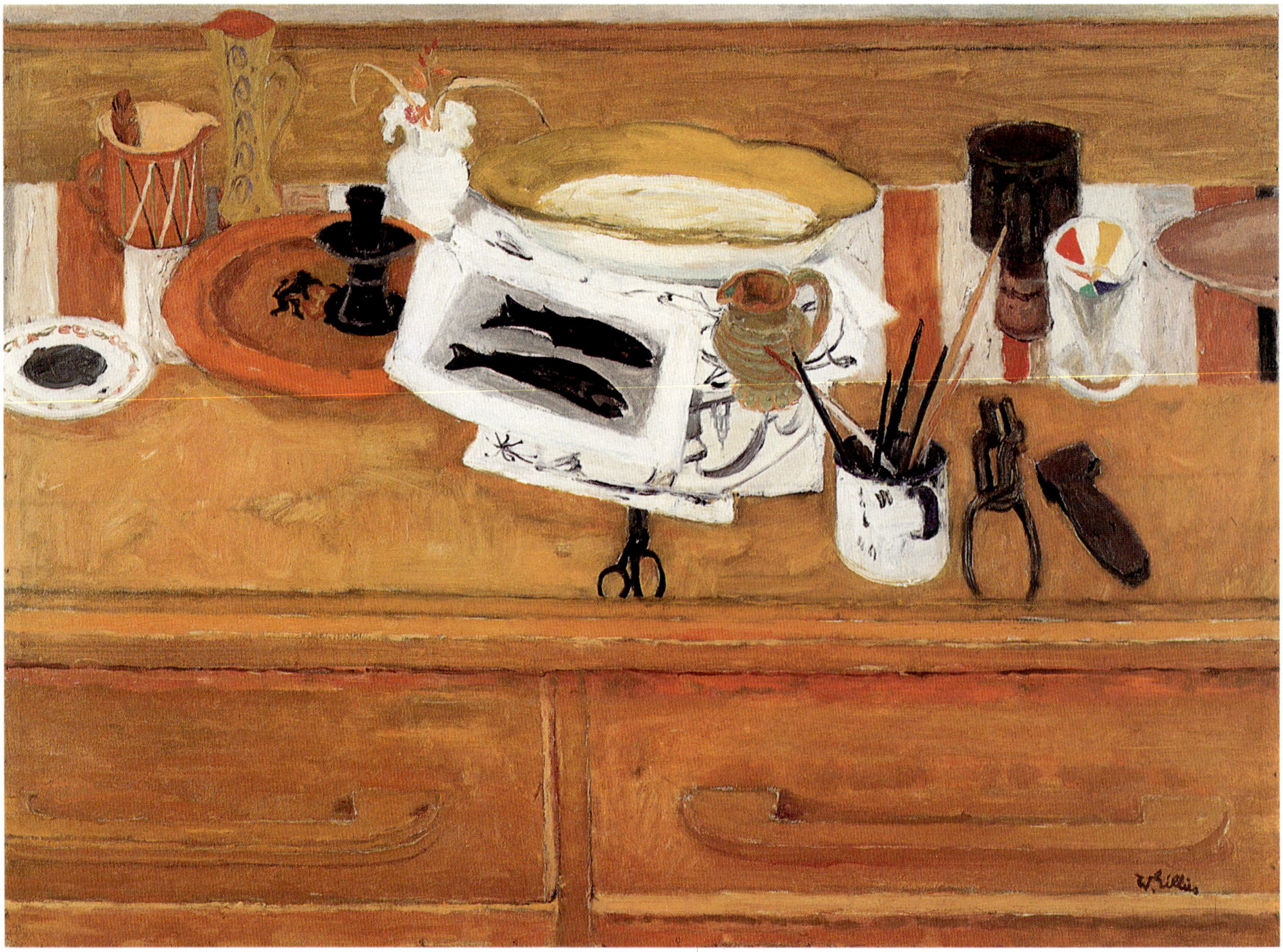

Still-life with Black Fishes 1965 oil on canvas 78 × 104 cm SNGMA

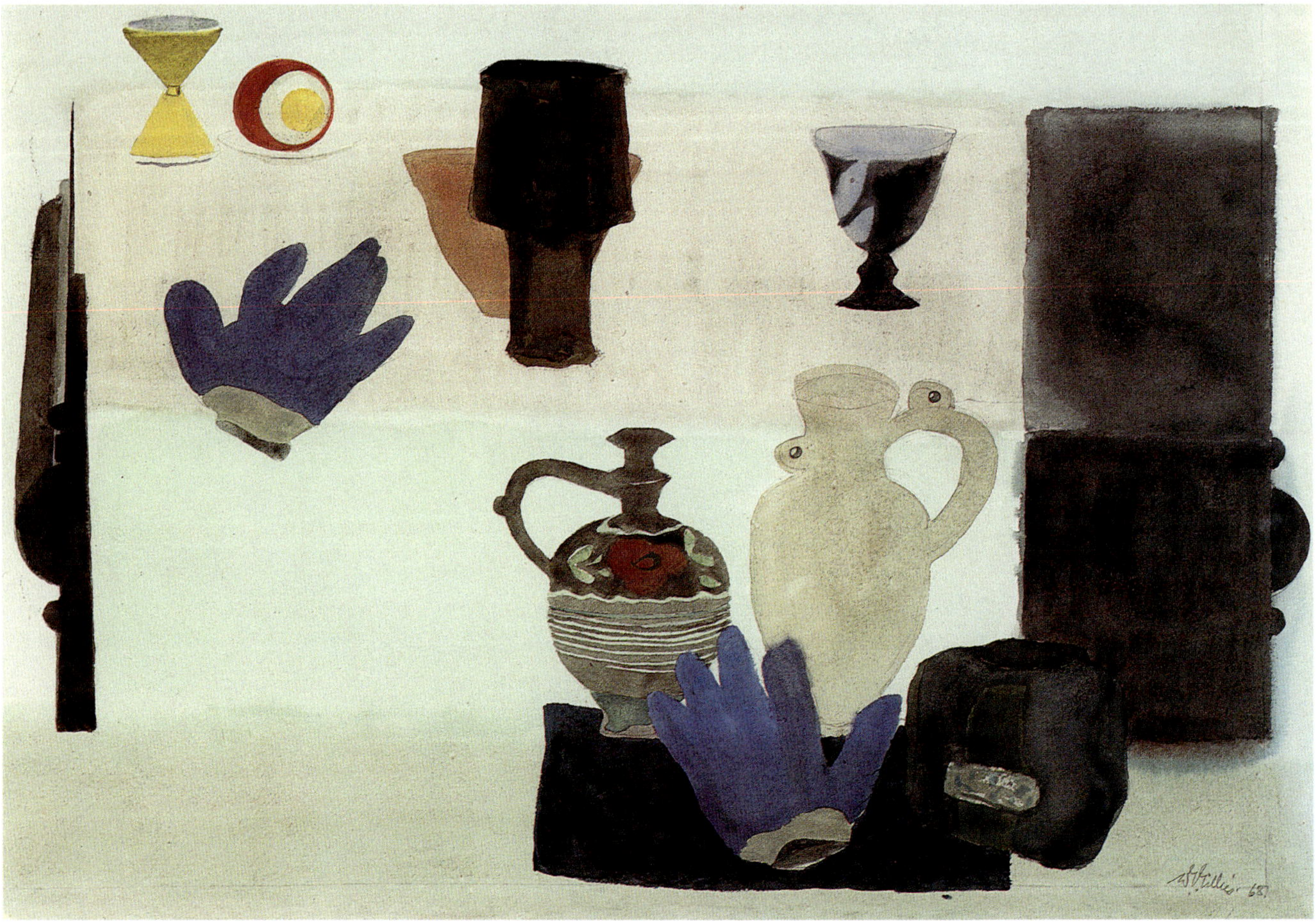

Still-life with Blue Gloves 1968 watercolour on paper 65 × 92 cm Tate Gallery

Chapter 10

Temple now became his entire world; drawing and painting – at last – his whole life. He pottered in what has been described as 'a poet's garden,' its wayward untidiness reflecting his affection for every growing thing. He continued to make gallons of 'Arniston Rosé' from the fruit of his raspberry canes. The self-discipline of a lifetime sent him to the studio every day and well into most nights. He might listen to police messages on an expensive radio until three in the morning. Mrs Napier became his cook. She thought he needed more nourishment and used him as a guinea-pig for daily experiments in haute-cuisine. He flourished on her diet. Friends detected a slight corpulence. If a visitor was coming from Edinburgh he told Mrs Napier: 'They're not getting any of my supper. I'll give them something out of a tin and have mine after they've gone.' On the few occasions when he left the village for a day or two he handed the Napiers a large manilla envelope bulging with hundreds of banknotes. 'Will you keep this until my return. If I do not, I want you to share it with another friend. I don't want the lawyers to get their hands on it.' These generous intentions of his should dispel any image of the miser and his hoard.

Many connoisseurs of Gillies' work believe that his Temple exteriors and late still-lifes, most of them painted during 1968 and 1969, represent the full flourish of his talent. *Still-life, Study in Grey* and the haunting watercolour now in the Tate Gallery, *Still-life with Blue Gloves*, are the logical synthesis of everything he has been trying to achieve – visionary design, a vocabulary of forms creating their own dynamic energy, and such poetic manipulation of space that these inanimate worlds are held in magical balance. No painter produced warmer or more colourful greys than Gillies. In his open landscapes they make curiously merry music, and close inspection reveals that they are not greys at all, but orchestrations of greens and blues and browns with tiny trumpeting notes of yellows and reds. *Temple-Dusk* is, however, a cantata in grey, that tombstone grey of the northern gloaming, when the pale cast of a full moon is about to supersede the last of the sunlight. The two grim tones of tarmac and pavement sweep the eye into their reciprocal greys in the sky. Sparks of colour sputter and falter in the dying sun. The vertical spars, a brilliant geometric device, suggest yet another view from a window. And we know that, any moment now, it will be time to draw the curtains and shut out the night.

For Gillies, however, the curtain was about to rise in 1970 on the most important event of his artistic life and the most comprehensive salute to a living painter Edinburgh had ever seen. The Scottish Arts Council had already begun to plan a major retrospective exhibition of his work under the direction of William Buchanan in close association with the artist. Over 100 oils, ranging through the years from the 1916 portrait of his mother to work that had just left the easel, would be shown at the RSA galleries at the Mound, and 87 watercolours would form a separate exhibition at the Arts Council gallery in Charlotte Square.

The retrospective was a huge popular and critical success. It toured to Aberdeen, Perth, Dunfermline and Dundee, then went to the Royal College of Art, London, before finishing at the SAC gallery in Glasgow. Over 30,000 people attended, some seeing the work for the first time, others – and particularly former students – lingering, then returning, awed by the scale of the man's achievement. This was Gillies' moment of revelation, confirmation, celebration. And he nearly missed it. On the icy road into Edinburgh for the formal opening his car skidded into a ditch. Friends following in another car contacted Robin Philipson who came and delivered him to the Mound on time. In a witty address Norman Reid, then Director

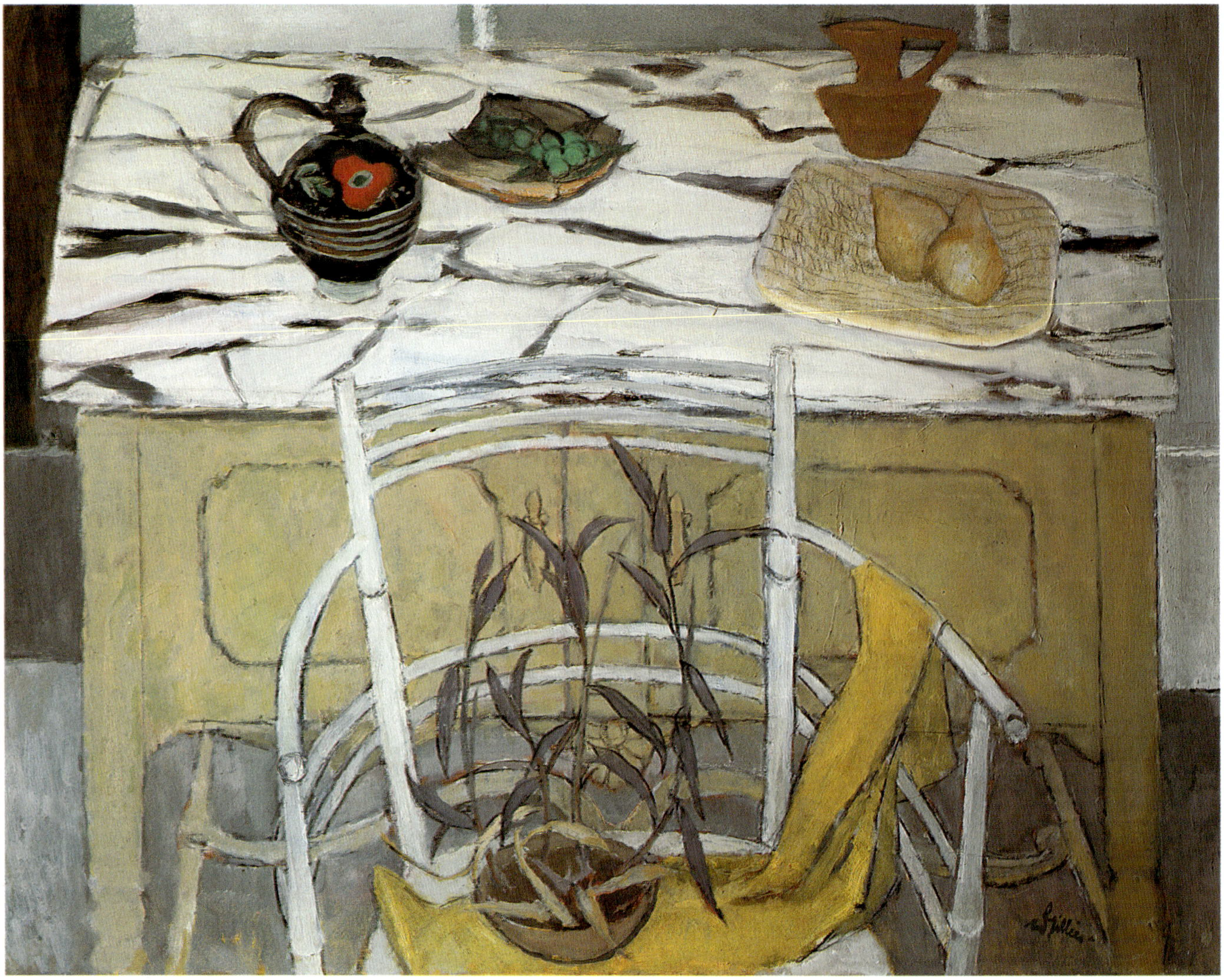

Studio Cupboard and White Chair 1972 oil on canvas 89 × 112 cm

of the Tate, former student and friend of Gillies at ECA, spoke about Jet providing 'a mobile dark account' in the predominantly high-toned Temple interiors. 'Jet has his own chair by the fireside and is fed, as far as one could judge, mainly on liquorice allsorts and Murray Mints, which seems to me a characteristically Scottish diet . . . We sampled the '63 Elderflower and several even older vintages. It was that evening that I began to understand the Scottish gift for colour.' Gillies, still shaken from his skid off the road, told his audience: 'I must be one of the very few painters who have had a retrospective while [only just!] still alive . . .'

That same year he was knighted for his contribution to Scottish art. At Buckingham Palace for the investiture the Queen Mother apologised to him; the Queen was in Canada, she would have liked to confer the honour herself. Sir William replied: 'That's all right, ma'am, you're more contemporary.'

The college had appointed him as the RSA representative on its Board of Governors, an ancient link with the old Academy school, and one that he could almost bridge in time and honoured as a duty to the future. He was elected to the Royal Academy, a rare distinction for any Scottish painter.

Back at Temple among his good neighbours he jokingly asked the Napiers if, now that he was a Knight of the Realm, he was still allowed to clean his own windows. It was generally agreed that he could – on condition that he kept off the roof.

Visitors – as many as a dozen in a week – kept up the pilgrimage to Temple. He, who would not have gone out of his way to see more than a handful of them, was nevertheless pleased to welcome them. He gathered their news – who's doing what? is he really? did he sell many? – and was always happy to hear good reports of former pupils and young painters who had aroused his interest. Many paintings were sold from the studio, and at generous prices to friends. Very good friends sometimes received a drawing as a gift, but with the professional proviso, 'Mind you, I'll have to charge you a pound for the mount.' Philip Napier said he could not 'hazard a guess at the amount of money he was owed for pictures he had sold on promise of payment which never materialised.'

One of his last paintings, *Studio Cupboard and White Chair*, is yet another departure in style. We are once again anchored in some sort of reality and not spinning in space. A domestic interior glows with subtle warmth. Even the marble top of the Victorian larder dresser, decorated with familiar objects, ceases to be a cold slab. And the chair, festooned with yellow and sprouting greenery, opens its arms wide and gathers us in.

He had his usual last-minute rush getting work ready for the 1973 RSA show. On Sunday, 15 April he joined the Napiers and called on another friend in the village for a pre-lunch drink. On the way home he said he was tired, but seemed cheerful enough. Mary McIver, out for a walk, saw him in the garden and called, 'Isn't it a lovely morning, Bill.' 'Aye, isn't it just,' he answered. Mrs Napier brought him his lunch and called back later to take Jet for a walk.

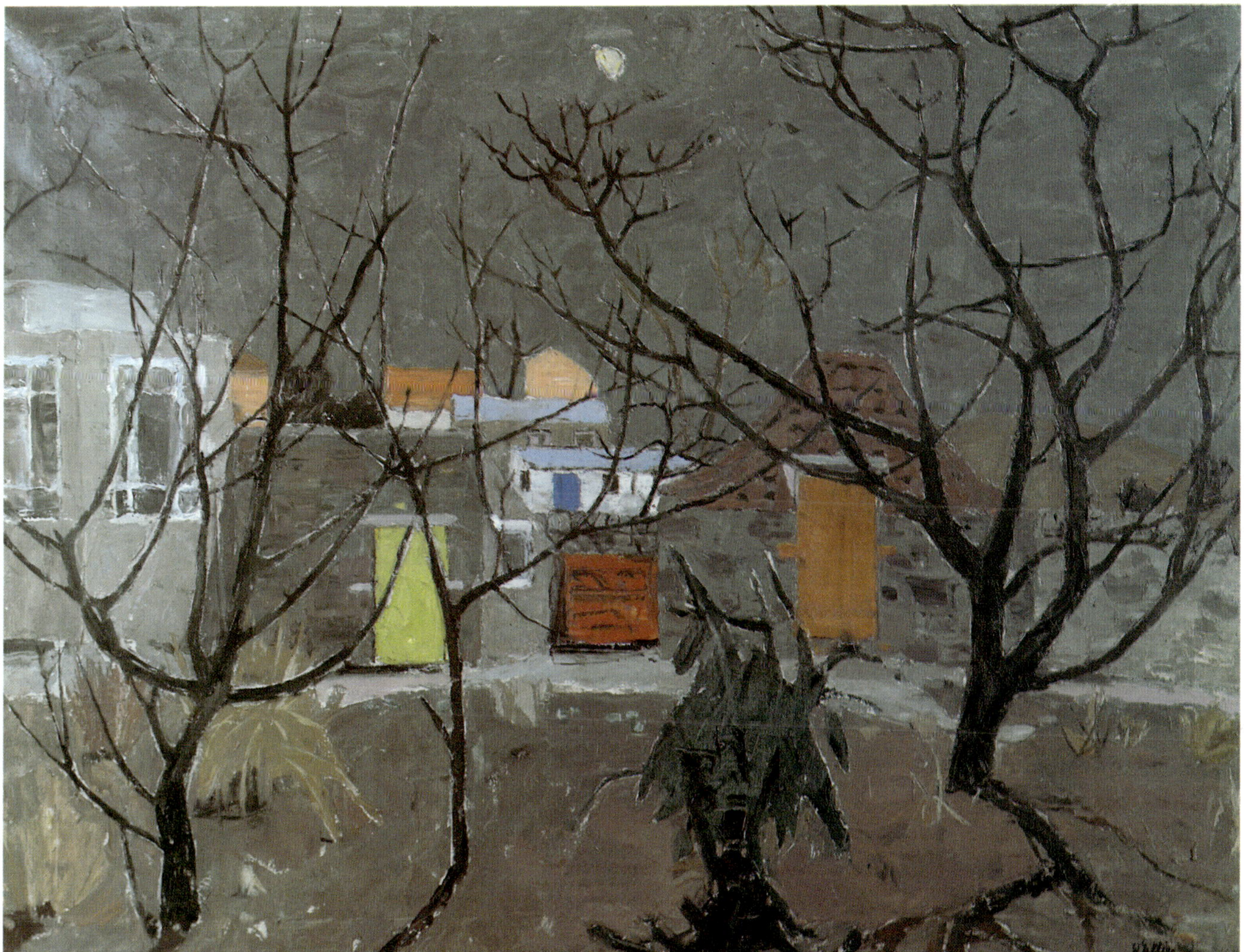

The Garden, Temple, Winter Moon 1961 oil on canvas 97 × 122 cm PAG

She found him slumped over the kitchen table, a spoon still in his hand. He had died in the act of raising food to his mouth.

He bequeathed the bulk of his estate and a houseful of paintings and drawings to the RSA, with the wish that the Academy would turn his cottage and studio into a sabbatical retreat for young painters. This was found to be impracticable and the house was sold. A prospective purchaser, viewing the property now bereft of its art treasures, fingered the muted grey, blue and yellow living-room curtains. 'Whoever lived in this house,' she declared, 'had nae taste.'

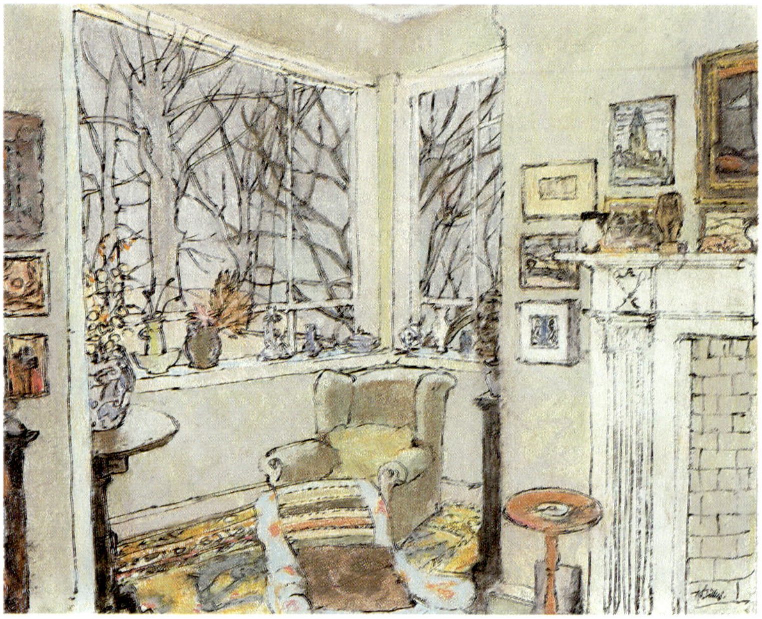

Interior, Temple c.1965 watercolour and pastel on paper 46 × 56 cm EDC

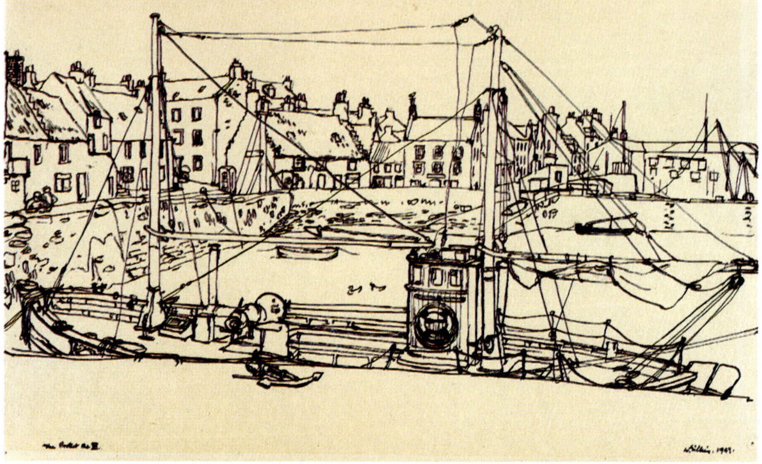

The Protect Me III, (St Monance) 1949 ink on paper 34 × 54 cm

Envoi

The funeral was so private and simple that nobody now remembers anything about it – no eulogy, neither pomp nor circumstance, just a quiet goodbye.

Maybe that was the way he wanted it – that shy, contented man, who kept the world at arm's length. But he had such a gift of conviviality, such generosity of spirit as an artist, that a wake might have been a good idea. It would have got rid of all that wine in an orderly fashion, and given his friends and colleagues, students and neighbours, the chance to say some of the things they felt about him, and have been thinking about him ever since.

PHILIP G. NAPIER
He gave away a lot of wine but, after his death, many dozens of bottles were found on shelves in his garage, some dating back 10 years or more. On the instructions of his executors we were asked to dispose of them to his neighbours. It was quite a sight – wheelbarrows, prams, push carts loaded with the stuff.

JACK KNOX
I still get as much enjoyment from his still-life in Kelvingrove [*Still-life, Blue and Brown*] as I did the first time I saw it.

SIR ROBIN PHILIPSON
I was always conscious of being in the presence of a singularly simple and straightforward man of massive intelligence. I think he made a deliberate effort to conceal that intelligence, but it appears in all his paintings. What is it that makes one of his landscapes – whether snowscape, height of summer, or coloured autumn – a thing so frequently of majestic abstract complexity? I think it's simplicity, and it's only afterwards that you think, 'God that's something!'

One time I was stuck. I hadn't painted for forty minutes. He said, in that helpful way he had, 'Sometimes if you're stuck it's enough just to turn it upside down, paint something out, and then everything else will re-arrange itself. And, if you have the courage, paint out the bit you like best.'

I don't think I ever had a conversation with him about God. But we didn't have any conversation about no God, either. He had in abundance whatever it is that inspires people to make the most of life. A quiet man, totally incapable of self-promotion. And there was never any chance that he would smother himself in dead language, leaving only a cipher or sign.

I know he was enormously proud of his decorations. He adored it when he became CBE. After one of our many chats round the fire at Temple – we had eaten the bacon, egg, and sausages at midnight to keep us going till 3 a.m. – I got up to go. He said, 'Got another letter from the Palace.' 'Not *it*?' I said. ''Fraid so,' he said. We had to get him a tail-coat.

He established a wonderful light touch in the running of the college. We often chatted about students who were showing promise and he was equally considerate of those who were struggling. Gillies could only operate in fairness. During the 60s – swinging London, permissiveness, a bit of turbulence, the odd sit-in – difficult years, I felt for him. If it had been anyone other than Gillies we might have had trouble, but he remained unruffled.

I think the way he suffered during the First World War indicates his capacity for suffering. He was not impervious to pain, but it was the very devil trying to get him to see a doctor.

He loved his home with all his ceramics – it was very much an artist's house. When people gave him things he looked after them. I've never kept the Christmas cards I make and send out every year. But I'm lucky, because Bill kept all mine and framed them, and as a trustee of his estate I gave them back to myself when he died. I remember pouring hundreds of bottles of wine down the drain. There must have been 600 jars of marmalade. We found 87 unframed paintings under his carpets.

Not long before he died he painted three pictures – impeccably laid down, controlled washes from edge to edge, and very different. I think he was still moving on. His handwork was so natural and simple. He reminded me of my mother in the simple things he did. In baking a cake she presented the back of her hand to the oven door to test the temperature – there was a little bit of that in Bill's simplicity and knowing.

He loved junk shops and second-hand clothes. He would say to me, 'Let's go down to the Grassmarket and look at the shops.' I hoped he meant the junk shops, because if it meant the clothes shops, I had to try everything on for him, and then hurry home for a bath.

WILLIAM J.L. BAILLIE
He was an outstanding and inspirational force in painting in Scotland in his lifetime. Much loved, revered and respected, his presence is still with many of us to this day. He always supported his school, students and staff against pressures from 'top brass.' A visionary stylist and technician. Not only a painter of the Scottish scene but an interpreter of the Scottish spirit. W.B. Yeats believed that an artist worked best among his own people and in his heritage. Gillies is a perfect example of this. Despite outside influences he retained his own integrity. He was a lyrical poet and absolute master of his craft. As a visionary he rose above the limitations of a national 'school' and remained true to his Scottish heritage. As a draughtsman and colourist he was a master of our time.

JAMES ROBERTSON
I held him in high regard. He was a perfect example of a painter who used landscape/still-life as a starting off point to create work of great imagination and charm. He never fell into the trap of being a 'victim' of the subject. His images were arrived at through his own personal vocabulary and deeply sensitive sense of colour. I always found him to be a perfect gentleman. I never heard him being pejorative about painters from my part of the country (unlike quite a few painters from the 'East.')

JEFFREY CAMP
Gillies worked beautifully and fast, moving the paint from palette to canvas in one continuous action, rather like the swift bowing of a violin.

HAROLD B. BELL
I remember saying to Willie Gillies, 'You know, I'm getting almost as much interest and pleasure in photography as I have in painting.' With his gentle smile he said, 'Aye, it's quicker, an' it's mair liker it.' On another occasion we were leaning on the upstairs rail in the Art College, looking down on some contemporary sculpture. One flamboyant piece immediately below us seemed to have little to commend it, and its energy seemed threatening. 'If you watered that,' I said, 'I believe it would come right up here.' He responded warmly, 'God forbid!'

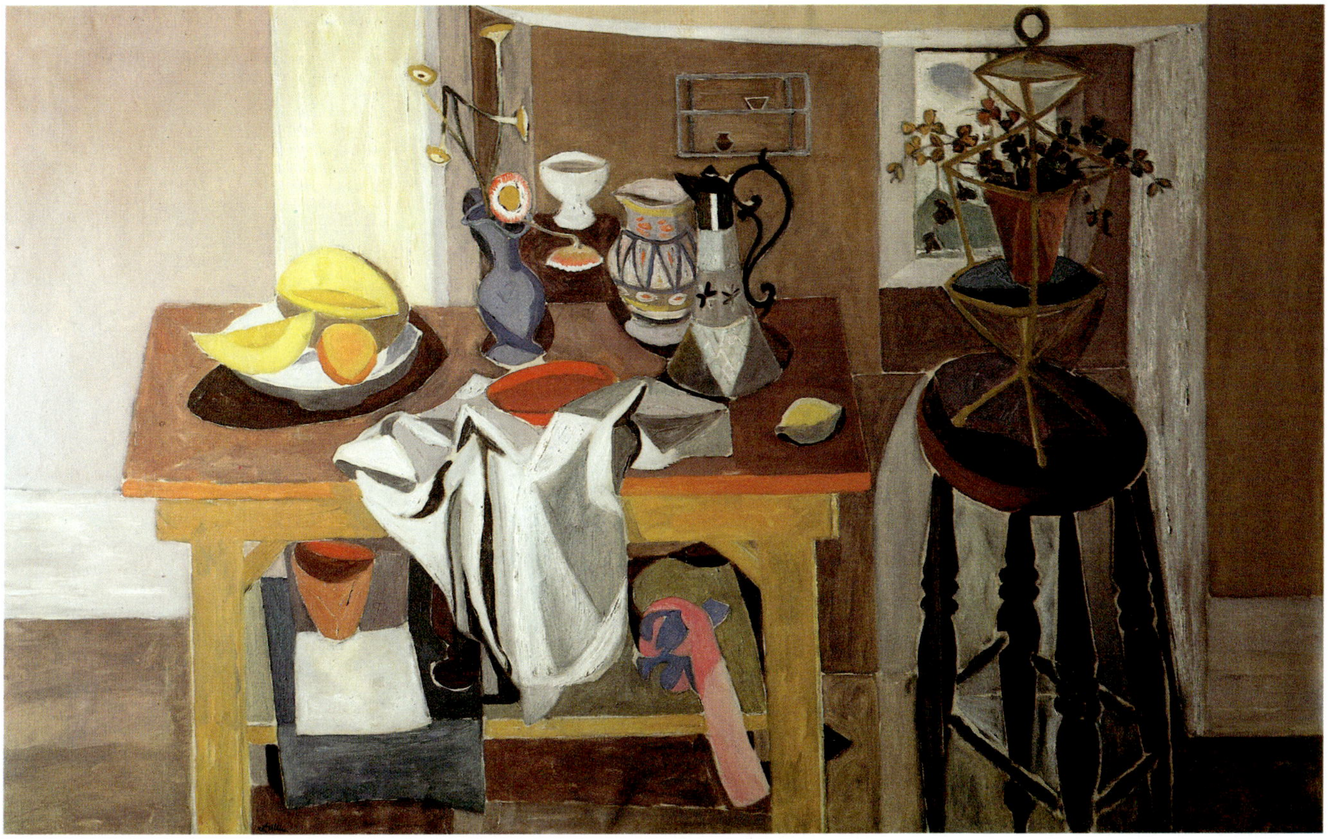

The Studio Table 1951 oil on canvas 117 × 215 cm A Fletcher

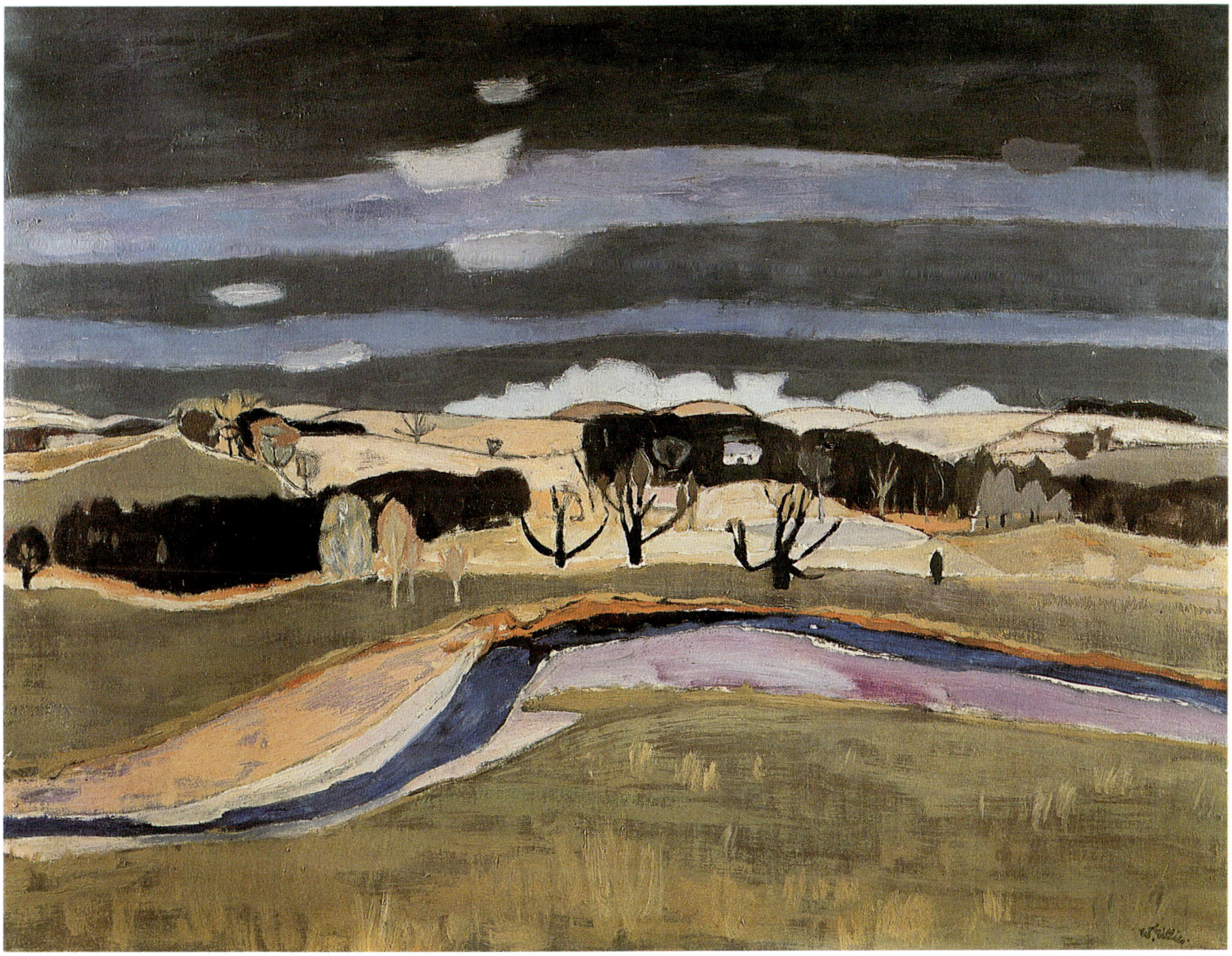

Dusk 1959 oil on canvas 71 × 92 cm AAG

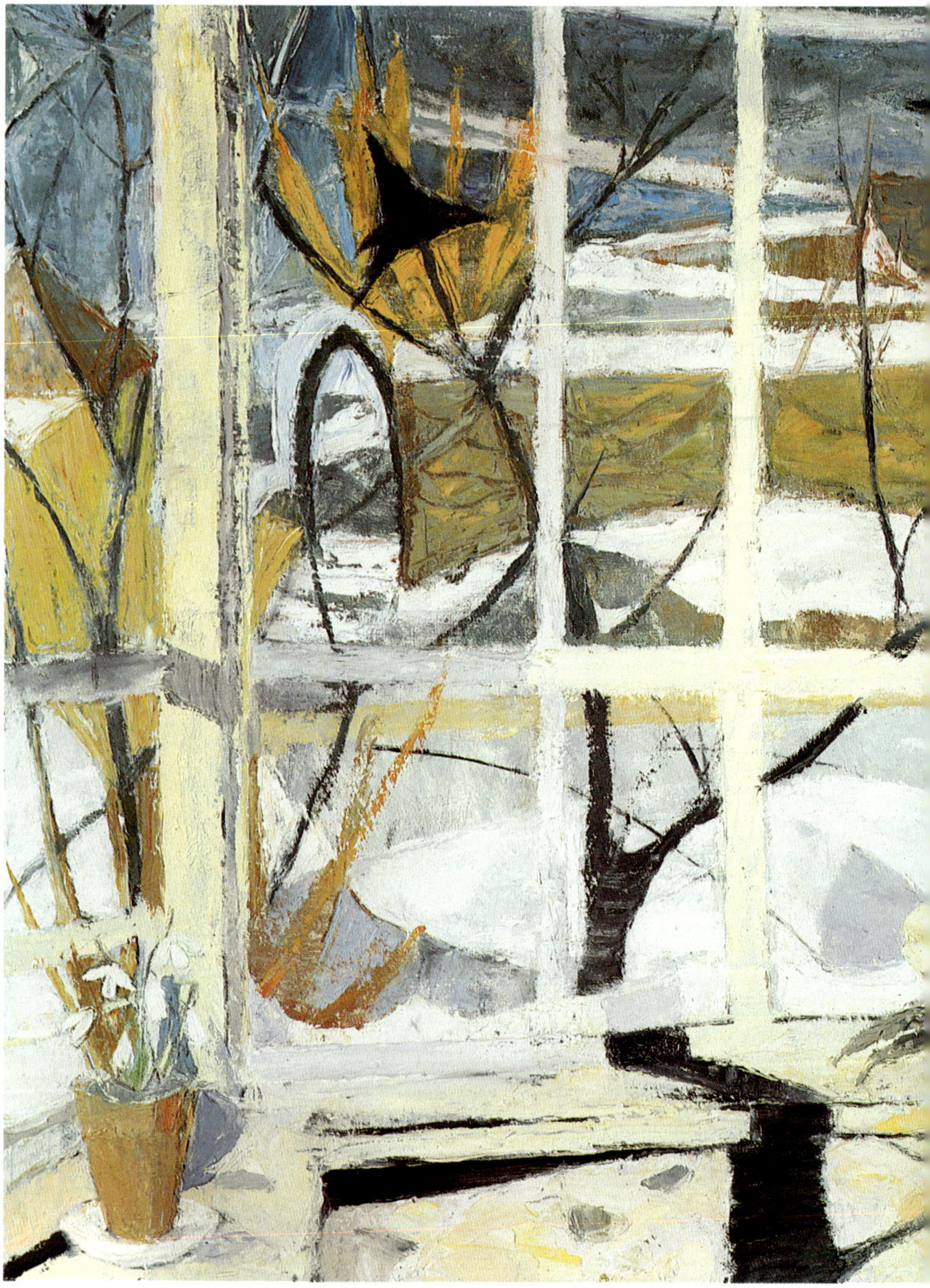

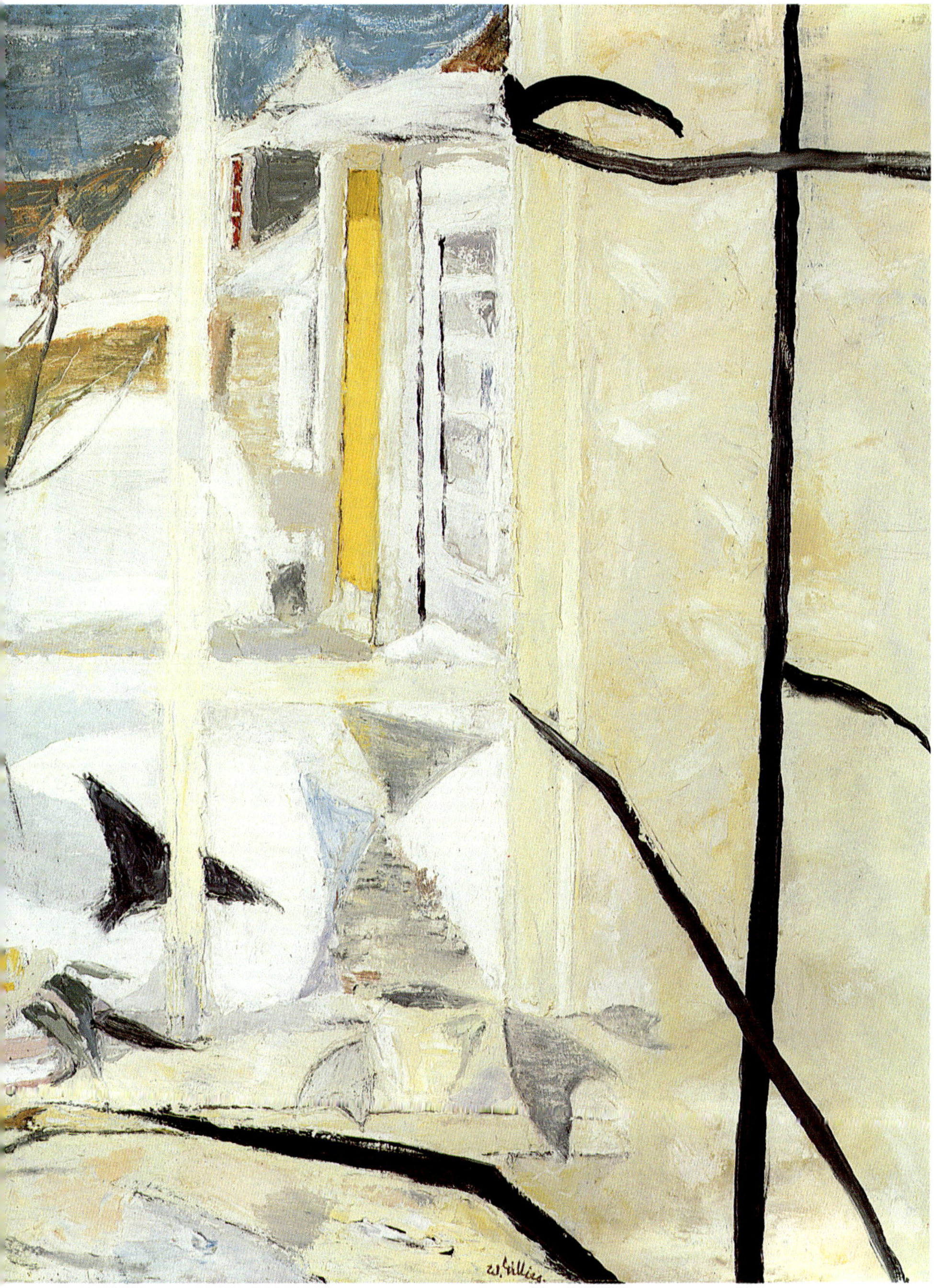

Garden, Winter Sunshine 1960 oil on canvas 102 × 152 cm

DAVID McCLURE

I have been trying to pin down my thoughts on the great man. I do not find it easy. In a way he remains an enigma. I was a student for five years while Gillies was Head of Painting and yet I had only three or four lessons from him in all that time. The first was when MacTaggart called for Bill Gillies to come and see a painting I had done. He admired it generously and commended it for its tonal values. I had on the easel a much more freely painted thing with apples and a jug. He looked at it and said 'Apples are not tennis balls. They have planes.' He then proceeded to push the wet paint around with his horny thumb, making the apples truly three-dimensional, and expressed in 'planes.' On another occasion I was propounding a theory I had come across about 'Organic Colour Values.' (Don't ask me now what it was about.) I asked him if he did not agree with this. His response was typically anti-intellectual. 'No. Nature always gets the colour wrong, so you have to try to improve it.' His criticism could be devastating, but 'nicely nicely.' In my post-diploma I had produced a lot of fairly robust figure compositions on a large scale, symbolist rather than realistic. When Gillies came round to give a crit I was completing a painting (a still-life) which I was trying to make as 'realistic' as I knew how. He reviewed the other works favourably but glanced at this still-life and said dismissively 'very prettily painted.' That painting went on the scrap-heap. At an opening of one of his one-man shows at Aitken Dott, Eileen Michie and my Joyce said to Gillies, 'we'd love to buy one of your paintings but . . .' His response was, 'Why would you want to do that? Your husbands can paint pictures for you.' He seemed to me to lead an asexual life and yet was not in any way 'pansy.' On one occasion a new model thought she should shave her pubis. When Gillies came to instruct the life class he looked at her rather prominent clitoris – and exclaimed, 'Just like a wee moose keeking oot of a hole!'

FRANCES WALKER

When I arrived at ECA in September 1947 the Food Office personnel were still removing themselves from their war-time quarters in the basement. I wore a skirt I had made from my picked-down gym tunic and my only pair of nylons – no tights then – instead of my white ankle socks. Most of the new students were ex-Service – articulate, eager, older and experienced – or so it seemed to me, straight from school and never been anywhere much. The word teenager had not been invented. There was no Arts Council, no network of galleries and exhibition opportunities, no subsidised studios, no residencies and very few opportunities to gain awards, bursaries and prizes – but there were teaching opportunities.

I first saw him when I went to do a drawing test. He appeared to be a janitor bustling around arranging antique busts for groups of anxious hopefuls to draw – then collecting our efforts. He wore a well-used smock overall belted round the middle. An unpretentious, practical, busy person – approachable but not likely to suffer fools or arrogant people gladly. He had a sharp, shrewd way of looking at people. I liked his direct, very Scottish, Lowland personality, his pawky dry humour and economy of words.

He was of small wiry build. His hair – so strong, upgrowing and crisp, full of vitality and energy – always seemed to me to epitomise the character of the man. It was nearly white but with that yellowed bloom from the nicotine of the cigarettes he smoked almost constantly. His voice was fairly high pitched, his speech slightly clipped and rapid with a narrow-vowelled 'educated' Scots accent. Sometimes he seemed to ham his own personality and accentuate his idiosyncracies of speech and phrase. He scampered round the room uttering words that got right to the point of any obvious, unresolved – or unnoticed flaw – 'the feet are too big' or, as he moved to the next student, 'the head's too wee.'

I know he had a strong influence on me – by example, in his dedication as an artist and by his work. The linear, lyrical quality of his work and his descriptive use of colour – and forget when he it was who proposed me as an Associate of the R.S.A.) I had somehow

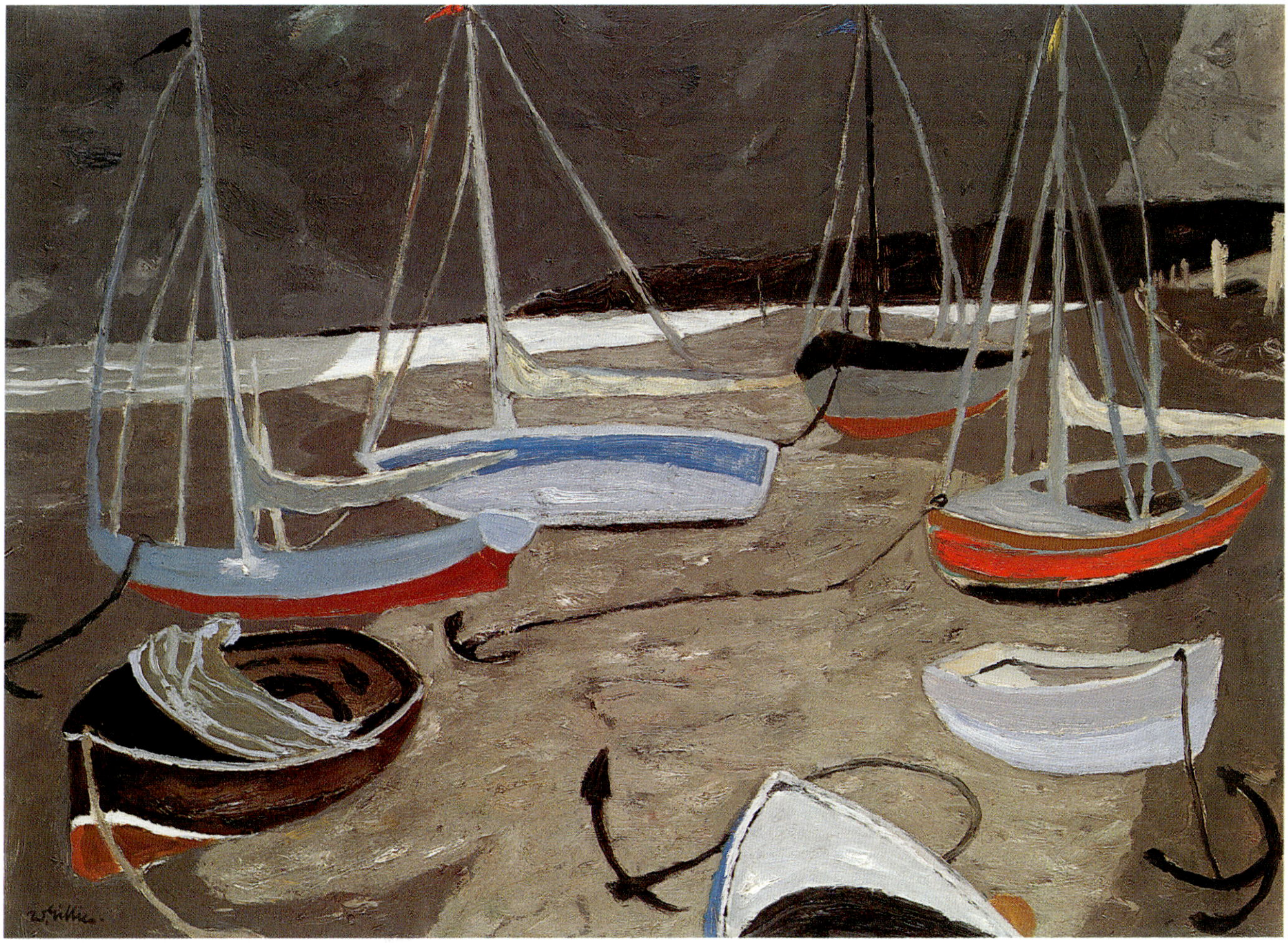

Beached Boats 1950 oil on canvas 62 × 84 cm

his whole vision – appealed to me. I felt instinctively that what I wanted to say in my work was more related to Gillies than the 'painterly' or 'stir the paint about more' gestural Scottish painting of the time. I envied his speed, facility and skill, and admired the fluidity and fluency of his pen-and-ink drawings and watercolours. His work reveals his continuous celebration and enjoyment of snow, rainbows, stormy skies, twilight, moonlight, sunlight.

He was working by a harbour in Fife and being watched over his shoulder by an old fisherman. As the painting evolved the fisherman said, 'You'd be better wi' a camera.' Gillies continuing painting and, without looking up, answered, 'Yes I know – but I havenae got a camera.'

I always thought of him going on into a great old age. I fully expected him to live into his nineties, he had always seemed so brisk and well.

PHILIP G. NAPIER

Jet got badly bitten by another dog and Bill rushed over to get my wife to go with him to the vet in Edinburgh. When they got there they were told it would be some time before Jet would be ready for collection, so they decided to do some shopping at Marks & Spencer. They looked at one another and burst out laughing. Bill was still wearing carpet slippers and my wife a kitchen apron.

ALBERTO MORROCCO

I studied not at Edinburgh, but at Gray's School of Art in Aberdeen (a circumstance that may not have been wholly in my favour although he was generously prepared to forgive

formed an impression of this lively, bird-like bachelor, who made his own jam, as a kind of unwordly innocent, and was shocked (as an unwordly innocent) to hear from his own lips that he possessed two powerful motor bikes and a highpowered car – and drove like a demon. Like all genuine artists he seemed to me to possess a mixture of diverse traits. Very biased about what constituted good painting, but open-minded about younger painters. Nervously hesitant and yet tenaciously strong in his opinions. A painter of immaculate taste, who would sometimes vote on selection committees for the most miserable amateur daub because it reminded him of some bit of country he loved.

One of his most endearing qualities was his complete lack of pomposity. As Head of Painting at Dundee, I sent a van through to ECA to collect a load of rather large student paintings – about 40 to 50 large works. When he arrived, the driver, one of our technicians, proceeded to the janitor's 'buckie' in the foyer, where he found an overalled janitor looking over some papers. He asked where the paintings were and he and the little janitor commenced to carry them out and load them on to the van. This hard work took them the best part of an hour. When they had finished, my technician, suspecting that the 'wee janitor' was perhaps the 'heid janitor,' asked who he was, and received the reply, "Bill Gillies – I'm the Principal ye know." It was said in that fey Temple accent which every painting student of the period learnt to imitate. The present President of the RSA, Bill Bailey, is an excellent exponent.

Gillies always seemed to me to be one of those fortunate painters who find themselves in perfect tune with their environment. All his early influences were French, but his work is

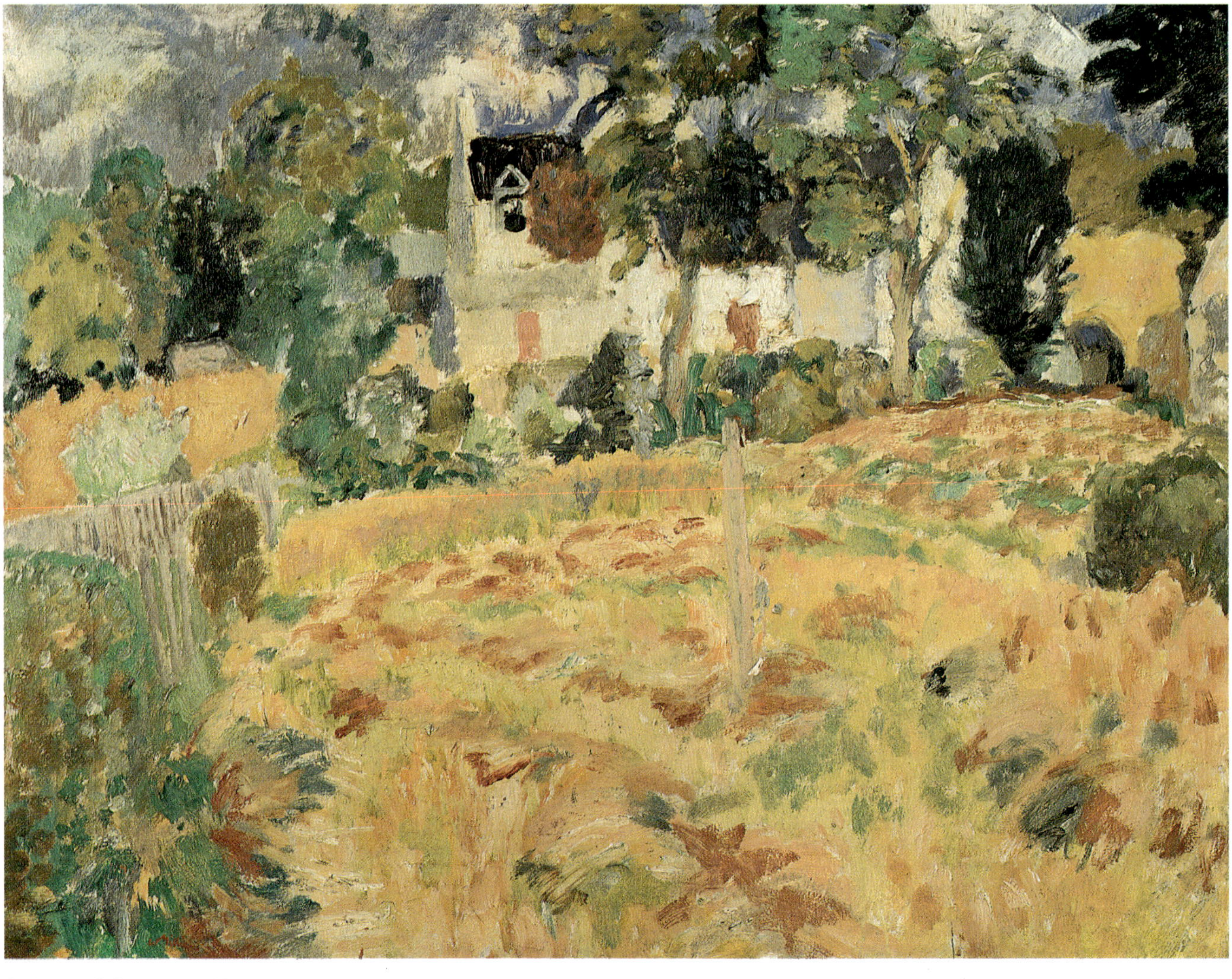

Spinningdale c.1940 oil on canvas 70 × 90 cm

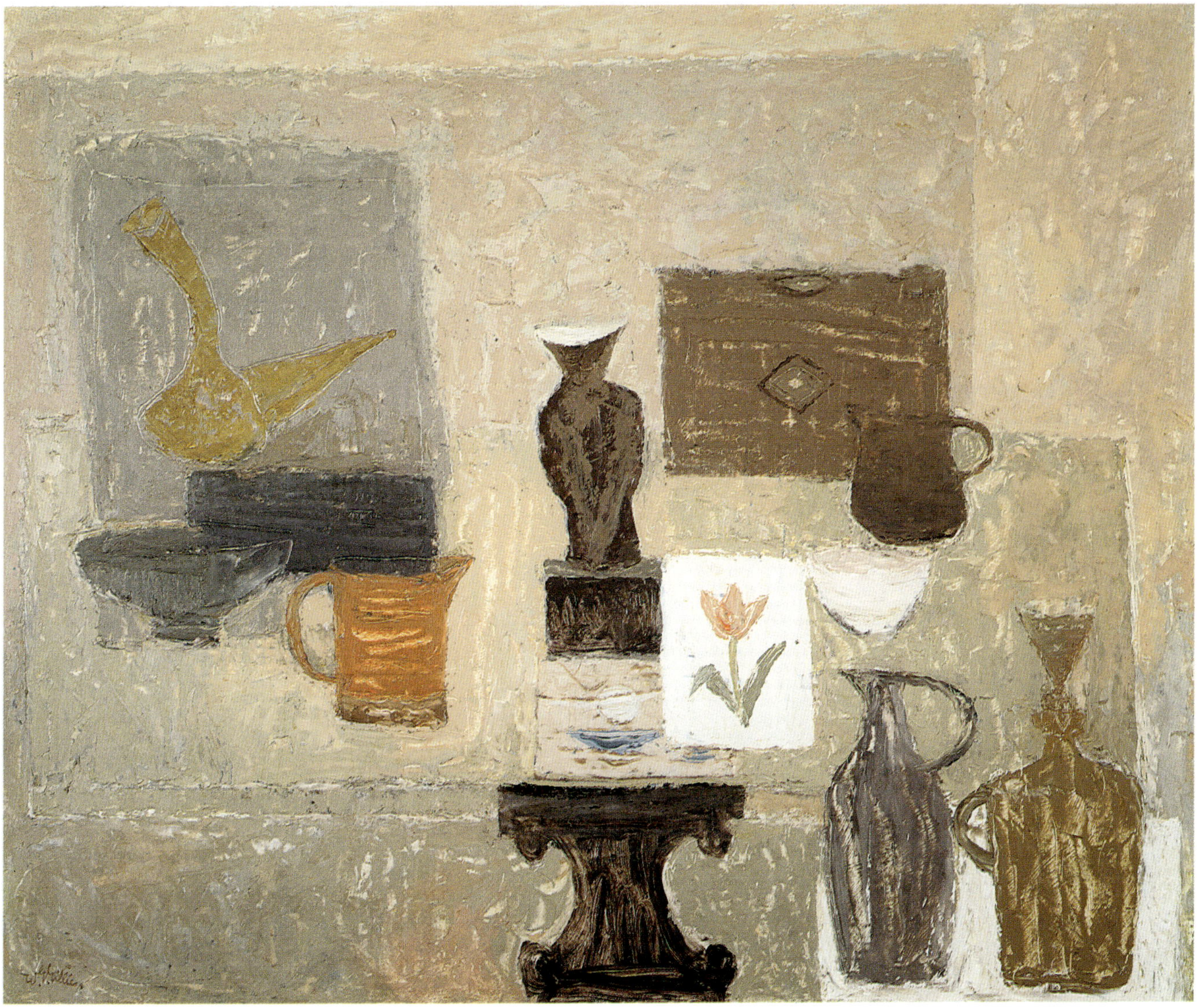

Still-life, Study in Grey 1968 oil on canvas 81 × 98 cm

nevertheless Scottish in taste and tempo, and never brash or vulgar, and never over-emphatic, never banging the big drum. He could make more impact with a group of soft greys and reduced pinks than most artists who use primary colours at full pitch. I don't think he responded strongly to the 'human condition' as a suitable subject for painting. There is no doubt of his position in Scottish painting, but as another painter I am not one to try to assess this nor, frankly, am I interested in doing so. I leave that to the art historians (who seem to be ten a penny these days) who must do something to occupy their time since they no longer seem to be interested in Art History.

MARGARET McLEAN

He had a terrific sense of fun – a puckish sense if you like. Once he was giving me a lift to Edinburgh and said the Temple pipes were frozen and he had to get water from the pub. I thought this was amusing and two weeks later I asked him if he was still getting water from the pub. He exploded into soft little chuckles all the way into town – and presently said, 'I had a very bad cold. It was the pump, not the pub.' Now that I think of it, I don't think there is a pub in Temple.

JOAN RENTON

His enthusiasm, especially for drawing and colour, carried you along with it. He would stand in front of your painting making little clucking noises and eventually say, 'That's a bonny wee bit of painting there. It's coming along very nicely.' If he had a criticism he would approach it in the same roundabout way. Before rushing off he would point to the offending part, perhaps a badly-painted mattress, and say, 'It looks like a grating,' then give a chuckle. He was very careful in his treatment of students. Being a very sensitive person he was never hurtful. Punctuality was one of his things. Staff, students, models alike were on the receiving end of a withering look if they arrived even a few minutes late for a class.

One year I bought a glass, antique firkin for my fiancé's Christmas. I loaned it to Willie for his beer at the studio party he always had during the Revels. He loved it so much I gave it to him and gave Ronnie something else. Willie was a traditional painter when these values were considered no longer acceptable. Yet he has always been seen as a liberating force in Scottish art, one which has influenced successive groups of young artists and art lovers. He carved the landscape into vertical and horizontal intervals in a style which is described as rhythm and counterpoint. He saw landscape in a series of almost abstract shapes and lines. Sky played an important part. He disliked too sunny weather as clouds were integral to the overall plan. Without them the subject wasn't as big as he would like. He was an inspired artist with an original and sensitive mind. He had the intuitive knowledge of a poetical painter who used colour with the spontaneity and freshness of the true impressionist. Colour took on a sensuous quality in his hands. He responded to the beauty of light and pattern in landscape and the inter-relationship of objects in his studio paintings. He struggled to maintain a balance between intellect and romantic impulse.

SANDY MOFFAT

Willie Gillies had just become Principal at ECA when I arrived there, a mere seventeen-year-old, in 1960. My first encounter with Principal Gillies took place about a year later after Robin Philipson had threatened to throw both myself and John Bellany out of the Painting School (our crime had been to attempt to paint like Alan Davie). We immediately knocked on the Principal's door and the genial old painter reassured us that Robin's bark was worse than his bite. Gillies told us he had been following our progress and considered us to be good students. We went away relieved and encouraged.

My only experience of Gillies in the studios was during the competition (in my second year) for an Andrew Grant Scholarship. I was working on a still- life (which included a photograph of Picasso) and Gillies seemed very pleased. Much later, I understood what he had meant

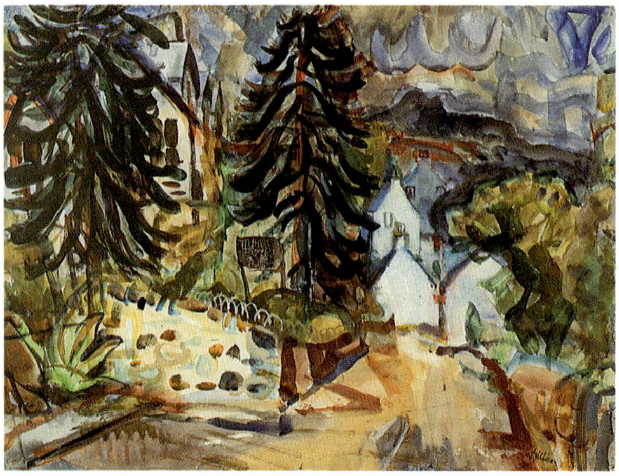

Down into Killin 1972 watercolour on paper 46 × 61 cm

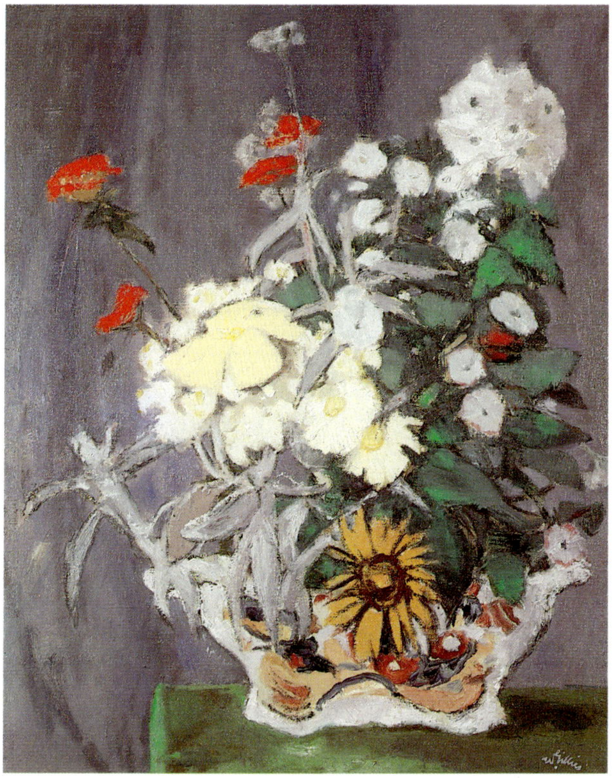

Flowers in a Tureen c.1950 oil on canvas 61 × 51 cm

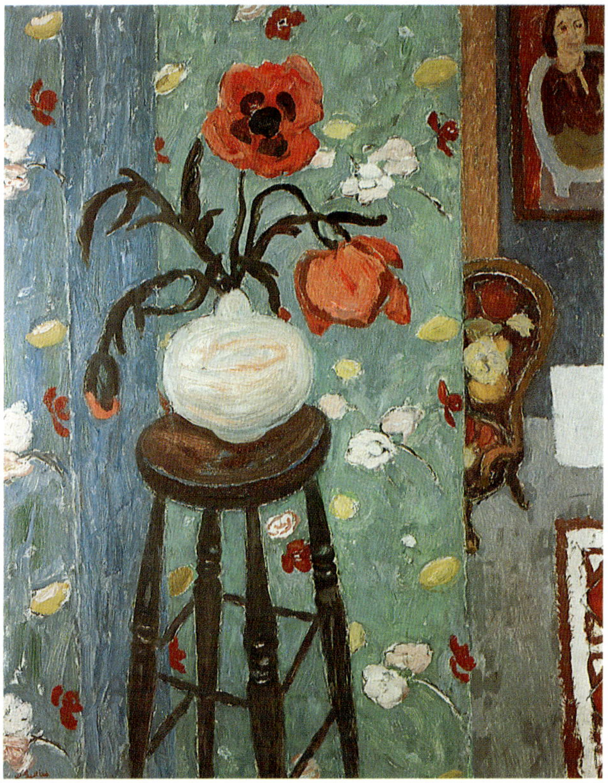

Studio Interior and Red Poppies 1939 oil on canvas 76 × 61 cm

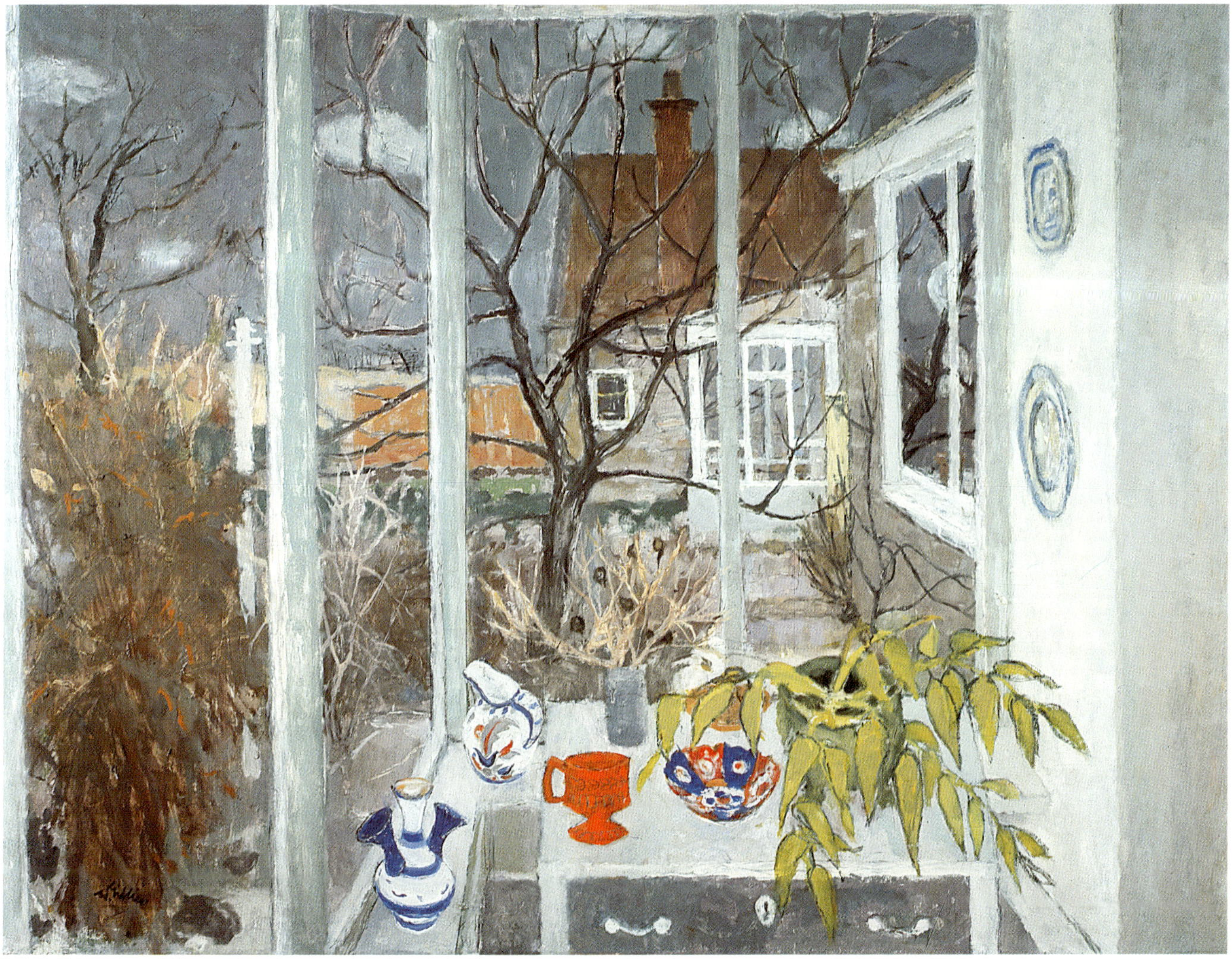

The Garden in Winter 1973 oil on canvas 76 × 102 cm

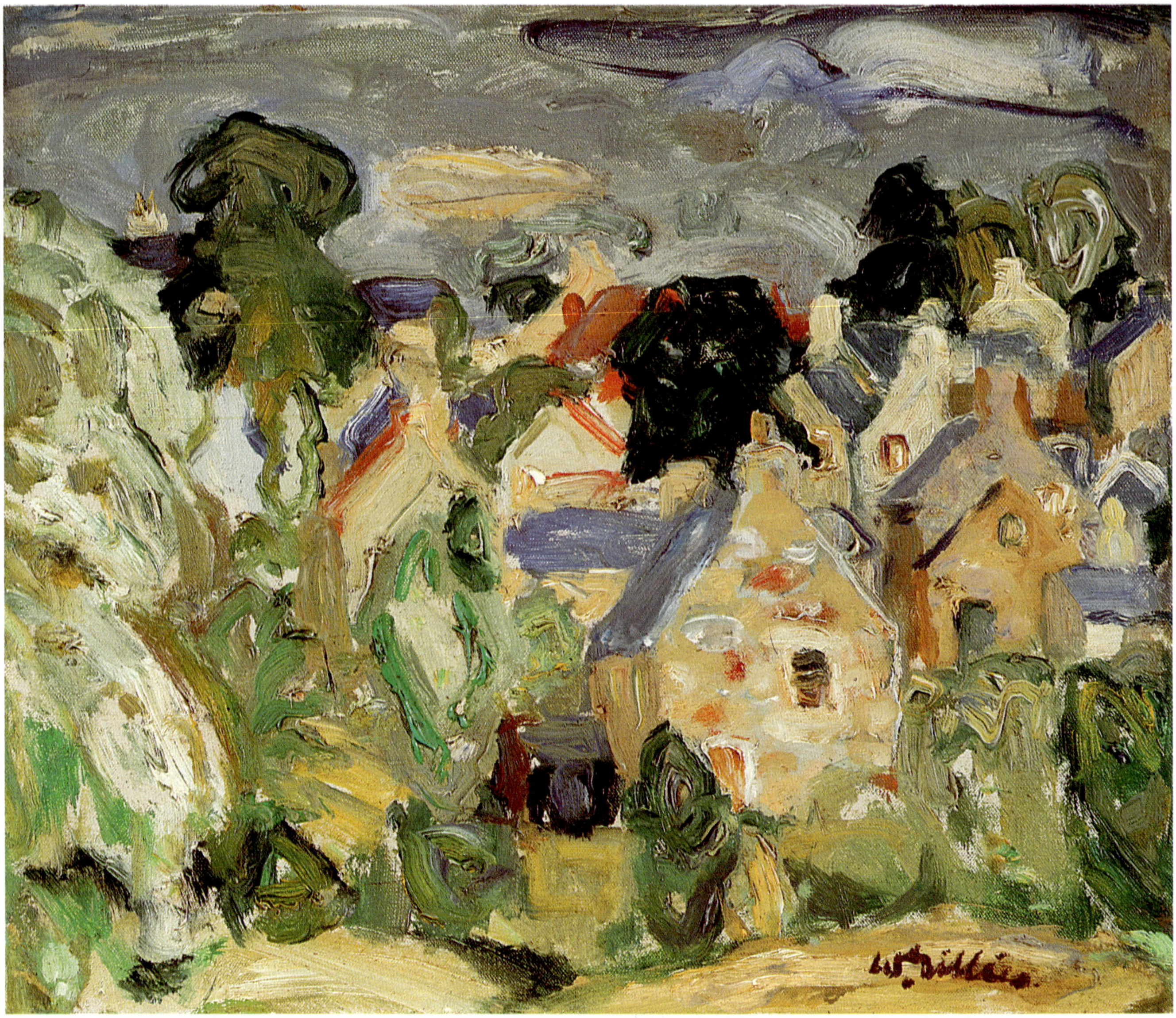

Newstead oil on canvas 30 × 36 cm

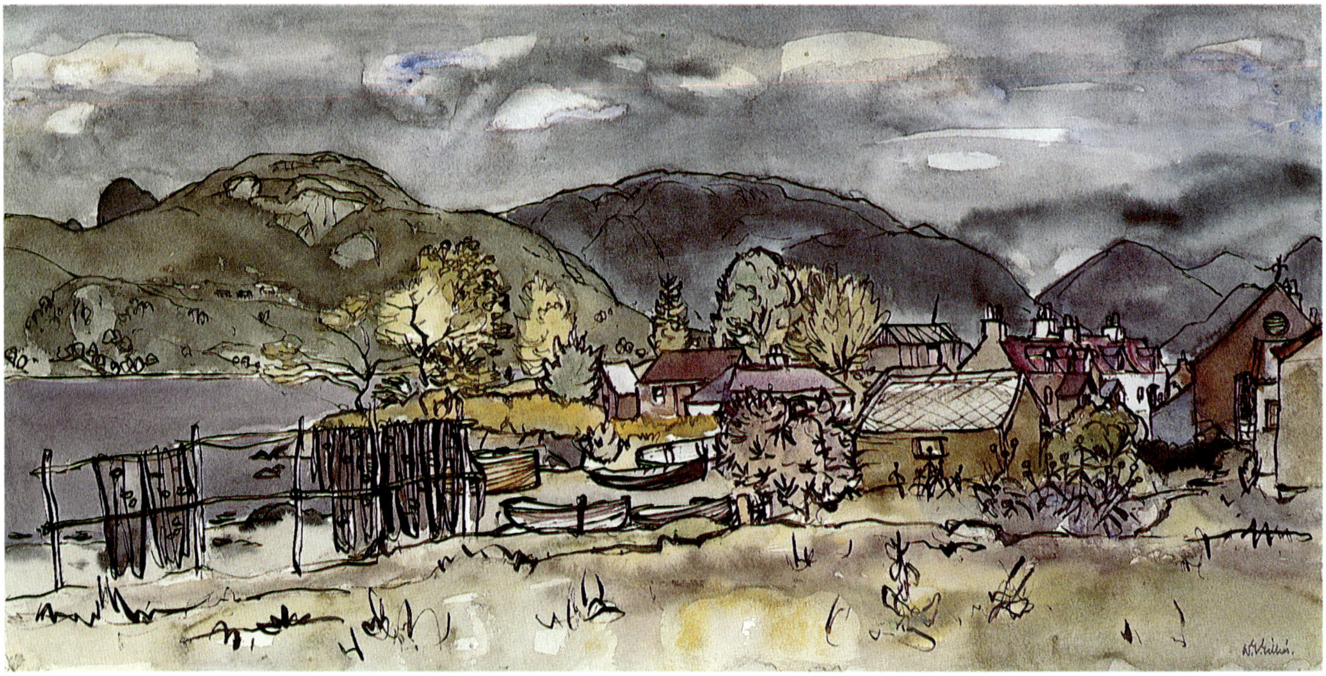

Letterfearn watercolour and ink on paper 34 × 65 cm

when talking about the qualities of paint, surface, colour, and so on, that I had stumbled upon that day.

But to be perfectly honest, it wasn't until the big retrospective in 1970 that I was able to grasp Gillies' full achievement as an artist. The exhibition was a revelation. (I had 'discovered' Bonnard in Paris in 1968 and this probably helped.) Here was a man whose inventiveness – as a composer and colourist, and as a painter and a draughtsman – was that of a master. The lessons learnt in Paris in the early 20s were clearly applied. A very special simplicity and quiet lyricism permeates his best work, and it is this clarity of vision with all inessentials removed (and magical touch) which makes Gillies a truly modern artist – a far more realised and greater artist than J.D. Fergusson and the Scottish Colourists, and McCance and Johnstone as well.

He's the best Scottish painter in the first half of the twentieth-century. I can hear John Bellany raving and ranting now. OK, the emotional range is limited, there's no angst, no alienation, no big issues explored. Sometimes the pictures are too nice, too easily arrived at. But there's a darker side to Gillies as well, and I agree with my friend Timothy Hyman that he shared certain things with Bonnard – not only his felicity but also some of Bonnard's abysses. What about his life with his sisters and mother (Morandi comes to mind)? Gillies' unpretentious manner and ability to get on with the day-to-day job of being an artist should serve as an example to all of us. He is the great natural, free of any aesthetic self-consciousness and all the ludicrous cant that engulfs the art world today.

JOHN BELLANY

Willie Gillies did not believe in verbiage – he was 'a man of the eye.' Although he did not actually teach me I was constantly aware of his presence as Principal when I was a student at ECA. When not 'office-bound' he was locked in his studio painting in his private domain. Only once was I allowed to enter the hallowed place and that was to help a janitor carry one of his paintings to a waiting van.

I remember him with a perpetual cigarette glued to his lower lip, singeing his minute ginger moustache. He had an angelic face with a mop of white hair giving him a Harpo Marx charisma, especially when wearing his white smock with flapping angel's sleeves. He was popular and much loved and respected by everybody. He was part of the auld alliance between France and Scotland and continued this tradition, although after his initial sojourn in France he seemed seldom to have crossed Hadrian's Wall.

He was in awe of the wonders of nature. He saw and portrayed nature tirelessly, with his own special freshness. He lived and breathed inside the landscape and with his alchemy could produce, from time to time, a masterpiece – sometimes with the innocence of a child and at other times the sophistication of a sage. He was a 'good artist.'

BARBARA BALMER [BAMMER]

His self-portrait in the National Portrait Gallery of Scotland reveals every aspect of the man as I knew him. Primarily alert and acutely aware visually; an impish mode of behaviour which concealed a powerful and serious dedication to his work and his concern for ECA and its role in Scottish painting.

On one occasion when giving a crit on the 'Summer Comps' (student work carried out over the vacation), he came to my endeavour and said, 'Miss Bammer is developing in a very interesting way' . . . and dissolved into confused giggles as the inevitable racket ensued from the assembled students. Another memory is of him at a Christmas Revel dressed as a Tour de France cyclist, peak-cap turned up at the front, the shortest of shorts revealing fine athletic legs, and a smiling welcome to us all for drinks in his studio.

Calling on him at Temple to buy a painting, it came to settling up. He turned the canvas round and said, 'Tut, tut. These fancy London prices,' and promptly made a huge reduction.

JOHN BUSBY

I did not know Gillies in private life or share any painting expeditions with him, but his work means more to me than that of any other Scottish painter. Though he never emphasised negative points he seemed to leave you knowing where improvements could be made. If he praised any particular painting you knew he really meant it and took pleasure in your work. I always felt that he 'read' my paintings and intentions well and was on my side in the struggle.

When I joined the staff at ECA in 1956, my admiration for this modest, efficient, and inspiring man increased, and I regard the time at ECA with Gillies as the vintage years of that establishment's history. With Gillies there was no pomposity, no attempt to impress, no political evasiveness. He disliked red tape and officialdom and any other excuses for not doing a job that needed doing. Faced with even janitorial awkwardness he could clear a studio or move furniture himself rather than waste energy arguing. I never knew him to pull rank; persuasion was usually enough.

Coming to Scotland very much under the influence of Paul Nash and Graham Sutherland I found in Gillies' work a similar deeply-felt vision of landscape, though the style was different. Much Scottish landscape painting struck me then as skin-deep – subject matter as an excuse for a painterly ego-trip. Gillies saw with a countryman's eyes and he understood the inner bones of landscape. His compositions and colour harmonies seemed to distil the essence of each experience of landscape and gave his work such a distinctive quality.

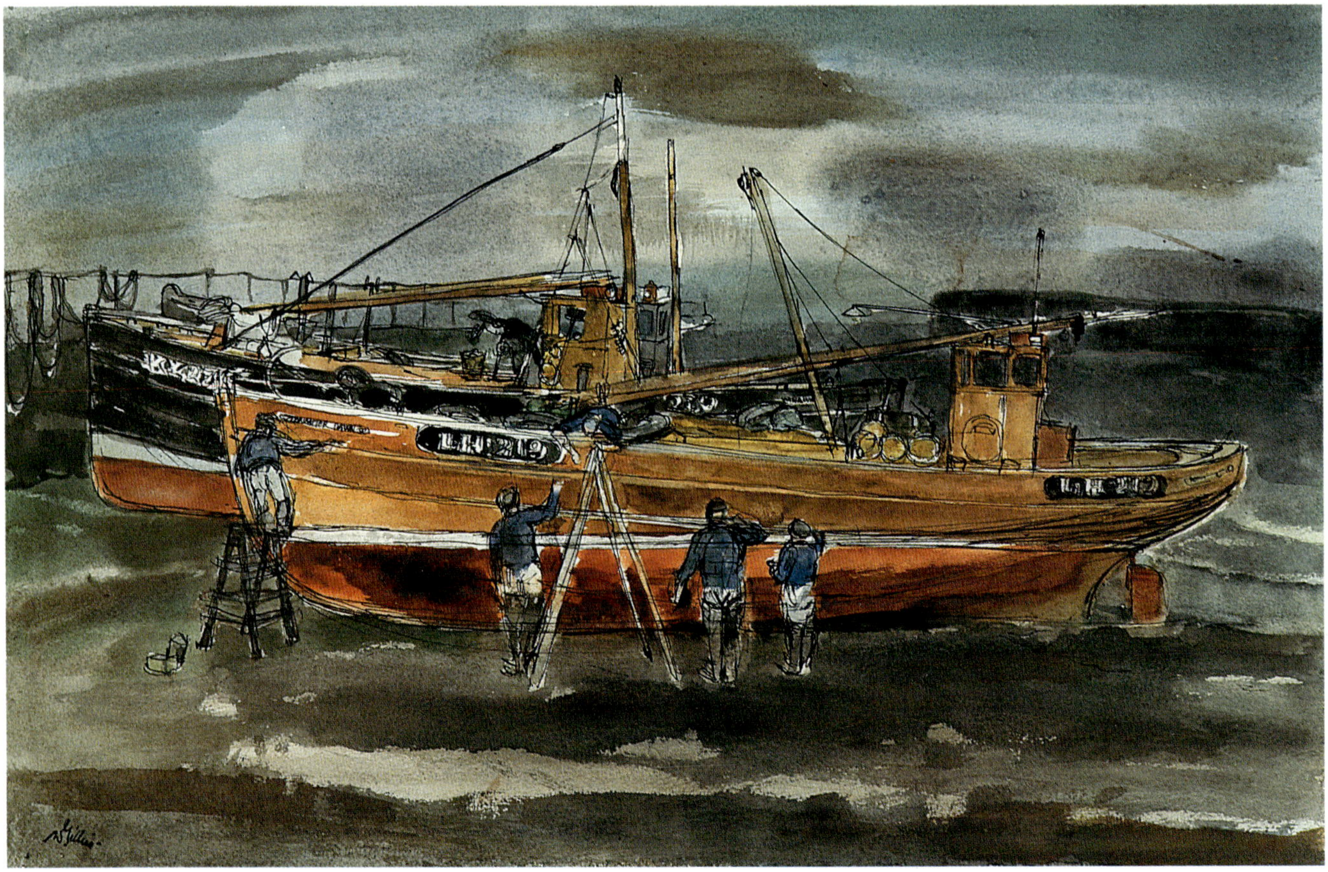

Painting the Boat, Anstruther 1950 watercolour and ink on paper 36 × 46 cm

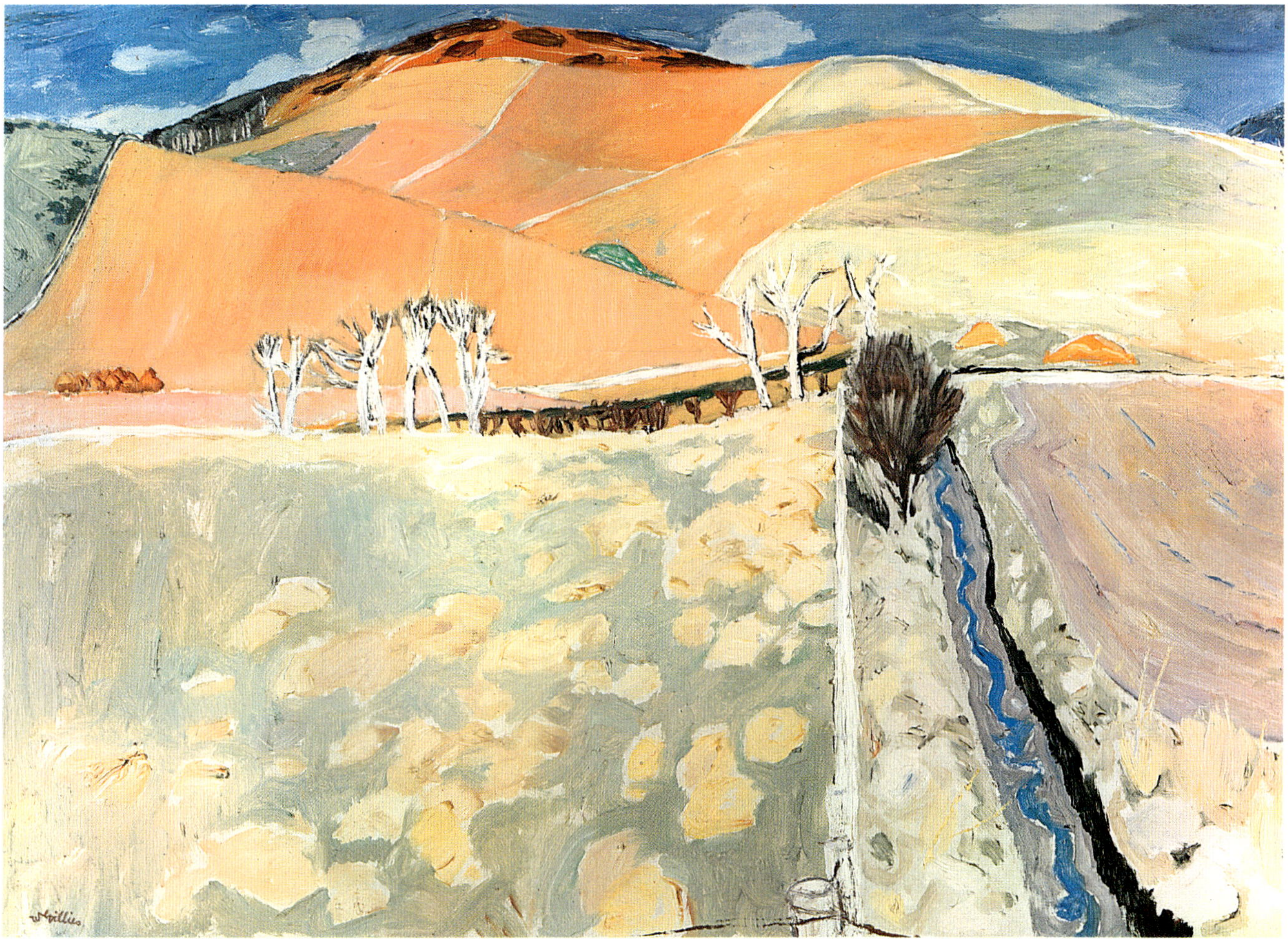

Heriot c. 1942 oil on canvas 71 × 92 cm

I often wondered whether the fact that he rode a fast powerful motorbike, accounted for the strong rhythmic lines of walls and fields in his paintings. At other times one sensed an inner stillness in the artist, enabling him to take insignificant bits of landscape detail – a scree slope, a winding hedgerow, village gable-ends – and turn them into pictorial magic. Other Scottish artists of his generation seem to receive more than their fair share of fashionable acclaim south of the Border. In Scotland, Gillies' paintings need no hype to recommend them. He made us see his beloved Lothian and Border landscape through his eyes and heart, and enriched our lives accordingly.

DAVID MICHIE
Gillies was a very remarkable artist – someone belonging to his time – a painter interested in the expressive qualities of shape, tone and colour for their own sake and 'seeing the significant in the ordinary.' Not much interested in painting which reflected social or political issues. I don't think he had much time for polemics in art. His 'backyard' provided enough in subject matter – objects he found in his domestic environment, his garden and the East Lothian landscape in particular, but sometimes with brief excursions to Aberdeenshire and the Fife villages.

When Robin Philipson returned from a visit to America, he enthusiastically described a trip to New Mexico and said that Bill Gillies would greatly like it. Gillies replied (rather drily) that he 'hadn't done the Glasgow area yet.' He had immense gift and flair for drawing and painting directly from nature. Very swift in execution, free flowing and absolutely true to the character of the subject. The late R. Henderson Blyth recalled pointing out to Gillies (as a joke really) that there were eight telegraph poles stretching along the side of the road where they were painting and not seven as Gillies had shown – so Gillies immediately added another pole.

His paintings reflected him – very unfussy, economical, unpretentious, without any pomposity and never heavily solemn. He didn't like pretentiousness in others. It was clear to all his students that he had integrity, cared about their wellbeing and the wellbeing of the school. He set high standards for himself and expected similar from those around him. He could be generous in praise and critical of slack work or behaviour by students and colleagues – quite fiercely.

His indulgences were simple – cars, motor bikes, chocolate biscuits and cigarettes whose smoke stained a wisp of a moustache. He sold me the first car I possessed – a Triumph Gloria with real leather upholstery – for £30. He was an enthusiastic maker of homemade wine (like his mother), responding to the flowers and fruits of the season – dandelion in early summer, gooseberry following. Raspberry was a favourite.

Gillies, Maxwell and Willie Wilson are an interesting trio to compare. All bachelors with idiosyncratic ways of relating to women. Gillies was very close to his mother and sisters. Apart from them women seemed to exert no fascination. In fact, Gillies seemed to be happily asexual. He had a great sense of fun and loved the fancy dress carnival of the college Revels. I remember him dressing up as Harpo Marx and on another occasion as a racing cyclist – padded body and arms giving him comic bulging muscles.

While he was a naturally modest person, he had a proper sense of his worthy qualities. He said of himself that he might be remembered as a 'little master'. However one describes him (I very much dislike 'ranking' artists) it is undoubtedly true that all who knew him and his work were enriched.

MARTIN BAILLIE

Water-colour may have been his forte but he handled oils with equal assurance, and though his still-lifes have been much admired, these seemed to me often mannered and I believe he was at his best in landscape, and his best period the late 40s and 50s. His emotional range was severely limited, as though he shrank from harsh reality, and this curtailed his subsequent development. Nonetheless there was poetry in the man and his best work will be remembered for a long time to come.

IAN FLEMING

I saw the painting of what we called the Gillies Tryptych [*Family Group – Willowbrae*], a painting of Gillies in the centre and figures to the right and left. Some wit in Edinburgh called it *Gillies Between Domesticity and Vice* – unaware that the figure on the left was his mother and on the right his sister. I have another memory of a journey with him from Edinburgh to Glasgow when he was Principal of ECA and I was Head of Gray's, Aberdeen. We were going through to Glasgow to select some works from a needlework exhibition. Sitting in the train Gillies said, 'It's an awful waste of time doing this on such a sunny afternoon.' I felt the obsession he had about painting was amplified by this. Such was Willie Gillies, a great and magnificent artist.

WILLIAM C.M. JACKSON

He was not a great innovator and certainly did not break new ground, but he might well prove to be one of the greatest natural painters this country has produced this century. I first visited Temple in the autumn of 1968. Here was this busy and amiable man who trotted everywhere

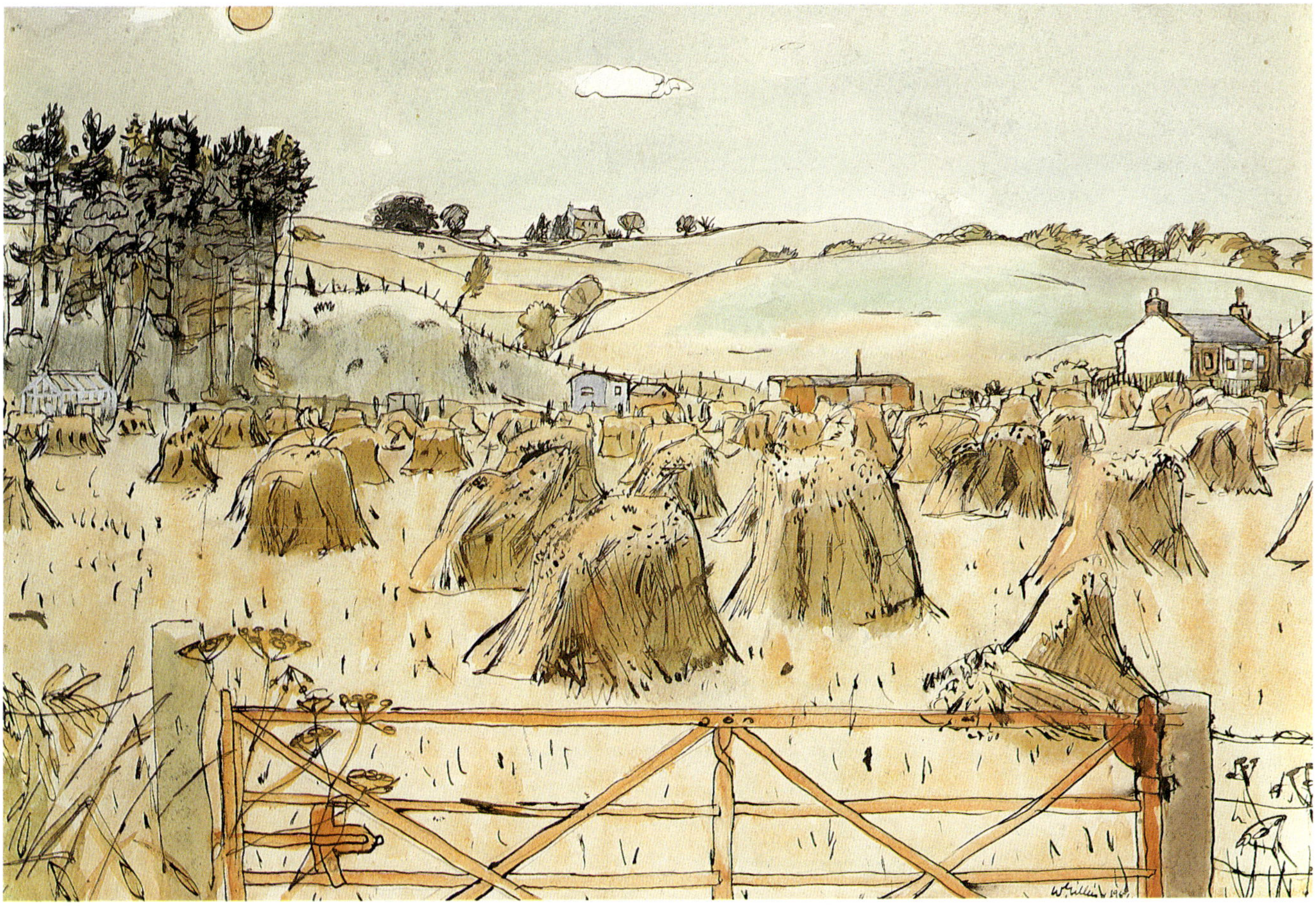

A Cornfield 1951 watercolour on paper 38 × 55 cm

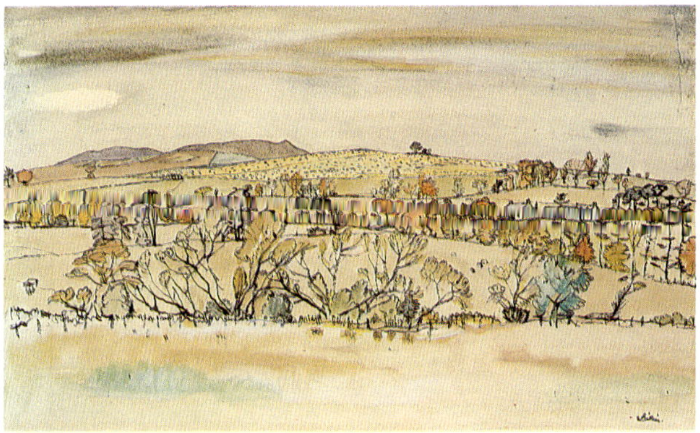

Near Romano Bridge Watercolour and ink on paper 36 × 57 cm

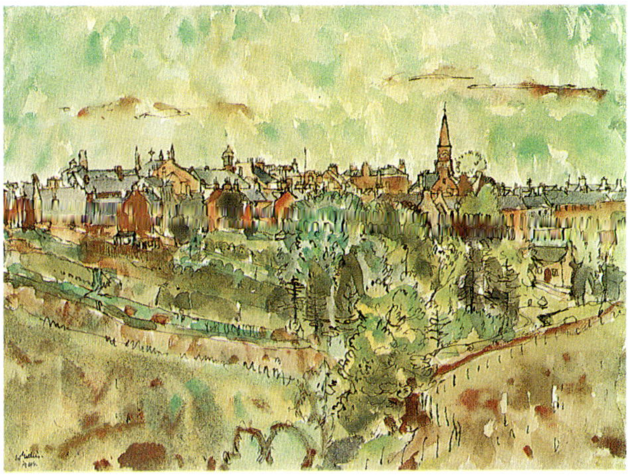

Kirriemuir 1946 watercolour and ink on paper 28 × 36 cm

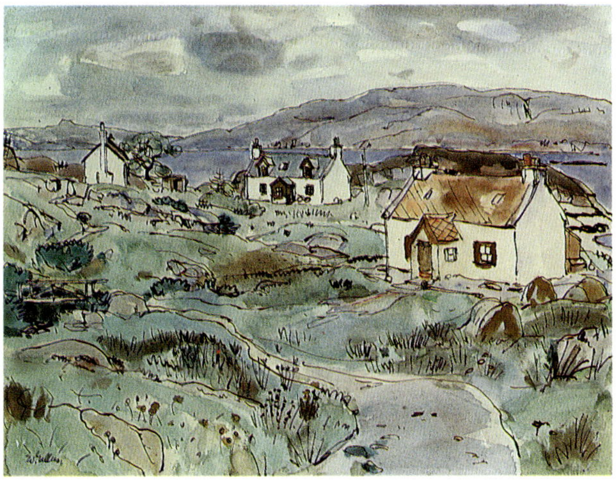

Durnish c1955 watercolour and ink on paper 25 × 32 cm

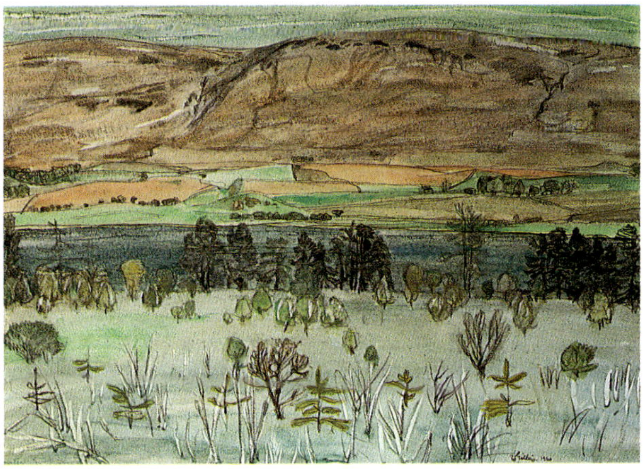

The Loch 1960 watercolour on paper 25 × 35 cm

with little, hurried steps. I remember the sitting-room at the back of the house, with its variety of wallpaper, and large key paintings which were astonishing to me in their brilliance. Then the studio, two large rooms with a wealth of works piled ten deep in every corner and against every wall. I was shown the garden and birch trees which he had just managed to save from the woodman's axe. The day was concluded with tea, toast and home-made apple jelly. There was also a bottle of elderberry wine, which is why I remember little of the return journey.

He was not a mean man, indeed he was exceedingly generous, and gifted many of his works to friends and charities. But he would take great pleasure in showing off a rather worn overcoat he had just bought in the Grassmarket. 'It cost me two-and-six.'

Perhaps there were situations where his judgment of students might have been viewed as narrow-minded. He was apparently furious when Alan Davie showed entirely experimental work for his diploma show. Gillies was eventually persuaded that it was in everyone's best interests for Davie to receive his diploma, at which point Davie promptly left for London, never to return to work in Scotland.

Gillies made few demands on his friends. He was not a deeply complex man who required continual intellectual stimulus, but he responded from the heart. His work had a passionate conviction about the values of commonplace things. He had the ability to produce something in total simplicity, which communicated a vision and idea with such force and integrity that one felt inadequate in his presence.

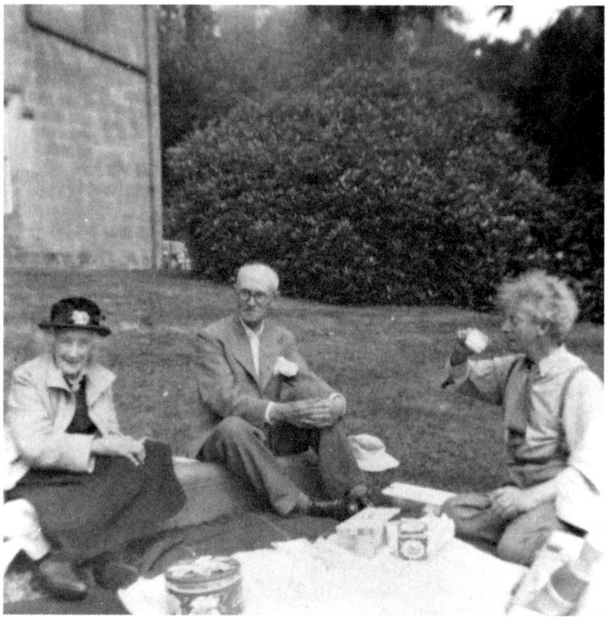

Mrs Gillies, Dr Robert Lillie and William Gillies, Wooplaw, 1948 (Photo: RSA Archives)

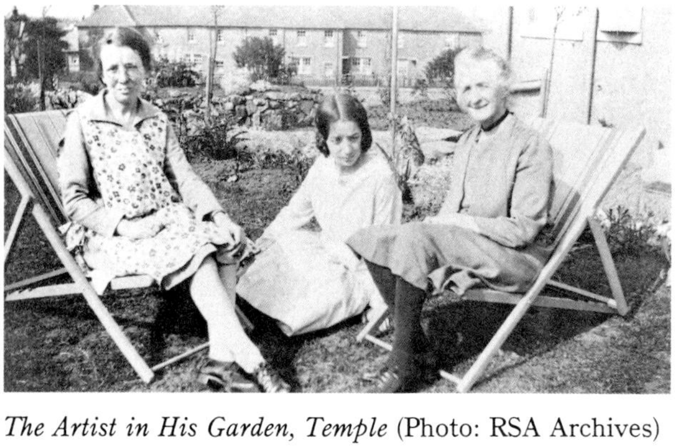

The Artist in His Garden, Temple (Photo: RSA Archives)

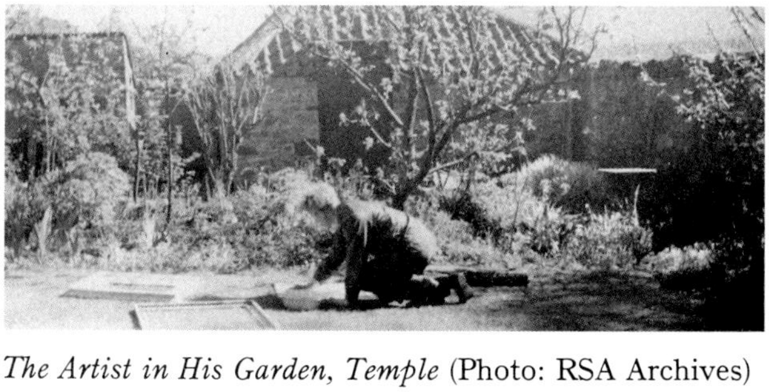

The Artist in His Garden, Temple (Photo: RSA Archives)

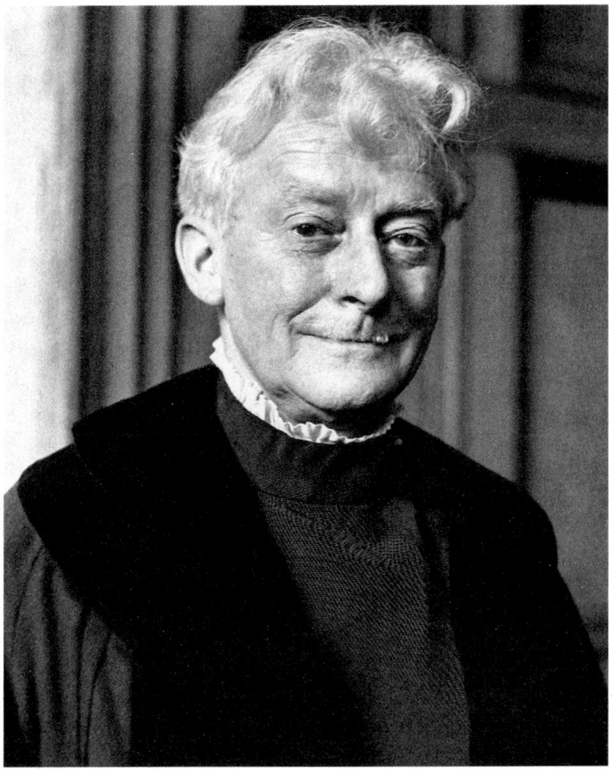

The Artist in his RSA gown (Photo: The Scotsman)

PETER COLLINS

An aesthetic of tone – herein lies the secret of the very personal (and influential) contribution Gillies made to Scottish painting. Such an aesthetic is far removed from the accurate observation and rendering of tonal values which is the hallmark of much traditional painting, and indeed a cornerstone of academicism. An aesthetic of tone is essentially abstract; a visual parallel to musical harmonies.

Harmony, in the world of music, demands perfect pitch as a sine qua non of its success, and in a broader etymological sense implies a 'working well' in a well-tempered inter-relationship. This is certainly true of the tonal harmonies found in most if not all of Gillies' paintings. Moreover, the analogy to music still holds good in the recognition that harmonies are subject to invention, and here we may concentrate on an invention most pertinent to Gillies' art: that of (surprise) inversion. The surprise is not too dissimilar to that of viewing a photographic negative, and an obvious illustration of Gillies' employment of inversion would be the frequency with which we find a landscape sky (normally, in Nature, of a high pitch of tone) rendered with a sonorous if not thunderous low-pitched tonality.

Tone is an integral quality of colour, and it is my belief that it is Gillies' mastery of tone which lies at the root of his abilities as a colourist. Significantly, he would seem to be at his happiest when his palette employs a muted range of hues; of tertiary colours usually described as 'neutral' – off-whites, blacks and coloured greys. His still-life paintings are *études* in composition, giving full rein to his powers as a designer, juggling with placement and pattern, balance and imbalance. The end product is often exquisite, revealing a sensibility of great delicacy. In their deceptive simplicity and dryness, but most of all in their sense of distillation, one is reminded of the *Gymnopédies* of Erik Satie.

In his landscapes this oriental sense of distillation pertains. His drawing is more 'naturalistic' than in his still-lifes only in the sense that he feels no need to revert to distortion. His line has both freedom and economy, combined with his aesthetic of tone and

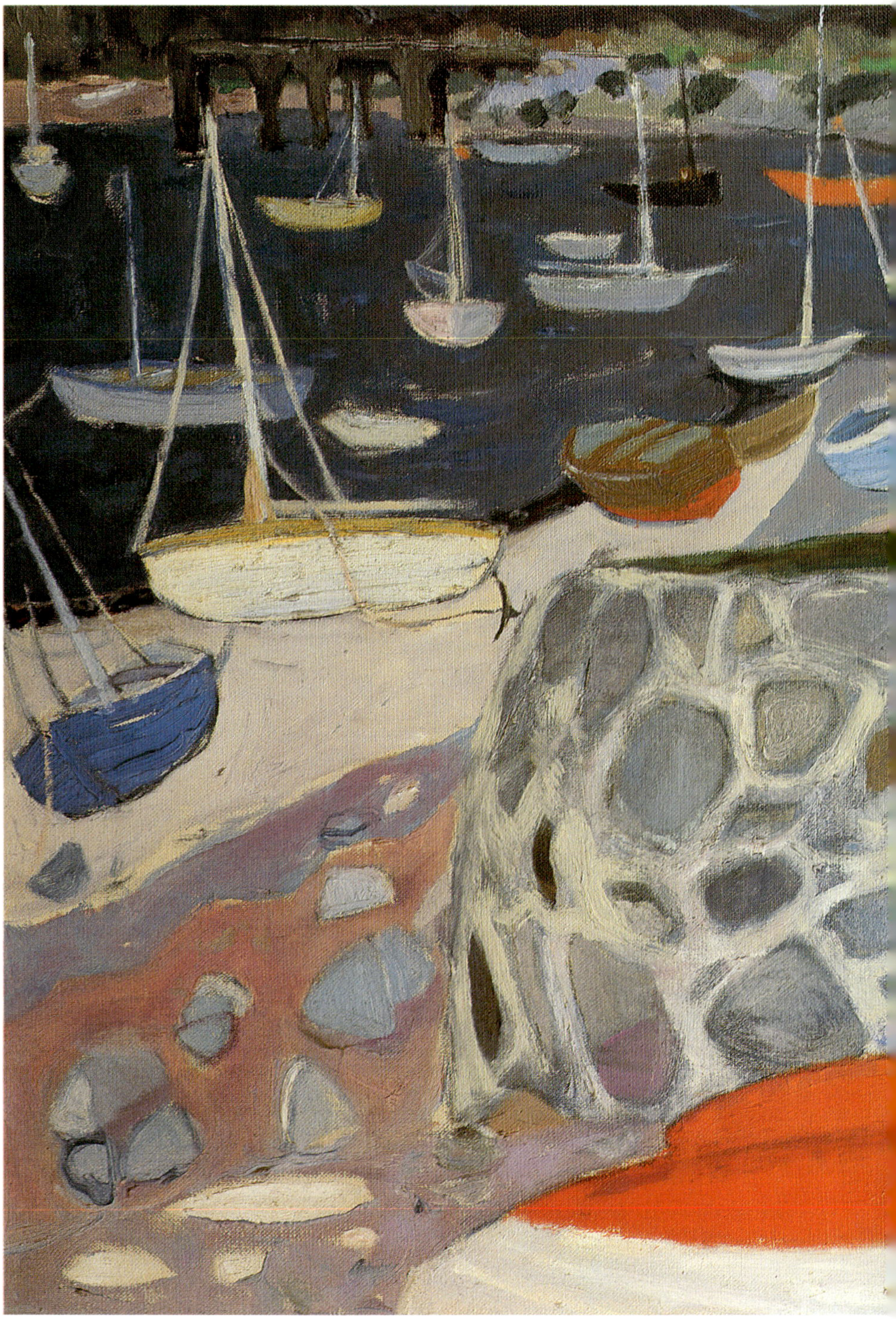

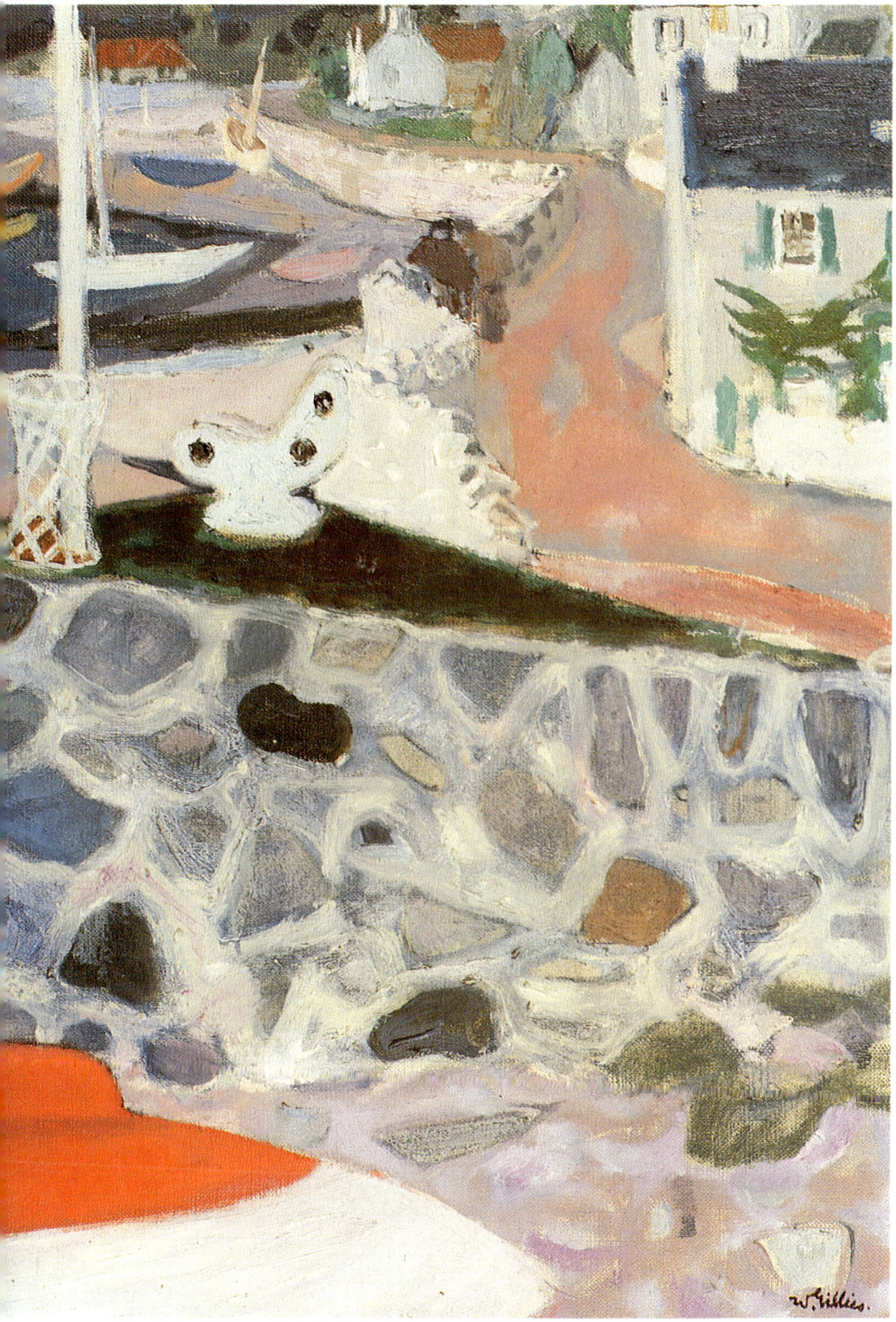

Kippford c.1950 oil on canvas 76 × 102 cm

colour. These 'impressionistic' mood paintings fully justify the adjective 'lyrical,' applied to them often enough to become a cliché. It is a lyricism with a French flavour, Fauré or Debussy perhaps, rather than the lusher romanticism of a Brahms or Schubert.

I have the strange feeling that I was never really 'taught' by Gillies. But that is unfair, for he taught me the lesson that as an artist one has to think for oneself, and have the courage of one's convictions. His teaching method was diagnostic and never prescriptive. The diagnosis would be delivered as a one-liner, more often than not employing simile, and so concise as to be cryptic. Nothing else was said beyond this one-liner, though there was undoubtedly an unspoken corollary: 'Really, it's up to you. Think about it, and then do something about it."

Gillies' legacy is not the bequest he left to the RSA, but rather a tradition of tonal aesthetic still fostered by the graduates of his *alma mater* in their own teaching. That it is a 'living' tradition there can be no doubt.

As part of a Christmas Revel, by the simplest of means, I transformed an antique mask into a portrait of Gillies by addition of a thin nicotine-stained moustache and a frizz of white hair employing 'tow' (fibres of jute). The mask was taken from Houdon's *Voltaire*. It was Willie Gillies, and Gillies much appreciated the joke.

JOHN HOUSTON

To me, he's one of the few Scottish painters I like – especially his watercolours. Somebody asked him how he thought the future would assess him. He said, 'Och, a very good minor Scottish painter.' He's always somebody you go back to and get a surprise – particularly by showing you what you can do with something you've seen a million times. And I like the very late work, just before he died.

It's amazing the respect he enjoyed, especially from these older people, they loved him – people like Adam Bruce Thomson and Donald Moodie. I always got the feeling that they thought he was special; they were pals, friends, but they honestly saw him on a different plane from themselves.

His administration was a bit of a joke. There were never any staff meetings. The only staff meeting was the day before term started. You went up and he said, 'Here, have a glass of sherry and a chocolate biscuit, and would you like to put that picture in a frame and hang it up somewhere,' That was your staff meeting. Oh, he knew what was going on – he was always round the studios, he knew all the students and what they were up to. The rest of the time it was just a chat over coffee, and that's how some of the business was done.

Out at Temple the hospitality mixture was something wonderful. You got home-made wine and then marmalade sandwiches. Then you could have the 'Store's' sponge washed down with Martel or Heine brandy – all on the kitchen table. And Marmite sandwiches, which I'd never had in my life before. So it really was quite an honour. Sometimes you even got a poached egg. He loved these great big frothy cream cakes.

I remember hearing about one of the painting-trips. They'd all split up, and Bobby [Henderson Blyth] was going back to wherever they were due to meet, and heard this voice asking, 'Is he around?' And there was Johnnie Maxwell hiding under a hedge, trying to keep out of the way.

I don't think Gillies ever bought anything new – the place was always chock-a-block with army greatcoats. They found all the early oils, the 20s and early 30s oils which the RSA fell heir to, stacked with newspapers under his carpets. He never threw anything away – boxes and boxes of string and brown paper.

I don't think he was a great teacher. He was very good at picking out something he could help and encourage. Actually the teaching was done by all the other people; he was the one who opened things up and made it possible.

ELIZABETH BLACKADDER

He was special to me. When I was a young student in 1949, and being a woman, I got no feeling from Gillies that I was in any way different – you were a painter, and it didn't matter what you were, man, woman, whatever. He just expected you to get on with it. That sense of there being no difference may not seem very much, but I think it was something very special to him and important to me as a painter, right from the beginning. I was very lucky to have such encouragement.

JIMMY MOWAT

As a first-year student at ECA in 1946, in my first week, I had occasion to go searching for a radial easel. I opened the door of a final-year studio and a fellow with a white coat asked if he could help. He tucked an easel under his arm and carried it the whole length of the balcony to where I was working. I remarked to my friend T.S. Simpson that the janitors were very obliging. The janitor in question was Head of Drawing and Painting.

When, later in life, I started exhibiting his work in my gallery in Lower Largo, I visited him on the last Sunday of every month. One day he remarked that his bank manager had been on the phone. I thought there might be some problem, but not really. The manager informed Bill that there was £40,000 in his current account. 'He took me out to lunch, and do you know, James, I'd already moved it into a building society.'

I had an arrangement with Cockburn, the village grocer, to deliver on every Christmas morning a bottle of whisky with an appropriate card. The bottle was to be left inside the door. Bill's comment to Robin Philipson that afternoon was: 'You know, James has been over again and left me a bottle of whisky.' I never disillusioned him.

For some reason or other I went to Temple on a Saturday accompanied by my younger son Robert. Arriving at the door just as Bill was coming out, I said that perhaps we had come at an inappropriate time. Not so, he was just on his way to Cockburn's for half-a-dozen eggs. I suggested young Robert would go. Bill thought about it; no it would be better if he himself went. 'I get them on tick till Thursday.'

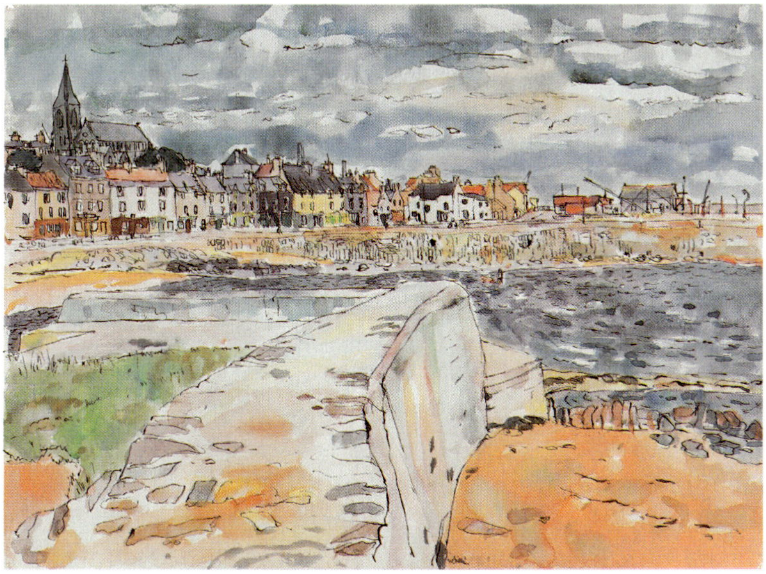

Anstruther, from the Harbour Wall c.1948/9
watercolour and ink on paper 46 × 62 cm SNGMA

A young doctor and his wife came to tea while he was acting locum in Lundin Links. A collection of Gillies watercolours was temporarily housed in our lounge, prior to an exhibition. The young doctor was much taken by a watercolour of Kessock Ferry, and as he was leaving early the next day, could he purchase it? We settled for the sum of £28. I phoned Bill to tell him I was now a painting less. He enquired who had bought it. I told him, 'A young doctor not too well off, so I charged £28.' 'Too much, give him four pounds back.' I returned four pounds to a very astonished medic at 8 am next day.

A Friday evening at the private view of the RSA. My wife and I were at the buffet when Bill arrived and my wife set about finding something for him to eat. A portrait by David Donaldson hung on the end wall. 'What do you think of it James?' 'Not at all bad,' says I, being cagey. 'I suppose not,' he says. 'Of course, it's from the other place.' Glasgow was always the other place.

I lost a very dear friend. I esteemed him as an artist and loved him as a man.

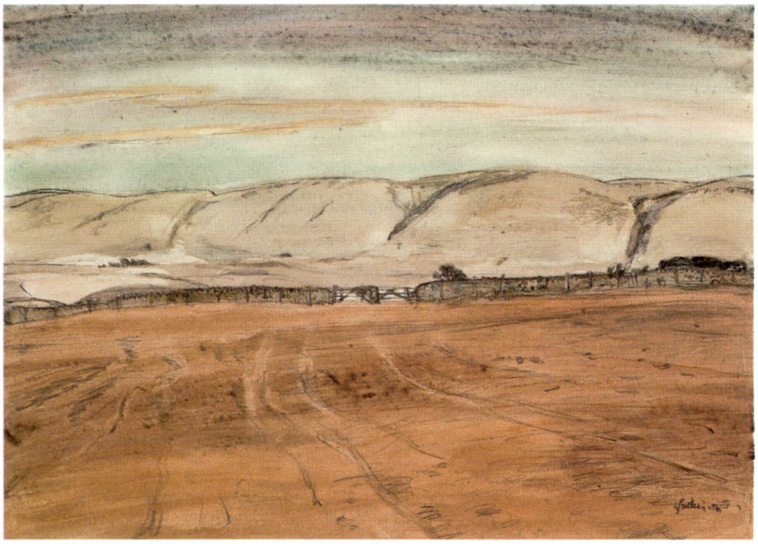

Borders Landscape 1961 watercolour and pencil on paper 23 × 35 cm
Sir Robin Philipson

JACK FIRTH

I knew him for over thirty years. I got all kinds of help from him, but it was never couched in memorable remarks or profound sayings – his criticism was practical rather than philosophical, the guidance of a professional. He just painted, all his life, like eating, and he avoided involvement with anything that did not have a bearing on art. He had, as far as I know, no romantic attachments and yet he was less a bachelor than a family man. His mother and sisters were the family proper, but the College was also part of his family. When you left you might be out of sight, but you could belong again just by going back and seeing him – you had never been away.

Someone once made the mistake of describing him as 'a mean man' while getting a lift in Jimmy Mowat's car. Jimmy stopped the car and asked the person to get out and walk, or withdraw the remark. Gillies could inspire that kind of loyalty. I know someone who went without lunch for months to buy a Gillies watercolour in the 1940s.

He was known to take his leave of social gatherings which he had felt bound to attend, in order to go home and paint (but usually after the food; he loved food). 'Going home to paint another picture Bill?' someone would call, 'What else would I do?' he would reply. I don't think he ever had a holiday from painting. He hardly ever destroyed work, preferring

St Valery en Caux 1938 pencil on paper 46 × 61 cm RSA

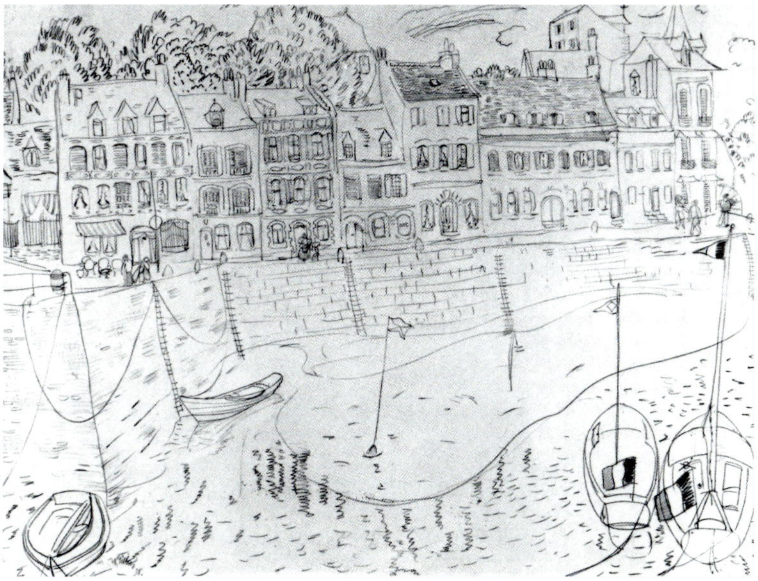

Kirriemuir, Houses on a Slope 1946 ink on paper 28 × 39 cm SNRMA

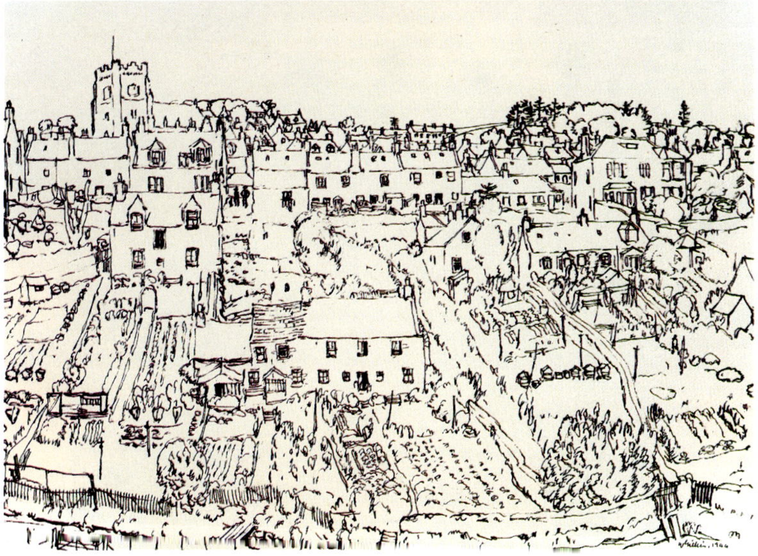

The Roods, Kirriemuir 1946 ink on paper 45 × 57 cm

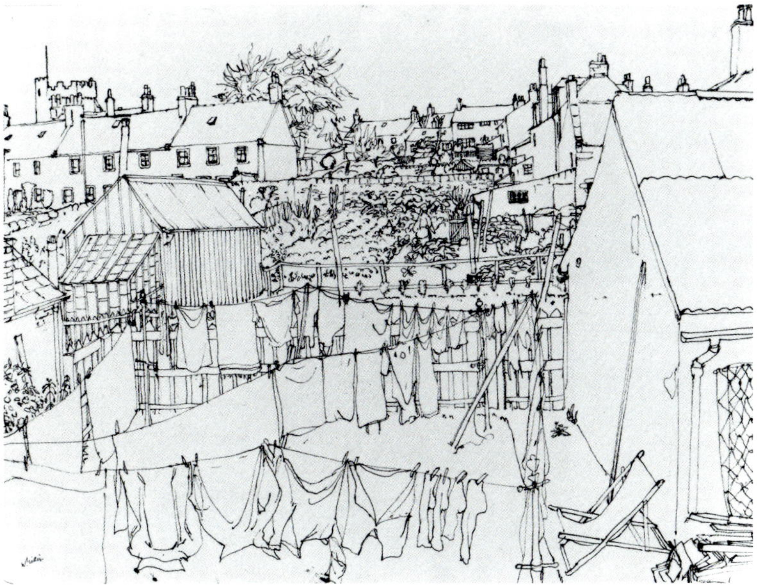

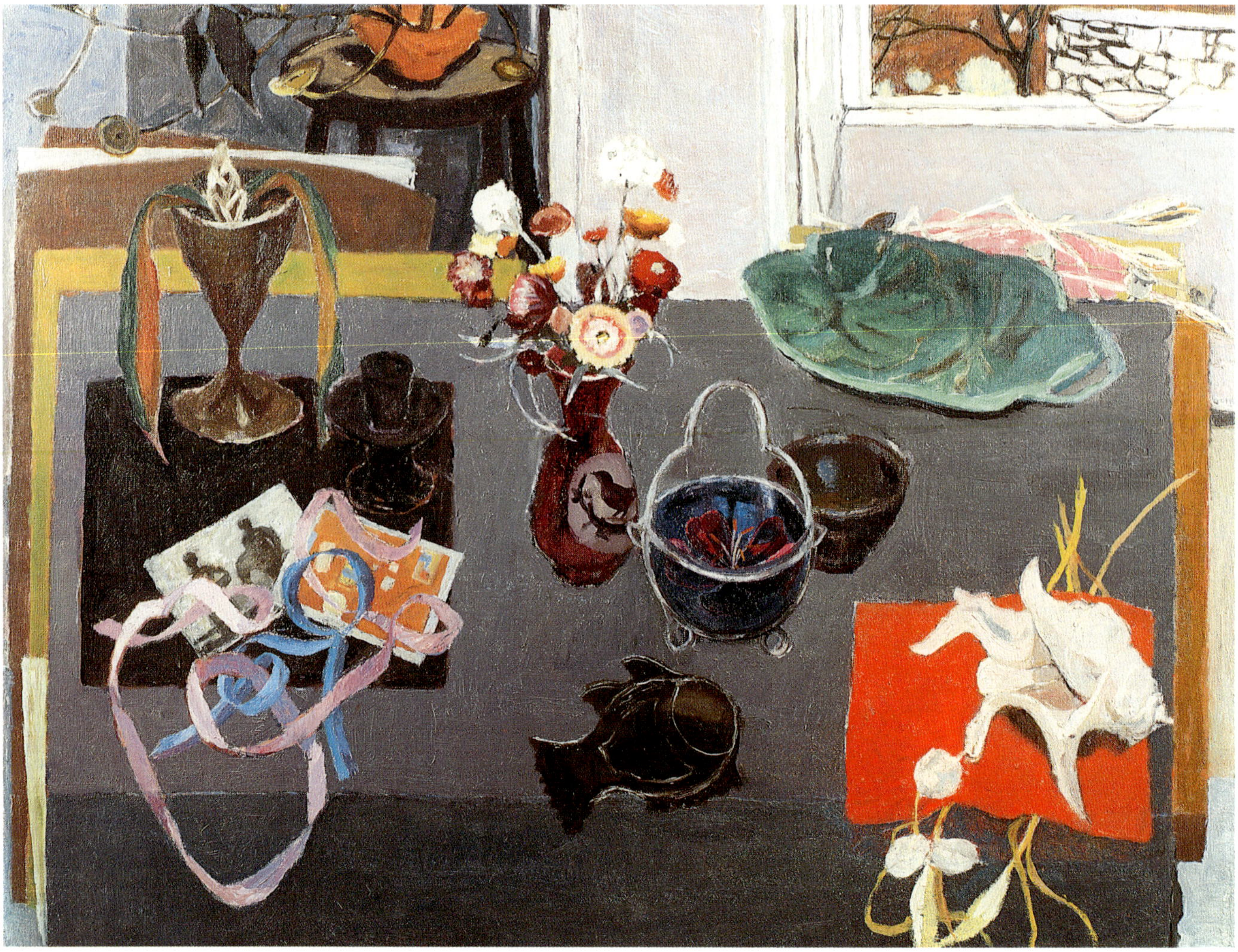

Still Life with Grey Table Cloth oil on canvas 84 × 112 cm

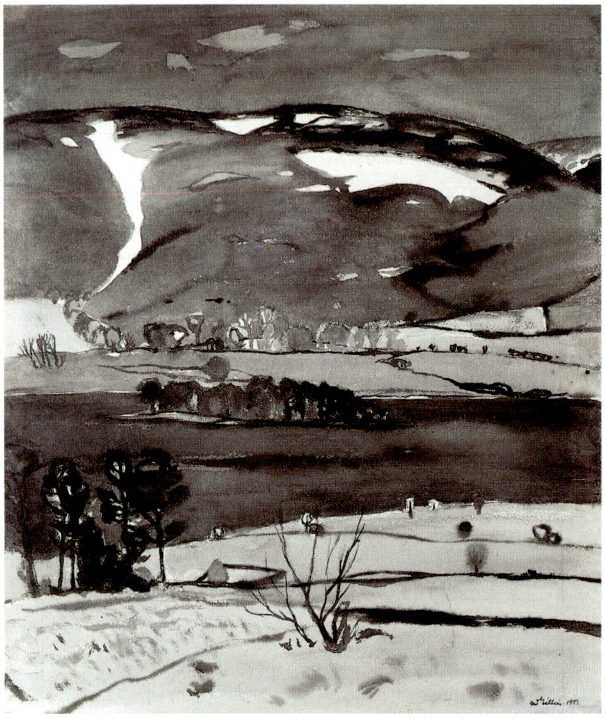

March, Moorfoot 1951 ink wash on paper 62 × 52 cm SNGMA

to keep it for another attempt – after all, one should learn from one's errors. 'It might come in handy some time.' Temple was like Anne Redpath's house in a way – it felt like being inside one of the artist's pictures (which, in a way, it was).

We were talking together in the long gallery of the RSA during the great Edinburgh Festival Braque Exhibition of 1956. It was the Academy's custom to retain a selection of Members' work from the annual exhibition and show this in back rooms while the Festival master was displayed in the front galleries. Not a good idea. Looking through an opening between the gallery and a back room, we both saw, framed between two superb Braques, a Gillies still-life with a passing resemblance to a Braque. Bill, who cheerfully acknowledged such debts, grinned suddenly at me and said, 'It looks awful *thin*.'

I remember him as a thirty-nine-year-old, scurrying about College from wardrobe to life room with armfuls of draperies for a pose. He was never still, his mousey hair rising in a shock above his high forehead like a halo. His tiny, pencil-line moustache was within reach of his tongue, and watching him draw was a revelation. Nothing clever or showy happened; he didn't revel in his line, like Donald Moodie, but instead, there was a slow, very economical use of the pencil, and out of a few considered marks – a searching, light line and some scribbled tone very sparsely indicated – the form of the model materialised from the centre of the torso outwards, solid, anatomically informed, but as a drawing, open.

Gillies was one of the great exhibition hangers – he perfected a system of treating the wall as the unit, with a smooth transition from one side across to the other; that wall then had to relate to the walls on either side of it, which themselves were hung as units. Finally, the last wall would complete the pattern, and the room would then become the finished presentation with, in all probability, a character of its own, different from other rooms in that gallery. The underlying idea behind a Gillies hanging was that each picture should get the best advantage. It is an extravagant way of hanging a show, but it is something to behold.

In my last student year I decided to paint a portrait, full-length, about three-quarters life-size. I must have been mad. I prepared a large canvas and asked a second-year student to pose for me. She was a small fluffy blonde, rather pretty but with indeterminate features – the most difficult kind of portrait subject, but I was Fourth Year, and knew no fear. I spent about three weeks on it. No one had seen it except my model. Gillies rushed past the open door one day and saw me painting, so he looked round the door with a shy enquiring smile. 'Can I have a look?' He gave the girl a winning smile and looked at the painting for ages. Then he turned to go, and said in a stage-whisper, 'It's awful like her.' A giggle and he was gone. I presented the portrait to my sitter and never saw it again.

Although he started no particular movements or styles in painting Gillies had a pervasive influence on many artists. His real influence was not in surface tricks, but in the way he taught his students to regard painting.

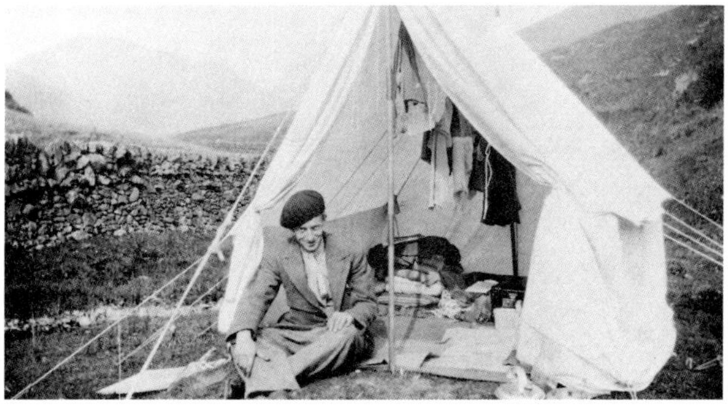

Camping in the Highlands (Photo: RSA Archives)

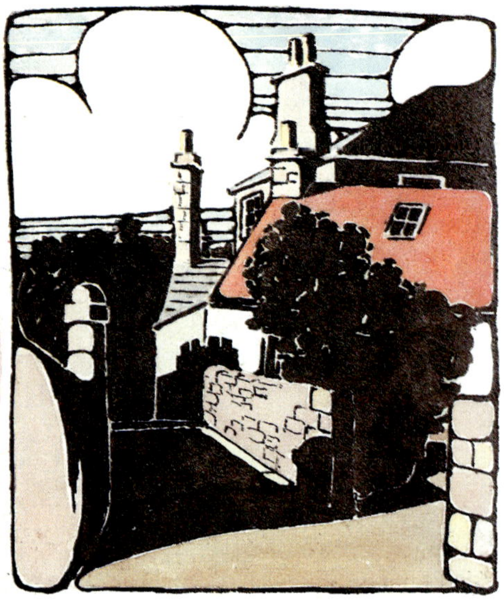

Broughty Ferry 1915 ink on paper 10 × 9 cm RSA

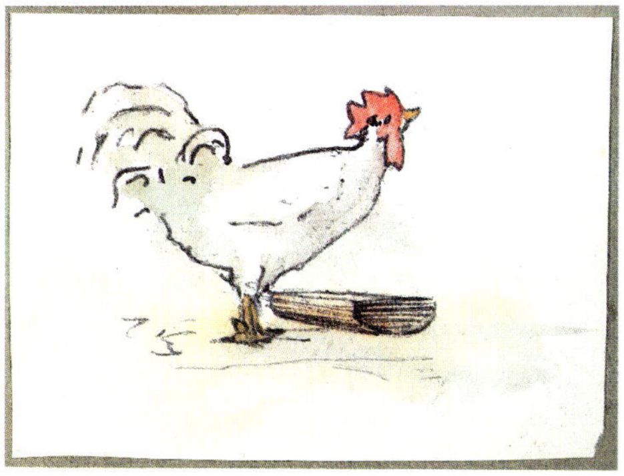

A Rooster 1914/15 ink and watercolour on paper 6 × 8 cm RSA

Acknowledgements

Artists, and particularly Scottish artists, are generous people. I have known this all my professional life and have had it confirmed by the way so many of them helped me to fill out the somewhat fugitive figure of Bill Gillies. Their contributions to my 'wake' for the artist's and the man add humour, affection, analysis, and insight to a scant Gillies archive. I thank them all for the readiness and warmth of their response, and apologise for some savage editing. Throughout the project several artists – Robin Philipson, Sandy Moffat, John Houston and Elizabeth Blackadder in particular – put time aside to steer my way and lighten the burden with advice and friendship.

The book owes an enormous debt to Gillies' old friend Jack Firth whose encyclopaedic knowledge of the man and his work is matched only by his enthusiasm and fellowship. I am grateful, too, to George Bruce for scholarly suggestions and permission to use his poem *Soup and Sherry*, written to celebrate his own eightieth birthday, as one of the book's most delightful decorations. Mary McIver graciously allowed me to quote from her recent book of memoirs *Pilgrim Souls* (Aberdeen University Press) and added other reminiscences of her time at Temple.

I have referred in the text to three monographs – on Gillies, MacTaggart, and Maxwell – published by University Press, Edinburgh, invaluable as reference sources and fascinating as chronicles of three important Scottish painters, their comradeship, and the times they lived through. Jack Firth's *Scottish Watercolour Painting* (Ramsay Head Press) is an informed analysis by a distinguished practitioner.

Various institutions – the Royal Scottish Academy, Edinburgh College of Art, the National Library and Galleries of Scotland, and Edinburgh City Libraries – co-operated with their customary efficiency and goodwill.

Gillies the painter is assured of his place in the pantheon of Scottish painting. If Gillies the man is less of a phantom because of this book I will owe a great deal to a host of people, and particularly to my partner Jay Flett, who has served me and the Gillies project with constant devotion.

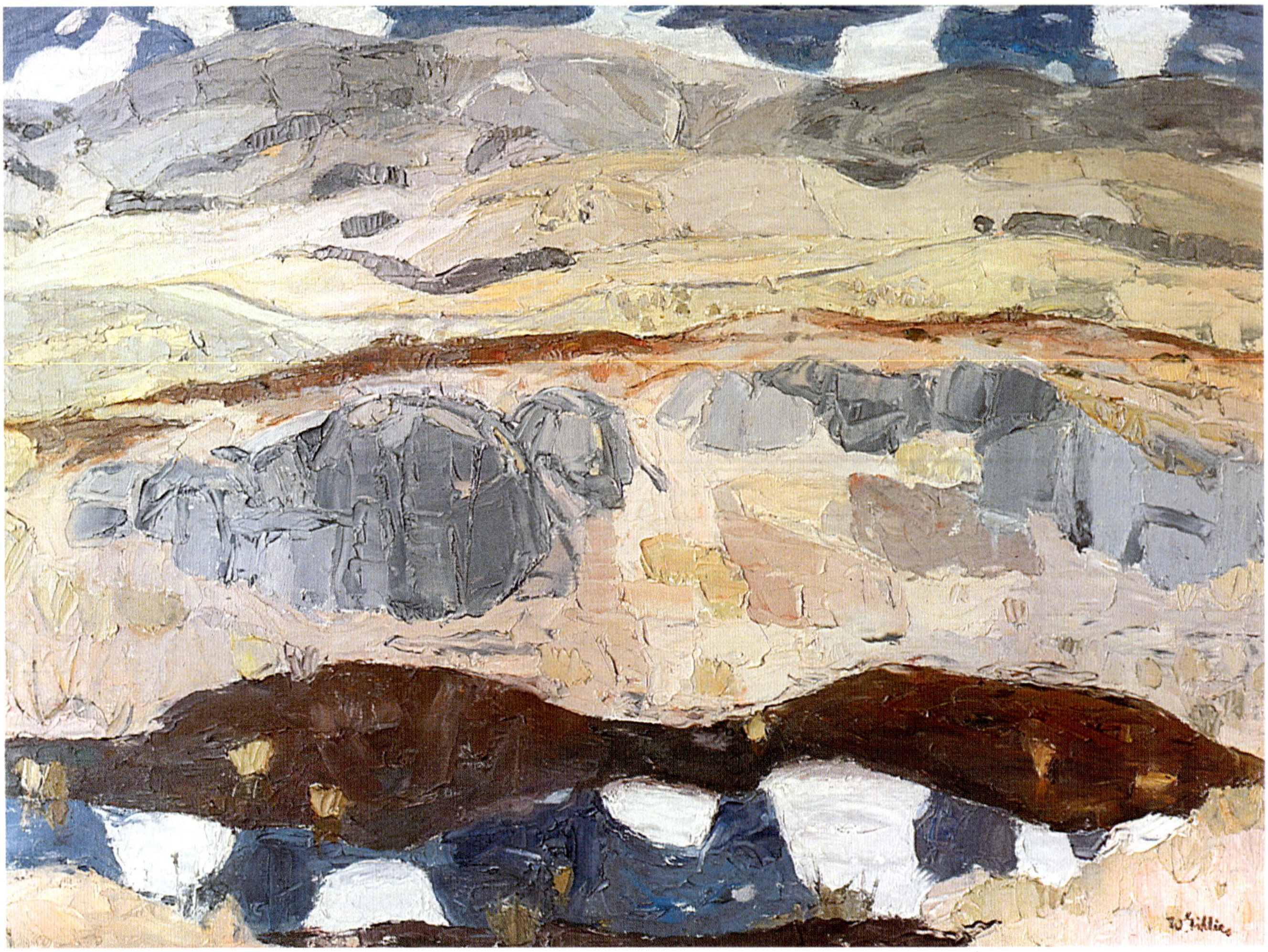

The Hill Pool 1960 oil on canvas 76 × 102 cm

INDEX

(Names indexed in capital letters have made personal contributions to *Envoi,* pages 85—111)

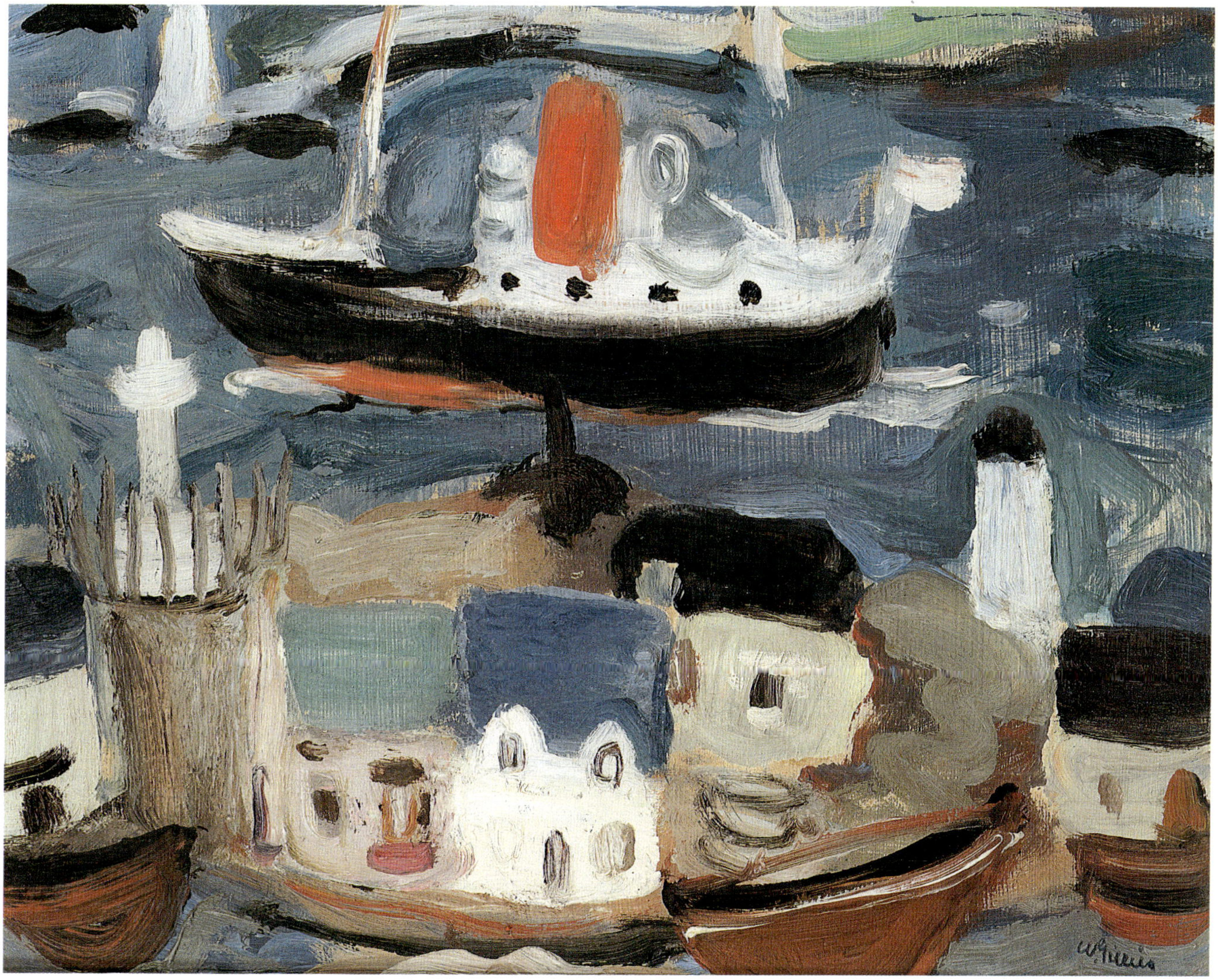

Kyleakin 1938 oil on board 18 × 26 cm

ABBREVIATIONS

RSA	Royal Scottish Academy
SAC	Scottish Arts Council
SNGMA	Scottish National Gallery of Modern Art
SNPG	Scottish National Portrait Gallery
ACGB	Arts Council of Great Britain
RA	Royal Academy
EDC	Edinburgh District Council Collection
GMAG	Glasgow Museums and Art Gallery
AAG	Aberdeen Art Gallery
PAG	Paisley Art Gallery

The publisher wishes to thank all the institutions and private collectors for their kind permission to reproduce their paintings.

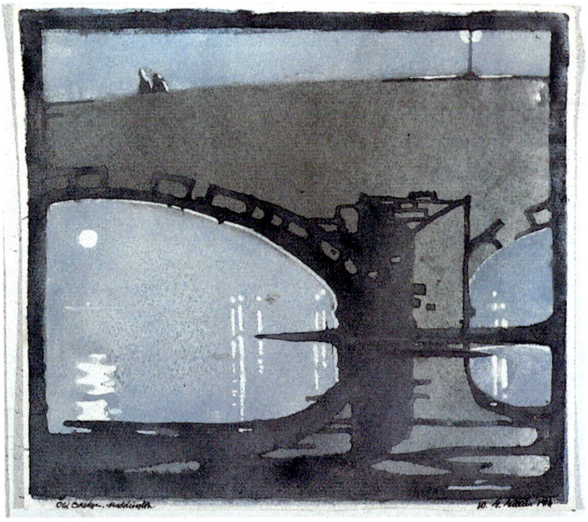

Nungate Bridge, Haddington 1916 linocut on paper 19 × 20 cm RSA

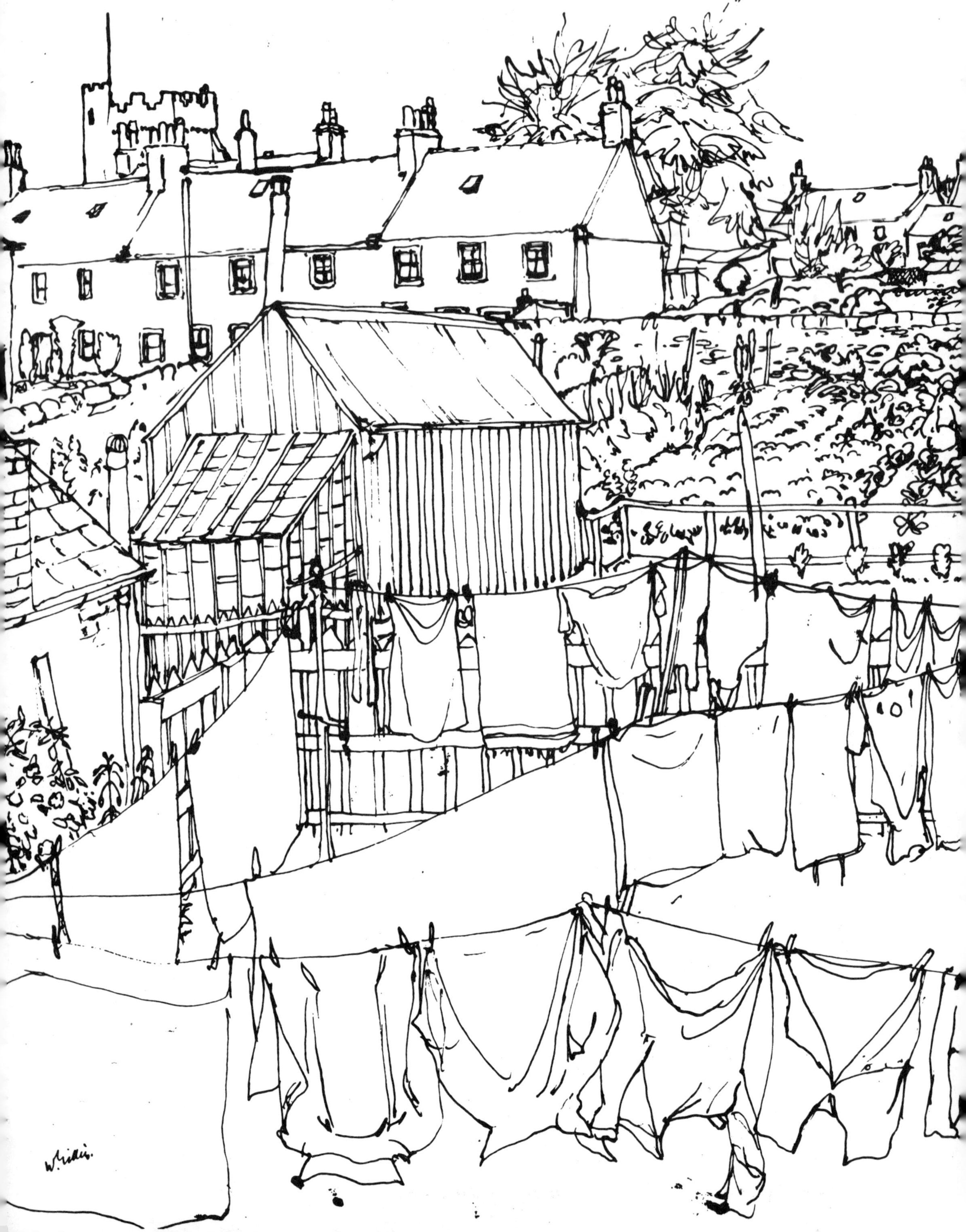